W9-DCO-669

THE BOOK OF
QUESTIONS
— AND —
ANSWERS

THE BOOK OF
QUESTIONS —AND— ANSWERS

BARNES
&NOBLE
BOOKS
NEW YORK

This edition published by Barnes & Noble, Inc.,
by arrangement with Horus Editions Limited

2003 Barnes & Noble Books

Copyright © 1998 Horus Editions Limited

ISBN 0-7607-4040-2

Printed and bound in Malaysia

10 9 8 7 6 5 4 3 2 1

CONTENTS

THE UNIVERSE

The Universe

WHAT DOES THE UNIVERSE CONTAIN? In the universe there are billions of star islands called galaxies; our own galaxy contains a hundred billion stars. Each star is a gigantic globe of hot bright gas. We live on a planet, the Earth, which travels around the Sun, our nearest star, once each year. Our closest neighbor is the Moon. It travels around the Earth once every 27 days.

▲ *The Solar System consists of the Sun and nine planets, of which the Earth is one.*

◄ *The Moon is 238,000 miles from the Earth. It travels around the Earth once every 27.3 days.*

WHAT IS A LIGHT-YEAR?

Light moves at a speed of 186,000 miles per second. A light-year is the distance that light travels in one year (about 5.8 billion miles). The nearest star to the Earth (apart from the Sun) is more than four light-years away.

HOW WERE ATOMS FORMED?

A millionth of a second after the beginning of time, particles called quarks joined together to make protons and neutrons. A single proton is the nucleus (central part) of a hydrogen atom. About a hundred seconds later, protons and neutrons linked up to form heavier nuclei of helium. Eventually, the universe became cool enough for nuclei to link up with lighter particles, called electrons, to form atoms.

HOW DID THE UNIVERSE BEGIN?

Most astronomers believe that the universe began in a tremendously hot dense explosion called the Big Bang, which took place between 10 and 20 billion years ago. As the universe expanded it cooled down, so that different kinds of atoms, then galaxies, stars, and planets, were able to form. The universe is still expanding, and the galaxies are rushing away from each other, just as spots stuck to the surface of an expanding balloon would.

HOW AND WHEN WERE GALAXIES FORMED?

As the expanding universe cooled down, huge clumps of gas formed. After a billion years or so, gravity had pulled the clumps together to form galaxies. Within each galaxy smaller clumps of gas collapsed, heated up, and became stars. Planets, like the Earth, formed from the clouds of gas and dust that surrounded the new stars.

► *At first, matter consisted of heavy particles (quarks) and light particles (electrons). Bunches of quarks formed protons and neutrons, which then formed atomic nuclei. Atoms were created when nuclei captured electrons.*

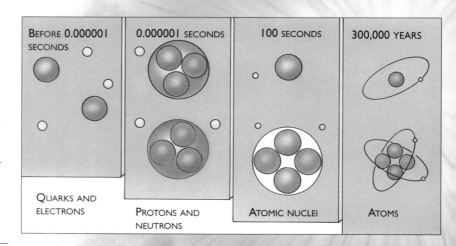

BEFORE 0.000001 SECONDS

QUARKS AND ELECTRONS

0.000001 SECONDS

PROTONS AND NEUTRONS

100 SECONDS

ATOMIC NUCLEI

300,000 YEARS

ATOMS

◀ The Sun is one of the hundred billion stars that make up our spiral-shaped galaxy.

50,000 LY

▼ Our Galaxy is near the outer edge of a huge supercluster of galaxies.

HOW DO WE KNOW THE AGE OF THE UNIVERSE?

The galaxies are rushing away from each other as the universe expands. Astronomers can measure their speeds and their distances, and from this information can work out how long it has taken them to reach their present distances. This tells us how long ago the Big Bang took place.

100 MILLION LY

WILL THE UNIVERSE EXPAND FOREVER?

If the pull of gravity is strong enough, the galaxies will eventually stop moving apart and will start to fall together, just as a stone thrown upwards eventually falls back to the ground. This universe (known as a 'closed universe') would then collapse until everything collided in a 'Big Crunch'. But if the galaxies are moving fast enough, gravity will never be able to stop them and the universe will expand forever (known as an 'open universe').

WHEN WAS THE SOLAR SYSTEM FORMED?

Most astronomers believe that the Solar System (the Sun and nine planets) formed all at the same time from the same cloud of gas and dust. The age of the Solar System can be worked out by studying radioactive elements in rock samples. These elements are substances that gradually change into other substances as time goes by. The radioactive element uranium, for example, eventually becomes lead. So, by comparing the amounts of uranium with the amount of lead in a piece of rock, scientists can calculate the rock's age. Measurements of the ages of rocks on the Earth, on the Moon, and in meteorites (lumps of rock that fall from space) have shown that the Solar System formed 4.6 billion years ago.

10 BILLION LY

▲ The Big Bang was a giant explosion, out of which came all the matter in the universe. Huge clumps of this matter eventually formed galaxies.

▶ The universe contains billions of galaxies. The farthest galaxies visible by telescope are about 10 billion light-years away.

Galaxies

THERE ARE BILLIONS OF GALAXIES BUT DO THEY ALL LOOK THE SAME? There are three main types of galaxy: spiral, elliptical, and irregular. A spiral galaxy has a central region, called the nucleus, which is packed with stars. The nucleus is surrounded by spiral-shaped 'arms' containing stars and gas clouds. Elliptical galaxies range in shape from spheres to flattened ovals and contain little if any gas. Irregular galaxies have no particular shape.

WHAT IS OUR GALAXY LIKE?

The Sun is one of the hundred billion stars that make up our galaxy, the Milky Way galaxy. It is a spiral galaxy that measures nearly 100,000 light-years across. If you could travel at the speed of light (186,000 miles per second) it would take 100,000 years to cross from one side to the other. The Sun is located near the edge of one of the galaxy's spiral arms, about 25,000 light-years from the center. It takes nearly 225 million years to orbit once around the center.

▲ *The Milky Way is a faint band of starlight that stretches across the sky.*

WHAT IS THE MILKY WAY?

The Milky Way is a faint misty band of starlight that runs across the sky. When the sky is very clear and dark it can be seen with the naked eye (without the help of a telescope or binoculars). The Milky Way is the combined light of billions of stars in the disc and spiral arms of our galaxy, which are viewed sideways-on from the Earth.

▶ *Seen sideways-on, our galaxy. is a flat disc of stars with a central bulge — like two fried eggs back to back.*

WHY DOES THE MILKY WAY STRETCH RIGHT ACROSS THE SKY?

Our galaxy has a central bulge, which is surrounded by a huge flat starry disc. The Earth is positioned in the disc, about three-fifths of the way between the galaxy's center and its outside edge. When we look at the Milky Way we are looking at the starry disc that stretches around the Earth, and see it as a starry band across the sky. When we look above or below the disc, we see far fewer stars.

◄ *The galaxies shown here include spirals (top and center right), an irregular (center left), and ellipticals (bottom). Most ellipticals are smaller than spirals, but some contain ten times as many stars as the Milky Way galaxy.*

▼ *Our galaxy's nucleus is surrounded by stars, gas clouds, and dust, bunched together in a spiral pattern. The Sun's position is shown by the yellow circle.*

How far away are the galaxies?

The farther away an object is, the fainter it looks. If we move a light bulb twice as far away, it will look only a quarter as bright as it did before. If we know how much light a particular kind of light bulb gives out, we can work out its distance by comparing the amount of light we see with the amount of light we know it gives out.

Astronomers can measure the distance of a galaxy in a similar way. They know how much light stars of particular types give out. If they can identify such stars in a distant galaxy, they can find out its distance by working out how far away the stars would have to be to appear as faint as they do. The nearest really large galaxy is the Andromeda galaxy, which is 2.2 million light-years away. Even though it is so distant, it can easily be seen with binoculars.

What are active galaxies and quasars?

Some galaxies, called active galaxies, have especially brilliant cores that vary in brightness. Often an active galaxy has jets of material shooting out from its core. Sometimes the jets point towards huge clouds of material that lie far beyond the visible galaxy. Many astronomers believe that a massive black hole lies at the center of each active galaxy. The energy that powers the active galaxy comes from gas falling in towards the black hole.

Quasars are particularly brilliant active galaxies, so bright that we can see their cores at distances of more than ten billion light-years.

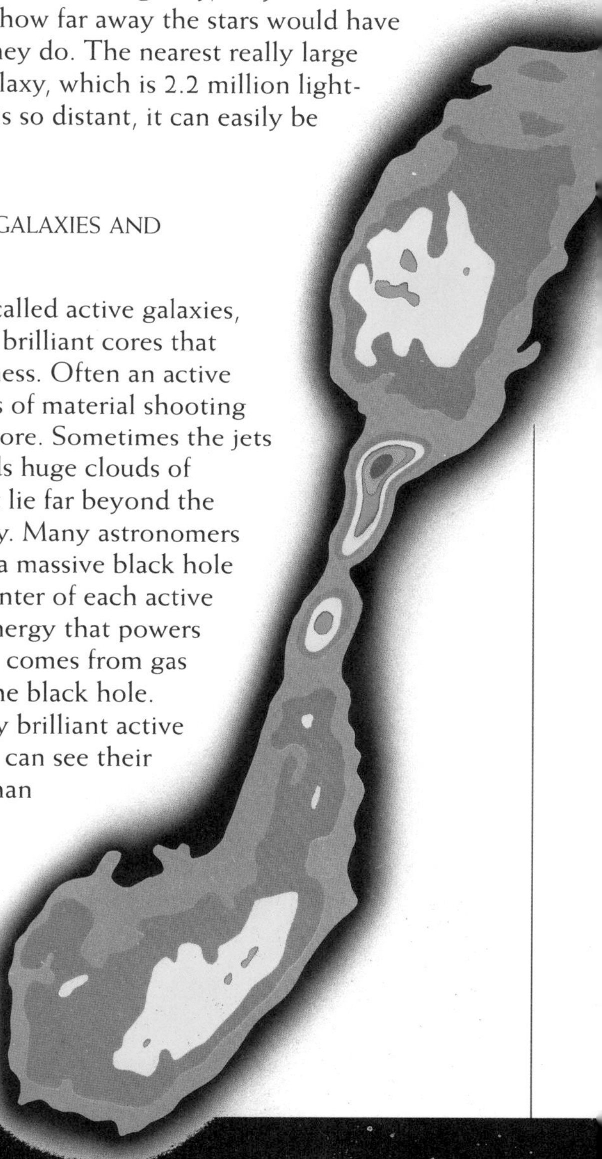

How spread out are the galaxies?

Galaxies exist in groups or clusters. The Milky Way galaxy is part of a small group of about 30 galaxies called the Local Group. Large clusters contain hundreds or even thousands of galaxies. Clusters tend to be grouped together into even larger superclusters, some of which are more than 100 million light-years across. The Local Group is at the outer edge of the Virgo supercluster.

► *Galaxies occur in groups or clusters. The Virgo cluster lies at the center of the Virgo supercluster, which contains about 5,000 galaxies.*

► *This active galaxy has a compact brilliant core connected to two huge clouds of material that emit radio waves.*

Stars

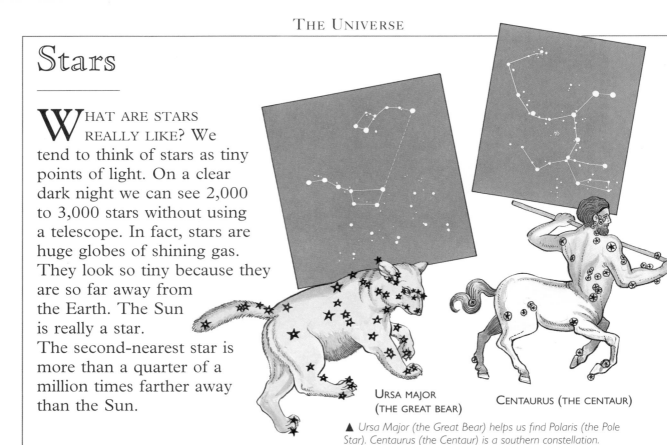

URSA MAJOR
(THE GREAT BEAR)

CENTAURUS (THE CENTAUR)

WHAT ARE STARS REALLY LIKE? We tend to think of stars as tiny points of light. On a clear dark night we can see 2,000 to 3,000 stars without using a telescope. In fact, stars are huge globes of shining gas. They look so tiny because they are so far away from the Earth. The Sun is really a star. The second-nearest star is more than a quarter of a million times farther away than the Sun.

▲ *Ursa Major (the Great Bear) helps us find Polaris (the Pole Star). Centaurus (the Centaur) is a southern constellation.*

WHAT ARE CONSTELLATIONS?

In ancient times, sky-watchers identified patterns of stars. These were named after people and creatures from myths and legends. Some of these star patterns, or constellations, are easy to recognize, but many require a lot of imagination. One of the finest constellations is Ursa Major, which represents a bear. The whole sky has been divided up into 88 constellations.

▼ *Because the Earth turns round, a long-exposure photograph shows stars as trails.*

WHAT IS THE CELESTIAL SPHERE?

The ancient astronomers thought that the stars were fixed to a huge sphere that turned round the Earth. Nowadays we know that the stars appear to move across the sky but that it is the Earth itself which is turning round. However, we still use the idea of a celestial sphere to describe the positions of stars. This imaginary sphere has an equator and poles, just like the Earth.

DO THE STARS MOVE?

Because the Earth spins round from west to east, stars appear to cross the sky from east to west. Stars near the imaginary celestial pole always stay above the horizon, appearing to move in circles round the pole.

WHAT IS THE ZODIAC?

If we could see the stars in daytime, we would see the Sun in front of the distant stars. Because the Earth moves round the Sun, the Sun seems to move round a band of sky called the zodiac. Ancient astronomers divided this band of sky into twelve sections, or 'signs', naming them after the main constellations through which the Sun appears to pass: Aries (the Ram), Taurus (the Bull), Gemini (the Twins), Cancer (the Crab), Leo (the Lion), Virgo (the Virgin), Libra (the Scales), Scorpius (the Scorpion), Sagittarius (the Archer), Capricornus (the Sea-goat), Aquarius (the Water-bearer), and Pisces (the Fishes).

▲ As the Earth moves round the Sun, the Sun appears to pass through a band of constellations called the zodiac.

HOW CAN WE MEASURE THE DISTANCE OF STARS?

Hold up one finger at arm's length. Close your left eye and line up your finger with a distant object, such as a chimney. Then, without moving your finger, open your left eye and close your right. Your finger will no longer be lined up with the object. This is because each eye is looking at your finger from a slightly different position. If astronomers look at a nearby star when the Earth is on one side of the Sun and again, six months later, when the Earth is on the other side, they can measure its tiny shift in position. Knowing the size of the Earth's orbit and the shift, called parallax, they can calculate the star's distance.

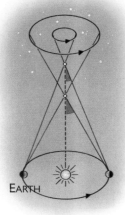

▲ A distant star has a smaller parallax (apparent shift in position) than a nearby one.

WHAT IS A STAR'S 'MAGNITUDE'?

The magnitude of a star is a way of describing its brightness. Very bright stars are of first magnitude and the faintest stars that can be seen with the unaided eye are of sixth magnitude. A few stars are even brighter than first magnitude.

HOW FAR AWAY ARE THE STARS OF ORION?

The constellation of Orion (the Hunter) contains seven particularly bright stars. Although these stars seem quite near to each other in the sky, they are each at very different distances from the Earth. Betelgeuse, the reddish star at the north-east (top left) 'corner', is at a distance of about 300 light years, but Rigel, the brilliant blue-white star at the south-west (bottom right) corner, is three times farther away. The three stars that make up Orion's 'belt', in the middle of the constellation, are even further away. Their names and distances are (from left to right): Alnitak (1,100 light-years), Alnilam (1,200 light-years), and Mintaka (2,300 light-years).

▶ The brightest stars in Orion lie at different distances from us. For example, Rigel (in the bottom right corner) is three times as far as Betelgeuse (in the top left corner).

Stars – Their Birth, Life, and Death

Stars are shining globes of gas, but are they all as hot and bright as the Sun, our nearest star? Their colors give a clue. Yellow stars like the Sun have surface temperatures of around 11,000°F, red stars are cooler (about 5,500°F), and blue stars are much hotter (54,000°F or more). Some stars are hundreds of thousands of times more brilliant than the Sun, others give out less than one ten-thousandth of the Sun's light.

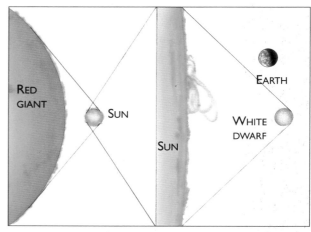

▲ A red giant is much bigger than the Sun, but the Sun is much bigger than a white dwarf.

▶ Betelgeuse, in Orion, is so large that it could easily contain all the planets out to and including Mars.

How big is Betelgeuse?

Betelgeuse is a red supergiant in the constellation of Orion. It is so big that if it were placed at the center of the Solar System, the orbits of the planets Mercury, Venus, the Earth, and Mars would fit well inside its huge globe. Betelgeuse is hundreds of times bigger than the Sun and gives out at least 14,000 times as much light. Some supergiants are even larger than Betelgeuse.

How massive are the stars?

Mass is a measure of the amount of matter that a body contains. When we weigh bodies, a more massive body is heavier than a less massive one. For example, a balloon filled with water is more massive, and heavier, than a balloon filled with air. Brown dwarfs are the least massive stars. At least 12 brown dwarfs would be needed to balance the Sun on a huge pair of scales. Nearly 100 Suns would be needed to balance the most massive supergiant star. A supergiant is so huge that its great mass is spread out very thinly. In white dwarfs and neutron stars – the tiniest stars – matter is squeezed very tightly.

How big are the stars?

Stars similar to the Sun have diameters of about half a million miles. Red giants and supergiants are huge cool stars, some of which are hundreds of times bigger than our Sun. White dwarfs are tiny, hot, compressed stars that are about one hundredth of the Sun's size, about the same size as the Earth. Neutron stars are amazingly small. They have diameters of 6–12 miles, smaller than a major city like London.

▼ On huge pairs of scales a piece of white dwarf material the size of a sugar cube would balance a small car. A 'sugar lump' of neutron star material would balance a small mountain!

HOW LONG DO STARS LIVE?

A star begins as a protostar, a shrinking cloud of gas that eventually becomes hot enough to shine. It is then a 'main sequence' star, which continues to shine because of nuclear reactions in its core. Towards the end of its life, it swells up to become a red giant or supergiant. It soon uses up its remaining fuel, and sheds its outer shell of gases to form a planetary nebula. It then shrinks and fades to become a white dwarf. A star like the Sun will take about ten billion years to reach this stage. A white dwarf finally becomes a black dwarf.

WHERE ARE STARS BORN?

Stars are born inside huge clouds of gas and dust. Some of these clouds, called giant molecular clouds, contain enough material to make a hundred thousand stars. If parts of the cloud are sufficiently dense and cool, gravity will cause them to fall together. As an individual clump of gas and dust collapses, it heats up and, in time, becomes hot enough for nuclear reactions to begin. These reactions turn hydrogen into helium and turn mass into energy. Once these reactions have started, the new arrival becomes a fully-fledged (or 'main sequence') star.

The Orion Nebula, a glowing cloud of gas, is part of a huge star-forming region. It shines because it contains some very hot stars. Astronomers believe that more new stars are also being born behind the visible nebula.

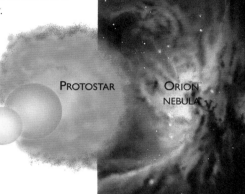

PROTOSTAR   ORION NEBULA

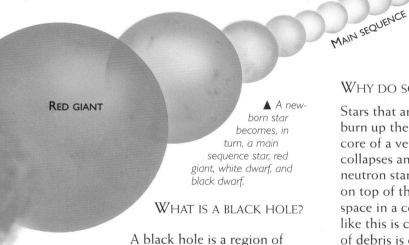

RED GIANT

MAIN SEQUENCE

▲ A new-born star becomes, in turn, a main sequence star, red giant, white dwarf, and black dwarf.

WHAT IS A BLACK HOLE?

A black hole is a region of space where gravity is so strong that nothing, not even light, can escape. A black hole may be formed when an extremely massive star runs out of fuel and collapses on itself. As it continues to collapse, the force of gravity at its surface becomes stronger and stronger until not even light can escape from it. The collapsing star then vanishes from sight and all of its mass falls to the center of the newly-formed black hole.

HOW CAN WE FIND BLACK HOLES?

Although a black hole gives out no light, it still has a gravitational pull. When astronomers find that a star that appears to be on its own is revolving, they know the star is revolving round an invisible companion – which may be a black hole.

WHY DO SOME STARS EXPLODE?

Stars that are much more massive than the Sun burn up their fuel much more quickly. When the core of a very massive star runs out of fuel, it collapses and is squeezed together to form a tiny neutron star. The rest of the star's material falls in on top of the core, rebounds and is blasted off into space in a colossal explosion. A star that explodes like this is called a supernova. The expanding cloud of debris is called a supernova remnant.

▼ The Crab Nebula is the remnant of a supernova that was seen by Chinese astronomers in the year 1054.

The Solar System

METEOROIDS

COMET

JUPITER

MARS

SATURN

VENUS

SUN

EARTH

MERCURY

ASTEROIDS

WHAT IS THE SOLAR SYSTEM? The Solar System consists of the Sun, nine planets and their moons, and a host of smaller bodies – comets, meteoroids, and asteroids. The Sun is by far the biggest and most massive member of the system. In order of distance from the Sun, the planets are: Mercury, Venus, the Earth, Mars (the 'terrestrial' planets); Jupiter, Saturn, Uranus, Neptune (the 'giant' planets); and Pluto.

▲ *The Sun is at the center of the Solar System. The planets, asteroids, comets, and meteoroids revolve around it.*

HOW BIG AND HOW FAR ARE THE PLANETS?

Jupiter, the largest planet, is 11 times the Earth's size. Pluto (the smallest) is smaller than the Earth's Moon. The distance between the Sun and the Earth is about 90 million miles. Mercury is at two-fifths of this distance, while Pluto is about forty times farther away.

JUPITER

▼ *Relative sizes of the Sun, planets, and some of the largest satellites, shown to scale.*

SATURN

MERCURY

VENUS

EARTH

MARS

URANUS

NEPTUNE

PLUTO

SUN

| 0.39 | 0.72 | 1.00 | 1.52 | 5.20 | 9.54 | 19.19 | 30.06 | 39.53 |

DISTANCE FROM SUN (GIVEN IN ASTRONOMICAL UNITS, 1 AU = 90 MILLION MILES)

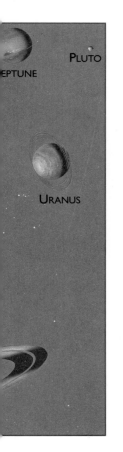

PLANET

PLUTO

EPTUNE

URANUS

WHAT IS AN ORBIT?

An orbit is the path which a planet, comet, or asteroid follows round the Sun, or a satellite (such as the Earth's Moon) follows round a planet. The orbit of a planet is an ellipse, an oval curve that looks like a squashed circle. The point where the planet is closest to the Sun is called perihelion and the point where it is farthest away is called aphelion. A planet moves fastest at perihelion and slowest at aphelion.

SUN

◀ About five billion years ago the Sun began to form at the center of a spinning disc of gas and dust.

◀ Lumps of matter collided with each other, forming planets.

HOW WAS THE SOLAR SYSTEM FORMED?

Nearly five billion years ago, a slowly-rotating cloud of gas and dust began to fall in on itself. As it collapsed, it spun faster and formed a flattened disc. The central part of the disc grew denser and hotter and eventually became the Sun. In the surrounding disc, small particles began to stick together to form larger lumps. These collided with each other to make planets. The giant planets gathered huge amounts of gas around their rocky cores.

▼ The remaining gas and dust blew away.

WHAT WILL HAPPEN TO THE EARTH?

In about five or six billion years, the Sun will swell up to become a huge red giant, 100 times larger and 1,000 times brighter than it is at present. The Earth will lose its atmosphere and the oceans will boil and evaporate into space. The Earth's surface will begin to melt as its temperature soars to over 2,000°F. Eventually, the swollen Sun will shrink, becoming first a white dwarf and then a black dwarf. Whatever is left of our planet by then will become a frozen relic in the weak light of the dying Sun.

FACTS

The Planets
Distance from the Sun
Time taken to travel round Sun

Mercury:	36 million miles
	88 days
Venus:	68 million miles
	224.7 days
Earth:	93 million miles
	365.26 days
Mars:	141 million miles
	687 days
Jupiter:	482 million miles
	11.86 years
Saturn:	885 million miles
	29.46 years
Uranus:	1,779 million miles
	84.01 years
Neptune:	2,788 million miles
	164.8 years
Pluto:	3,658 million miles
	247.7 years

The Sun

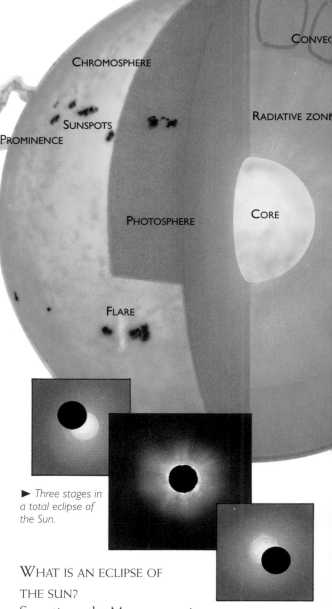

WHAT MAKES THE SUN SO BRIGHT? The Sun is a huge globe of searingly hot gas. With a diameter (width) of 863,000 miles, it is big enough to contain well over a million planets the size of the Earth. Less dense than the Earth, it is composed mainly of the lightest gases – hydrogen and helium. Its dazzling surface, which is called the photosphere, has a temperature of 9,900°F. The photosphere is surrounded by a thin layer of gas called the chromosphere and a huge, faintly glowing atmosphere called the corona.

HOW DOES THE SUN GENERATE ENERGY?

At the center of the Sun, the temperature is so high (nearly 27,000,000°F) that nuclear reactions take place. These reactions release vast amounts of energy. This energy flows out from the Sun's core, through the surrounding gas, to the photosphere and then escapes into space.

WHAT IS THE SOLAR WIND?

Atomic particles (mainly protons and electrons) escape from the Sun's atmosphere and rush out into space at speeds of hundreds of miles per second. This flow of material from the Sun is called the solar wind.

▶ *Three stages in a total eclipse of the Sun.*

WHAT IS AN ECLIPSE OF THE SUN?

Sometimes the Moon passes in front of the Sun. When part of the Sun's surface is covered by the Moon there is a partial eclipse. When the Sun is completely hidden, a total eclipse occurs, and the corona can be seen.

WHAT ARE SUNSPOTS?

Sunspots are patches on the Sun's surface that appear dark because they are cooler than their surroundings. The number of spots increases and decreases over an 11-year period.

◀ *The Earth's magnetic field deflects most solar-wind particles away from our planet but some can get into our atmosphere near the poles. When the particles strike the atmosphere, auroras appear.*

◄ The Sun's core is surrounded by two layers of gas: the radiative zone and the convective zone. Bubbles of hot gas rise through the convective zone to the surface, or photosphere. Sunspots, flares, and prominences are different kinds of short-lived activity on the Sun's surface.

FACTS

Mean distance from Earth 92,800,000 miles	**Composition** 73% hydrogen 25% helium 2% heavier elements
Diameter 863,000 miles (109 times Earth)	**Luminosity** (energy output) 386 million million million million watts
Mass 332,946 Earth's mass	
Mean density 1.409 times water	**Age** 4.6 billion years
Temperature surface 1,000°F center 27,000,000°F corona more than 1,800,000°F	**Distance from center of galaxy** 25,000 light-years
Rotation period at equator 25.38 days	**Time taken to orbit the galaxy** 225,000,000 years

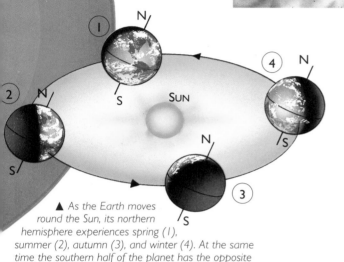

▲ As the Earth moves round the Sun, its northern hemisphere experiences spring (1), summer (2), autumn (3), and winter (4). At the same time the southern half of the planet has the opposite seasons.

WHY DO WE HAVE SEASONS?

The seasons occur because the Earth's axis (the line joining the north and south poles) is tilted. When the Earth is on one side of the Sun (late December), the north pole is in darkness and the south pole has continuous sunlight. This means it is winter in the northern hemisphere and summer in the southern hemisphere. Six months later, when the Earth is on the other side of the Sun, the reverse happens. Spring and autumn occur half way between these two positions. Around 21 March and 22 September (spring and autumn) the Sun is directly overhead at the equator and day and night are exactly equal in length everywhere on the Earth's surface.

WHAT ARE PROMINENCES AND FLARES?

Prominences are huge streamers of hot gas that surge up and down from the Sun's surface or sometimes hang like clouds in the solar atmosphere. Some prominences reach heights of 186,000 miles. Flares are violent explosions that occur above the Sun's surface and release atomic particles, light, X-rays, and other kinds of energy into space.

WHAT ARE AURORAS AND WHAT CAUSES THEM?

Auroras are shimmering patterns of faintly-colored light that are seen when bursts of atomic particles from the Sun strike the thin gases of the upper atmosphere. Sometimes they appear as shapeless glows, but at other times they look like rays, curtains, or curved arches of light that brighten, fade, and shift around. Auroral displays are usually seen in polar skies and are called the northern lights (aurora borealis) or southern lights (aurora australis). Sometimes, after a really big flare on the Sun, bright auroras can be seen near the equator.

▼ Auroras are seen when electrons and protons from space enter the upper atmosphere.

The Earth and Moon

▲ *Seen from space the Earth is mainly blue, showing its predominant feature – water.*

WHY IS THE EARTH SO SPECIAL? The Earth is the third planet in order of distance from the Sun and is the only one that has oceans of liquid water on its surface and large amounts of oxygen in its atmosphere. Above all, it is our home, and the only planet which we know of that supports life of any kind on its surface. It is accompanied on its journey around the Sun by the Moon, the Earth's only natural satellite.

MAR
IMBRI

ARISTACHUS

COPERNICUS

OCEANUS
PROCELLARUM

HOW DO THE EARTH AND MOON COMPARE?

Unlike the Earth, the Moon is a barren, hostile, rocky world with no air or water. It has about a quarter of the Earth's diameter and 0.012 of the Earth's mass.

WHAT IS THE MOON'S SURFACE LIKE?

The most obvious features of the Moon's surface are the dark lava plains, which were called 'seas' by the early astronomers. The Moon is peppered with craters that were produced billions of years ago when asteroids and giant meteorites rained down on its surface.

▼ *The largest rise and fall in the sea's level (spring tides) occurs at New and Full Moon, the smallest (neap tides) at First and Last Quarter.*

WHY DOES THE MOON HAVE PHASES?

The Moon seems to change its shape, or phase, as it moves round the Earth. At New Moon, the Moon's far side is lit up and its Earth-facing side is dark. When the Moon has traveled a quarter of the way round the Earth we see a half-lit Moon (this is called First Quarter). The Earth-facing side is fully illuminated at Full Moon and then the phase begins to shrink.

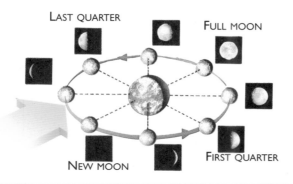

LAST QUARTER

FULL MOON

NEW MOON

FIRST QUARTER

WHAT CAUSES THE TIDES?

The pull of the Moon's gravity causes bulges in the Earth's oceans, one on each side of the planet. As the Earth spins round, every place on its surface passes through two tidal bulges and the sea level rises and falls twice a day. The biggest tides occur when the Sun, which also pulls at the Earth, is in line with the Moon.

► Apollo 15 landed near Mount Hadley in July 1971. The battery-powered Lunar Rover is in the foreground with the landing craft, or Lunar Module, beyond.

MARE SERENITATIS

MARE CRISIUM

APENNINES

MARE TRANQUILLITATIS

MARE FOECUNDITATIS

CLAVIUS

CRUST

CORE

OUTER CORE

MANTLE

▲ The Moon's core is surrounded by several different layers of rock.

WHERE AND WHEN DID PEOPLE FIRST REACH THE MOON?

The first piloted spacecraft to reach the Moon – Apollo 11 – touched down in July 1969 on one of the Moon's dark plains, the Sea of Tranquillity (also known by its Latin name of 'Mare Tranquillitatis'). On July 21, astronauts Neil Armstrong and Edwin Aldrin stepped down onto the lunar surface, collected samples, and set up scientific instruments.

WHY DOES THE MOON KEEP THE SAME FACE TURNED TO THE EARTH?

The Moon spins round on its axis in 27.3 days – exactly the same length of time that it takes to orbit once round the Earth. This means that the same side of the Moon always faces the Earth. To see how it works, get a friend to be the Earth and sit on a chair in the middle of a room while you (as the Moon) walk right round the chair facing the chair all the time. To do this, you will also have to turn steadily round to face each wall of the room in turn.

WHAT IS THE MOON LIKE INSIDE?

Astronomers think that the Moon may have a small iron core surrounded by an outer core of partly molten rock. This, in turn, is surrounded by a thick rocky mantle and a crust made up of less dense rocks.

FACTS

The Moon

Distance from the Earth (center to center):		Diameter:	2,155 miles
mean	238,328 miles	Mass (Earth = 1):	1/81 = 0.012
greatest	252,152 miles	Surface temperature:	
least	220,974 miles	highest	243°F
Orbital period (time		lowest	−261°F
to go round Earth):	27.3 days	Strength of gravity at the Moon's	
Rotation period (time		surface compared to Earth =	
to spin round):	27.3 days	0.165 (multiply your Earthly	
Period of phases (New Moon		weight by 0.165 to see what you	
to New Moon):	29.5 days	would weigh on the Moon)	

Mercury, Venus, and Mars

▲ *Mercury's surface is covered with craters.*

WHAT ARE THE TERRESTRIAL PLANETS? Mercury, Venus, Mars, and the Earth itself, are called the terrestrial ('Earth-like') planets because they resemble the Earth in a number of ways. They are all small dense planets composed of rocks and metals, such as iron and nickel, and they all have solid surfaces on which a spacecraft could land. Despite these similarities, there are also very great differences between them.

WHICH PLANETS SHOW PHASES?

Like the Moon, Mercury and Venus show phases. When either planet passes between the Sun and the Earth its dark side faces us, just like New Moon. As the planet moves away from the Sun it appears as a thin crescent. The phase steadily grows until, when the planet is on the far side of the Sun, we see a fully-lit disc, just like Full Moon.

WHY IS VENUS THE BRIGHTEST PLANET?

Venus is the brightest planet in the sky because it is the closest to us and because it is covered in thick clouds that reflect a lot of sunlight. Its dense atmosphere is mainly made up of the heavy gas carbon dioxide. This acts like a huge blanket, keeping the temperature on the planet's surface as high as 900°F – hot enough to melt lead.

▼ *Venus is covered in clouds that reflect most of the incoming sunlight. The clouds, composed of sulfuric acid droplets, revolve around the planet in about four days.*

WHAT DOES MERCURY LOOK LIKE?

Mercury is the nearest planet to the Sun. With a diameter of 3.024 miles, it is the second-smallest planet in the Solar System. It is a rocky, airless world, with a surface that is completely peppered with craters. Being so close to the Sun, the temperature can rise as high as 800°F near its equator at midday but, with no air to keep in heat, the night-time temperature can drop to –290°F.

WHAT IS IT LIKE ON VENUS?

Most of its searingly hot surface consists of gently undulating plains, but there are some high mountains, deep valleys, and shallow craters, too. The tallest mountains rise to heights of around 7 miles. Venus has some huge volcanoes and many smaller volcanic features. Some of the volcanoes may still be active and, close to them, flashes of lightning may brighten the gloomy cloud-laden sky.

OLYMPUS MONS

THARSIS MONTES

ASCRAEUS MONS

PAVONIS MONS

ARSIA MONS

VALLES MARINERIS

SOLIS PLANUM

WHY IS MARS 'THE RED PLANET'?

Mars looks red in color because its surface is covered with red dusty soil. With about half the Earth's diameter and a tenth of its mass, Mars is a small world. It has a thin atmosphere and no liquid water on its surface, but it does have icy caps at its north and south poles.

▼ *A future Mars lander carrying astronauts is likely to use parachutes and rocket motors to slow down its descent.*

▶ *This region of the martian surface includes volcanoes, valleys, and craters.*

WHAT IS OLYMPUS MONS?

Olympus Mons is the name of the largest volcano on Mars. Long since extinct, this huge volcano is 15 miles tall and 373 miles wide. Mars has several similar volcanoes, many craters, a huge valley system (the Mariner Valleys) that is 2,790 miles long and, in places, 4 miles deep, and some winding channels that look like dried-up river beds. Up until a few decades ago, people thought that life of some kind might exist on Mars, but spacecraft have found no sign of life, not even bacteria in the soil. Mars seems to be a completely lifeless world.

WILL ASTRONAUTS EVER LAND ON MARS?

Several unpiloted craft have already landed on Mars. Space crews are likely to land there in the 21st century as a first step towards setting up a permanent base.

FACTS

Mercury
Closest planet to the Sun (36 million miles)
Orbital period (round Sun): 88 days
Rotation period (on its axis): 59 days
Diameter (across equator): 3.024 miles

Venus
Second planet from Sun (67 million miles)
Orbital period (round Sun): 225 days
Rotation period (on its axis): 243 days
Diameter (across equator): 7,504 miles

Mars
Fourth planet from Sun (141 million miles)
Orbital period (round Sun): 687 days
Rotation period (on its axis): 24 hours 37 minutes
Diameter (across equator): 4,212 miles
Two moons

Jupiter and Saturn

WHICH ARE THE LARGEST PLANETS? Jupiter is the largest planet in the Solar System, with a diameter eleven times that of the Earth. Jupiter's swirling clouds form colorful belts and zones that stretch right round the planet. Saturn, the second-largest planet, has nine times the Earth's diameter. It is surrounded by a beautiful system of rings that can be viewed with quite small telescopes.

◄ Beneath Jupiter's atmosphere are two layers of liquid hydrogen. The inner layer is like liquid metal. It surrounds a hot rocky core.

WHAT IS JUPITER MADE OF?

Jupiter is mainly made up of the elements hydrogen and helium. Apart from a central core of rocks and metals, the planet is a globe of liquid hydrogen and helium, spinning so fast that it bulges out at its equator and is flattened at its poles. Its liquid interior is surrounded by a cloudy atmosphere that is about 600 miles deep.

HOW MANY MOONS DOES JUPITER HAVE?

Jupiter has sixteen moons in all – four large ones and twelve smaller ones. The four largest are Io, Europa, Ganymede, and Callisto. Io and Europa are similar in size to the Earth's Moon, Callisto is larger, and Ganymede, the largest satellite in the Solar System, is bigger than the planet Mercury.

WHICH MOON HAS VOLCANOES?

Io has violently active volcanoes that throw plumes of sulfur-rich material to heights as great as 180 miles. The eruptions have covered Io's entire surface with this material, giving it a yellowish color.

WHAT DID THE GALILEO SPACECRAFT DO?

Launched from Earth in 1989, Galileo reached Jupiter in December 1995. One part of the spacecraft went into orbit round Jupiter to study the planet and its moons while the other plunged into the planet to study its atmosphere and clouds.

▼ Galileo's atmospheric probe parachuted down through Jupiter's cloud layers on 7 December 1995 and transmitted a host of valuable data which was relayed to Earth by the Galileo orbiter.

▼ Jupiter's moons: Ganymede and Callisto are made of rock and ice, Europa is coated with ice, and Io is a rocky world with active volcanoes. The outermost satellites are probably captured asteroids.

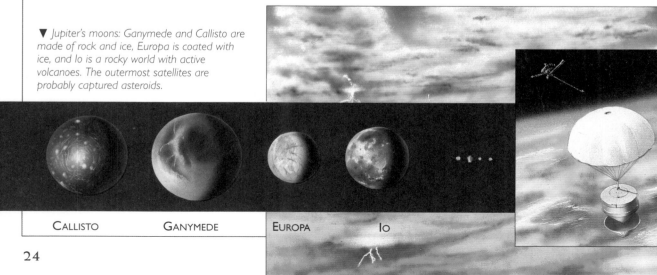

CALLISTO   GANYMEDE   EUROPA   Io

WHAT IS SPECIAL ABOUT SATURN?

Saturn is the most distant planet that can be seen without a telescope or binoculars. Like Jupiter, this giant world is composed mainly of liquid hydrogen and helium and its deep atmosphere contains belts and zones of swirling clouds. The most amazing thing about Saturn is its huge system of rings, the main part of which is 169,000 miles in diameter but less than one mile thick. Saturn has at least eighteen moons. Titan, its largest moon, has a dense atmosphere that is composed mainly of nitrogen.

▲ Around Jupiter's cloud-streaked globe is a faint, thin ring of dust.

▼ Saturn's cloud belts are not as varied and colorful as those of Jupiter. The prominent gap in the rings is called the Cassini division.

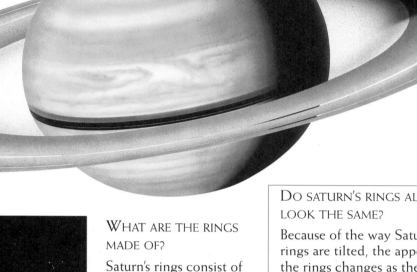

WHAT ARE THE RINGS MADE OF?

Saturn's rings consist of billions of orbiting particles that are made of rock or ice. The ring particles vary in size – some are as small as grains of dust while others are as big as houses.

DO SATURN'S RINGS ALWAYS LOOK THE SAME?

Because of the way Saturn and its rings are tilted, the appearance of the rings changes as the planet moves round the Sun. Every 14 or 15 years, the rings are sideways-on to us and are so thin they appear to vanish. At other times we see the north or south face of the rings.

FACTS

Jupiter
Fifth planet from the Sun
(482 million miles)
Orbital period: 11.86 years
Rotation period: 9 hours 55 minutes
Diameter (at equator): 88,650 miles
Diameter (pole to pole): 82,894 miles
Mass (Earth = 1): 317.9
Density (water = 1): 1.33
Sixteen moons

Saturn
Sixth planet from the Sun
(885 million miles)
Orbital period: 29.46 years
Rotation period: 10 hours 39 minutes
Diameter (at equator): 74,732 miles
Diameter (pole to pole): 67,411 miles
Mass (Earth = 1): 95.2
Density (water = 1): 0.71
Eighteen moons

Uranus, Neptune, and Pluto

WHICH ARE THE MOST DISTANT PLANETS? Uranus, Neptune, and Pluto are the outermost planets in the Solar System. Too faint to be seen without a telescope, Uranus was discovered in 1781, Neptune in 1846, and Pluto in 1930. Uranus and Neptune are giants, each four times the size of the Earth, but Pluto is smaller than the Moon.

▼ The core of Uranus is surrounded by layers of ice, water, and gas.

DOES URANUS HAVE RINGS?

Uranus has ten narrow rings, composed of rocky boulders, and one broader, dusty ring. The rings, which are all rather dark and faint, were discovered in 1977 when Uranus passed in front of a distant star. The star's light flickered several times before it disappeared behind the planet and again after it reappeared. Each dip in brightness was caused by one of the rings. Detailed images of the rings were transmitted by the *Voyager* 2 spacecraft in 1986.

▼ It takes Uranus 84 years to go through a cycle of seasons.

2028 2007 SUN 2049 1986

WHAT IS ODD ABOUT URANUS?

The axis of Uranus is tilted over at an angle of 98 degrees so that the planet rotates almost on its side. Because Uranus takes 84 years to go round the Sun, each pole experiences nearly 42 years of sunlight followed by nearly 42 years of darkness!

WHAT ARE URANUS AND NEPTUNE MADE OF?

Uranus and Neptune are mainly made up of hydrogen, helium, and ices of various kinds. The rocky core of each planet is probably surrounded by a mantle of water or slushy ice and a deep, hazy, hydrogen-rich atmosphere.

WHAT IS SPECIAL ABOUT TRITON?

With a temperature of −391°F, Triton's icy surface is one of the coldest places in the Solar System. Triton has a very thin atmosphere that is mainly made up of nitrogen gas and strange volcanoes, or geysers, that eject plumes of gas, ice, and dust.

WHAT IS NEPTUNE LIKE?

Neptune has cloud belts that lie deep down in its hazy blue atmosphere. The planet is surrounded by two narrow and two broader rings, each of which is very faint. Neptune has eight moons. Triton, its largest moon, has a diameter of 1,677 miles and, unusually, travels round the planet in the opposite direction to the planet's spin. The other moons are small irregular bodies that are between 30 and 260 miles in size.

▲ Geysers eject dusty plumes of nitrogen which drift downwind in Triton's thin atmosphere.

WHAT IS STRANGE ABOUT PLUTO'S ORBIT?

Pluto is so far away that it takes nearly 248 years to go round the Sun. Because its orbit is an elongated ellipse (oval shape), its distance from the Sun varies between 2,745 million and 4,570 million miles, and when it is near perihelion (its closest point to the Sun) it is actually closer to the Sun than Neptune is. Pluto crossed inside the orbit of Neptune in 1979, and did not regain its title of 'most distant planet' until 1999. Pluto's orbit is tilted at an angle of 17 degrees so that it passes above Neptune's orbit at each crossing and there is no chance of a collision.

PLUTO'S ORBIT

▲ At perihelion, Pluto is closer to the Sun than Neptune is.

NEPTUNE'S ORBIT

FACTS

Uranus
Seventh planet from the Sun (1,779 million miles)
Orbital period: 84.01 years
Rotation period: 17 hours 14 minutes
Diameter: 31,693 miles
Mass (Earth = 1): 14.6
Density (water = 1): 1.27
Fifteen moons

Neptune
Eighth planet from the Sun (2,788 million miles)
Orbital period: 164.8 years
Rotation period: 16 hours 6 minutes
Diameter: 30,707 miles
Mass (Earth = 1): 17.2
Density (water = 1): 1.76
Eight moons

Pluto
Ninth planet from the Sun (3,658 million miles)
Orbital period: 247.7 years
Rotation period: 6.4 days

Diameter: 1,427 miles
Mass (Earth = 1): 0.0022
Density (water = 1): 2.0
One moon

WHAT WOULD IT BE LIKE ON PLUTO?

Composed of rock and ice, Pluto is a frigid world whose surface is probably coated with frozen methane. When it approaches perihelion, some of this methane evaporates to give a very thin atmosphere. We do not have any images of Pluto's surface because no spacecraft has ever been there, but many astronomers believe it will look rather like Triton. Seen from the surface of Pluto, the Sun would be so small that it would look just like a dazzling star.

◄ The bluish globe of Neptune, viewed from above Triton. The dark streaks on Triton's icy surface are made by the dust from its geysers.

DOES PLUTO HAVE A MOON?

Pluto has one moon, Charon, which revolves round the planet once every 6.4 days. With a diameter of 735 miles, it is just over half the size of Pluto itself. This is much larger than any other moon when compared to the size of its planet. Pluto spins round on its axis in 6.4 days and so keeps the same side turned toward Charon all the time.

▲ A rare event – Charon passes between Pluto and the Sun causing an eclipse and casting its shadow onto the planet's icy surface.

Asteroids, Meteorites, and Comets

▼ Ceres, the largest asteroid, is about a quarter of the size of the Moon. Some are little bigger than the Empire State Building in New York City.

MOON

CERES

WHAT ARE ASTEROIDS, METEORITES, AND COMETS? Asteroids are small bodies that travel round the Sun like tiny planets, while meteorites are lumps of rock or iron that can strike a planet's surface. Comets are icy bodies that develop a glowing head and tail when they approach the Sun.

HOW BIG ARE ASTEROIDS?

The largest asteroid, which is called Ceres, has a diameter of 580 miles. Most are very much smaller. There may be half a million asteroids that are a little less than a mile in diameter and many more that are even smaller.

WHAT DO ASTEROIDS LOOK LIKE?

Although Ceres is spherical, most asteroids are irregular in shape. The Galileo spacecraft produced images of two asteroids, Gaspra and Ida. They showed that these asteroids were irregular bodies with cratered surfaces.

WHERE DO METEORITES COME FROM?

Most meteorites are believed to be fragments of rock or iron that are produced when asteroids collide. Some of these fragments are thrown into paths that collide with the planet Earth.

▲ When asteroids crash into each other, fragments are scattered. They still orbit the Sun but may crash into planets.

WHAT HAPPENS WHEN A METEORITE HITS THE EARTH?

Meteorites enter the atmosphere at speeds of between 25,000 and 60,000 miles per hour. Small meteorites slow down as they pass through the atmosphere and land in one piece or in fragments, but very massive meteorites hit the ground so violently that they blast out craters. The best-known meteorite crater is in Arizona. Produced about 25,000 years ago, it is 4,149 feet wide and 574 feet deep. Some scientists think that the dinosaurs were wiped out when a 5-mile asteroid struck our planet about 65 million years ago.

◄ Meteor Crater in Arizona is believed to be the result of a 50,000-ton iron meteorite blasting out the ground.

HOW DOES A COMET BEHAVE?

A comet usually follows a very elongated orbit. As it approaches the Sun, gas and dust evaporate from the surface of the nucleus (the main body of ice and dust) and spread out to form the coma, the 'head' of the comet. Gas and dust are further driven out of the coma to form one or more tails. As the comet is moving toward the Sun, it continues to brighten and its tail grows larger. As it moves away again, the comet fades and its tail shrinks. The tails of comets always point away from the Sun.

▼ *As a comet approaches the Sun, its gas is driven out by the solar wind to form a long narrow tail and its dust is pushed out by sunlight to form a broad curving tail.*

WHICH COMET COLLIDED WITH JUPITER?

Comet Shoemaker-Levy 9 (named after the astronomers who discovered it) collided with Jupiter in July 1994. The comet had previously been captured into an orbit round Jupiter and, in 1992, passed so close to Jupiter that its nucleus was broken into about 20 fragments. When the fragments fell back, they plunged one by one into the giant planet's atmosphere in a series of spectacular impacts. Each explosion released as much energy as half a million megatons of TNT. Although the impacts happened on the far side of the planet, astronomers could see huge fireballs rising beyond the edge of the planet's globe, and Jupiter's rapid rotation soon brought into view the dark 'scars' that had been left in the planet's cloud layers. This amazing event has told astronomers a lot about the nature of comets and the make-up of Jupiter's atmosphere.

◄ *Giotto hurtled through Halley's comet at around 155,000 miles per hour. The spacecraft had a shield at the front because, at that speed, even tiny bits of dust or ice could have caused a lot of damage.*

▶ *Because meteoroids travel in the same direction, meteor showers appear to spread out from a single point in the sky.*

◄ *A meteor shower takes place when the Earth passes through a stream of meteoroids.*

WHAT WAS THE *GIOTTO* PROBE?

Giotto was the name of a European spacecraft that flew past the nucleus of Halley's comet, the most famous comet, in 1986. Halley's comet is named after Edmond Halley, the seventeenth-century astronomer who was the first to realize that comets actually travel in orbits round the Sun. Images taken by *Giotto* showed that the nucleus of Halley's comet was an irregular lump of ice with a dark dusty skin. It measured 9 by 5 by 5 miles. Jets of gas and dust escaping from cracks and craters in the nucleus provided material for its coma and tail.

WHAT IS A METEOR?

A meteor is a short-lived streak of light that is seen when a tiny particle – a meteoroid – plunges into the atmosphere and is destroyed. Meteoroids orbit around the Sun and most of them are smaller than a grain of sand. A meteor shower is seen when the Earth crosses a stream of meteoroids.

Astronomy – Early and Modern

HOW HAS ASTRONOMY CHANGED OVER THE YEARS? For thousands of years, people had to study the heavens with their eyes alone. When the telescope was invented, nearly 400 years ago, it enabled astronomers to see much fainter, more distant, objects in far more detail than the eye alone could see. Throughout the twentieth century, astronomers have built bigger and bigger telescopes.

WHICH IS THE WORLD'S LARGEST TELESCOPE?

The largest telescope in the world is the Keck telescope, which is located at an altitude of 13,776 feet on the summit of Mauna Kea, a high mountain in Hawaii. Its main mirror is 33 feet across.

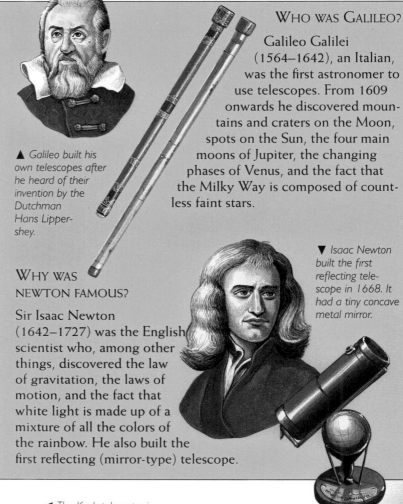

▲ Galileo built his own telescopes after he heard of their invention by the Dutchman Hans Lippershey.

WHO WAS GALILEO?

Galileo Galilei (1564–1642), an Italian, was the first astronomer to use telescopes. From 1609 onwards he discovered mountains and craters on the Moon, spots on the Sun, the four main moons of Jupiter, the changing phases of Venus, and the fact that the Milky Way is composed of countless faint stars.

▼ Isaac Newton built the first reflecting telescope in 1668. It had a tiny concave metal mirror.

WHY WAS NEWTON FAMOUS?

Sir Isaac Newton (1642–1727) was the English scientist who, among other things, discovered the law of gravitation, the laws of motion, and the fact that white light is made up of a mixture of all the colors of the rainbow. He also built the first reflecting (mirror-type) telescope.

◄ The Keck telescope is housed in a huge dome. Its main mirror consists of 36 segments that are linked together and are controlled by computer to give the correct shape. The telescope weighs nearly 270 tons.

WHAT IS THE HUBBLE SPACE TELESCOPE?

The Hubble Space Telescope, named after the American astronomer Edwin Hubble, is the largest optical (visible-light) telescope ever to be put in space. A reflecting telescope with a 11-foot mirror, it orbits the Earth at a height of 370 miles.

WHAT IS A RADIO TELESCOPE?

Many distant objects in space give out radio waves that travel through space at the speed of light and can penetrate down through our atmosphere. A radio telescope collects these waves, often using a huge concave metal dish that focuses the waves onto a radio receiver. By studying these radio waves, astronomers can build up a picture of what a radio source in the sky looks like. Sources of radio waves include the Sun, the planet Jupiter, gas clouds in space, supernova remnants (the debris of exploded stars), and active galaxies.

► The largest steerable radio telescope is at Effelsberg, in Germany. Its dish is 330 feet across.

HOW ARE ASTRONOMICAL IMAGES PRODUCED?

Astronomers use photography or electronic devices to record images (pictures) of distant objects. A photograph can record thousands of star images at one time and can 'see' stars much fainter than the human eye can. But photographic emulsions (the light-sensitive material on films or plates) are not very efficient. They record only a tiny fraction of the light that falls on them. Electronic devices are much more efficient and so can detect much fainter objects than photography can. Electronic information can easily be processed by computers to give sharper images or to bring out details that photographs cannot show.

▼ Light from the Hubble Telescope's main mirror bounces off a smaller mirror onto a bank of instruments.

WHY DO ASTRONOMERS USE SATELLITES?

Many kinds of radiation (waves) from space cannot get through the atmosphere and can only be studied from orbiting satellites. These radiations include gamma rays, X-rays, ultraviolet light, and infrared radiation (the faint heat from distant objects). Satellites also study atomic particles and magnetic fields.

WHAT CAN AMATEUR ASTRONOMERS DO?

Looking at the night sky and identifying stars and planets is great fun, even without a telescope or binoculars. A good pair of binoculars will show craters on the Moon, the main moons of Jupiter, star clusters, and the Orion nebula. A telescope will show fainter objects and much more detail. Amateur astronomers sometimes make important discoveries such as new comets or novae (stars that suddenly flare up in brightness).

►Useful observing equipment includes a star map, a red torch (to avoid dazzle), binoculars, a telescope, and a camera.

Space Travel

HOW FAST MUST A SPACECRAFT GO? The faster you throw a ball, the higher it will rise before it falls back. If you could throw it faster than 25,000 miles per hour, it would never return. This speed is the Earth's escape velocity, the minimum speed that an interplanetary spacecraft must reach.

▶ The Saturn V consisted of three sections, or stages, stacked on top of each other. Each stage dropped off when it ran out of fuel.

▶ This map shows the landing sites of each of the Apollo spacecraft. The first landing was in the relatively smooth Sea of Tranquillity. Later missions explored rougher terrain.

A15 A17
A12 A11
A14
A16

WHAT WAS THE WORLD'S BIGGEST ROCKET?

The Saturn V, which was used to launch the Apollo missions to the Moon, was the longest and most powerful rocket ever built. With an Apollo spacecraft mounted on top, it stood 360 feet tall – as long as a football pitch – and weighed 2,900 tons.

HOW MANY APOLLOS LANDED ON THE MOON?

Six crewed missions have landed on the Moon: Apollos 11, 12, 14, 15, 16, and 17. Apollo 11 touched down July 20 1969. Apollo 13 suffered damage on the way to the Moon, did not land, but returned safely to Earth. The last mission, Apollo 17, landed on the lunar surface on December 11 1972.

WHAT IS THE SPACE SHUTTLE?

The American Space Shuttle is a reusable spacecraft that takes off vertically, like a rocket, but lands on a runway like an aircraft. At launch, the delta-winged orbiter is attached to a huge external tank (ET) that supplies fuel to its main engines. Two solid-fueled booster rockets (SRBs) fixed to the ET provide extra thrust for the first two minutes of the flight and then drop off. The ET drops off soon afterward. The orbiter's cargo bay measures 59 feet by 15 feet and can carry up to 29.5 tons of cargo, such as satellites, spacecraft, or a crewed laboratory.

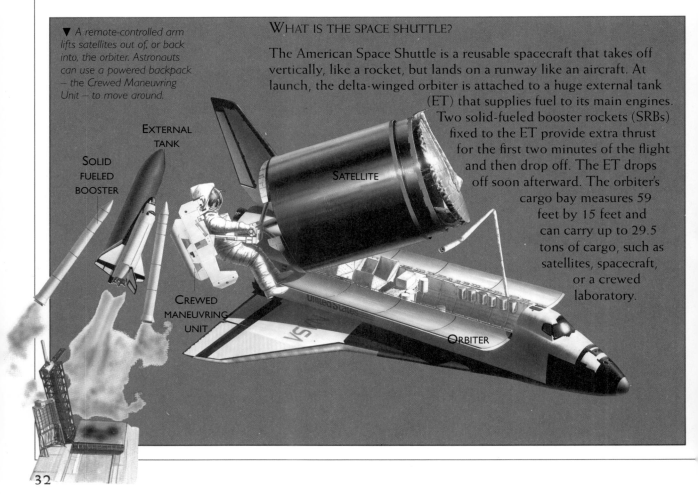

▼ A remote-controlled arm lifts satellites out of, or back into, the orbiter. Astronauts can use a powered backpack – the Crewed Maneuvring Unit – to move around.

EXTERNAL TANK

SOLID FUELED BOOSTER

SATELLITE

CREWED MANEUVRING UNIT

ORBITER

▶ Voyager 2 flew past Jupiter in 1979, Saturn in 1981, Uranus in 1986, and Neptune in 1989

WHAT ROUTE DID *VOYAGER* 2 FOLLOW?

When the giant planets were lined up in a special way that would not happen again for about 180 years, the *Voyager* 2 spacecraft was able to fly past Jupiter, Saturn, Uranus, and Neptune on a single mission. Each time *Voyager* passed a planet it used the planet's gravity to pick up extra speed. Launched from Earth in 1977, it flew past Neptune in 1989 and is now heading towards interstellar space (the space between the stars).

▼ Space station (ISS) will have living and experimental areas. Electrical power will be supplied by solar panels.

CASSINI

HUYGHENS

TITAN

▲ The Huyghens probe will be released when Cassini makes the first of many fly-bys of Saturn's moon, Titan.

WHAT IS A SPACE STATION?

A space station is a large orbiting structure in which crews can live and work for long periods of time. Among other things, it can be used as a space observatory for studying the Earth and the universe, as a laboratory for carrying out experiments in zero gravity, and as a servicing center for satellites and spacecraft. The United States and Russia, together with Europe, Japan, and Canada, are joining forces to build an international space station, (ISS). Work on assembling the station began in 1998.

WHAT IS THE *CASSINI-HUYGHENS* MISSION?

The *Cassini* spacecraft was launched in 1997 to begin a four-year study of the planet Saturn and its moons. It should enter orbit around Saturn in 2004. In 2005 it will drop a probe called *Huyghens* through the atmosphere of the giant moon Titan onto its surface.

FACTS

1957 (Oct 4): Launching of Sputnik 1 (USSR), the first artificial satellite
1959 (Oct 7): Luna 3 (USSR), takes first images of far side of the Moon
1961 (Apr 12): Yuri Gagarin (USSR), on board Vostok 1, is first human in space
1962 (Dec 14): Mariner 2 (USA), first Venus fly-by
1965 (Jul 14): Mariner 4 (USA), first Mars fly-by
1966 (Feb 3): Luna 9 (USSR), first soft-landing on Moon
1968 (Dec 24): Apollo 8 (USA), first crewed craft to orbit the Moon
1969 (July 20): Apollo 11 (USA), first crewed landing on Moon

1970 (Dec 15): Venera 7 (USSR), first soft-landing on surface of Venus
1971 (Nov 14): Mariner 9 (USA), first Mars orbiter
1973 (Dec 3): Pioneer 10 (USA), first Jupiter fly-by
1974 (Mar 29): Mariner 10 (USA), first Mercury fly-by
1976 (Jul 20): Viking 1 (USA), first Mars lander
1979 (Sep 1): Pioneer 11 (USA), first Saturn fly-by
1986 (Jan 24): Voyager 2 (USA), first Uranus fly-by
1989 (Aug 25): Voyager 2 (USA), first Neptune fly-by
1995 (Dec 7): Galileo (USA), first Jupiter orbiter and atmospheric probe

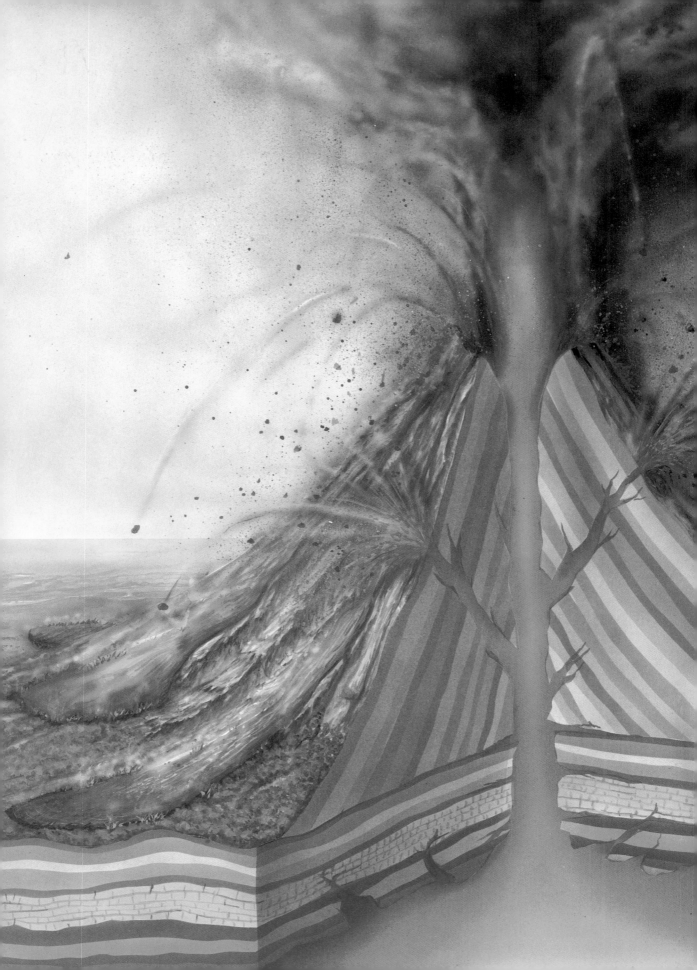

Part 2

THE EARTH

Dynamic Earth

WHAT DO WE KNOW ABOUT THE EARTH? The Earth is the third planet from the Sun. As it is our home it is the planet that is best-known to us. Even so, we are only really familiar with the outer surface, the part that we can see. Deep below our feet there are layers and structures that we only know about indirectly. Volcanoes and earthquakes are signs of the huge, slow-moving forces at work within the Earth.

WHAT IS INSIDE THE EARTH?

The Earth is made up of layers. Its center, or core, is made of iron. The inner core is so tightly packed that it is a solid mass, even though it has an incredibly high temperature. The outer core, however, is molten (liquid) iron. Between the core and the crust, making up the bulk of the Earth, is the mantle. This part is made of a stony material and is solid, although there is a softer area near the crust. Mantle rocks are very dense and heavy.

WHY ARE THERE MOUNTAINS?

The crust is the portion of the Earth's structure that we can see and sample directly. It is not an even surface covering, but forms hollows that are full of water, which are the oceans, lumps that form the continents, and ridges and wrinkles that are the great mountain chains. The outer surface of the Earth is constantly moving, and this movement produces the mountains and the oceans.

INNER CORE

OUTER CORE

OCEANIC CRUST

LOWER MANTLE

UPPER MANTLE

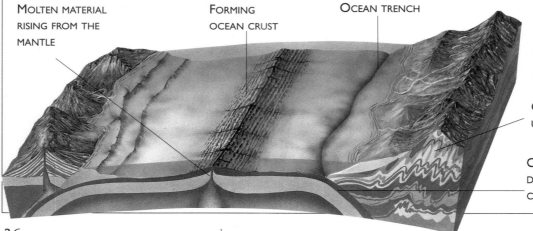

MOLTEN MATERIAL RISING FROM THE MANTLE

FORMING OCEAN CRUST

OCEAN TRENCH

◀ *The ocean crust grows outward from the oceanic ridges. As it grows, some parts of the crust push against others, building up mountains.*

CONTINENT CRUMPLING UP INTO MOUNTAINS

OCEAN CRUST GRINDING DOWN BENEATH CONTINENTAL CRUST

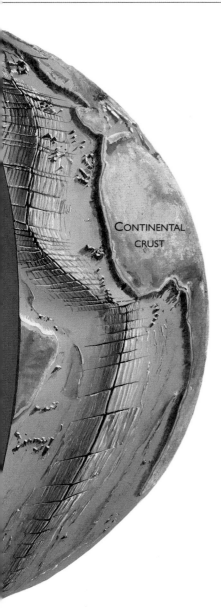

CONTINENTAL CRUST

IS THE EARTH'S SURFACE MOVING?

Scientists have been able to work out that the Earth's continents were in different positions in the past. This movement is called plate tectonics and it is a result of the Earth's surface being constantly created and destroyed. Imagine that the surface of the Earth consists of individual plates, like the panels of a football. They are made up of the crust and the upper mantle. Each plate is growing along one edge and being destroyed along another. The growing edges lie along the oceans. They produce the volcanic ridges that run along the floor of every ocean. The edges being destroyed are the deep ocean trenches that lie along the edges of some continents.

DO ROCKS BEND OR BREAK?

Rocks, hard as they look, cannot remain solid and unmoving for long. The moving continents compress them as one plate pushes against another. The various layers also crumple up on each other to form 'folds'. This process gives rise to fold mountains. When the continents are pulled apart they split into blocks, which drop or rise to different positions along cracks called faults.

▲ At the beginning of the age of dinosaurs, 200 million years ago, all the continents were together as one vast landmass.

▲ At the height of the dinosaurs' reign, 100 million years ago, this supercontinent had begun to break up.

▲ When the age of mammals had begun, 50 million years ago, the continents were drifting toward their present positions.

WHAT HAPPENS WHEN A FAULT MOVES?

The movement of rock masses along a fault can be sudden and very dangerous, and can be experienced as an earthquake. The forces that move the continents can build up to such an extent that the rocks cannot take the strain any more. They crack and shift to a new position. The shock waves sent out can bring down cities, send giant sea waves crashing over coastal towns, and cause great loss of life.

▲ As rocks are compressed they crumple up forming 'folds' that rise and fall in different positions along faults.

► Shock waves can destroy cities and crack roads.

Volcanoes

WHAT GOES ON INSIDE A VOLCANO? We have all seen pictures of volcanoes erupting. Smoke and gas belch out of a crater while molten rock bursts upward from the Earth's interior spreading deadly hot lava over the landscape. At every moment there is volcanic activity taking place somewhere on the Earth's surface, mostly where the Earth's surface plates are meeting or pulling apart.

▲ Glowing basaltic lava spurts out of a volcano, forming a spectacular fire fountain.

CAN ERUPTIONS BE GENTLE?

Some volcanic eruptions are more spectacular than dangerous. Where the Earth's plates pull apart rather than collide, the molten material comes straight up from the Earth's mantle. Usually the eruption is from the ocean floor. The molten rock is relatively low in a mineral called silica, leaving it soft and runny. As a result the lava flows for long distances before becoming solid. This kind of lava is called basalt, and the volcano shape it produces is broad and low. The volcanoes of Iceland, a country lying on the

WHEN ARE VOLCANOES MOST DANGEROUS?

Wherever two of the Earth's plates are colliding, one slides beneath the other and melts. This molten plate material eventually rises through the plate above and bursts through to form a volcano. The molten material of these volcanoes is rich in silica, which makes it stiff and sticky. It often solidifies before it can burst out, blocking an eruption. However, pressures build up beneath the plug that has formed and when the eruption finally comes it does so with a great explosion. The kind of lava it produces is called andesite. Andesitic volcanoes are high and steep-sided and have very dangerous eruptions. They are found in mountain chains and in island arcs around the edges of oceans.

▶ A cut-out section of an andesitic volcano shows it formed out of a series of explosions and a build-up of ash and lava.

THICK CLOUDS OF HOT ASH

THE VENT IS OFTEN PLUGGED BY A SOLID MASS OF ROCK

VOLCANIC CONE BUILT UP FROM LAYERS OF ASH AND LAVA

ERUPTIONS COME FROM THE SIDES AS WELL AS THE TOP OF A VOLCANO

IS VOLCANIC ASH DEADLY?

Lava ash is the great volcanic killer. Vesuvius is a typical andesitic volcano. It is in the Mediterranean where the African and European plates meet. Its cone rises from the remains of a huge crater that was formed by an ancient explosion. In AD59 it erupted throwing masses of hot smothering ash over the towns of Pompeii and Herculaneum. An andesitic eruption usually involves ash rather than lava. In 1908 the town of St. Pierre in Martinique was flooded by white-hot ash from the nearby volcano Mont Pelée. The pressure built up in the volcano until the hot ash finally burst out fizzing with compressed gas. It flowed down the mountainside like water, destroying everything in its path. A total of 29,000 people died.

◀ A dog, caught in the tortured moment of death, as it suffocated in the ash that fell from Mount Vesuvius in AD59.

WHAT EFFECT CAN VOLCANOES HAVE UNDERGROUND?

Water circulating through rocks underground is often heated by volcanic action. It may then return to the surface in the form of hot springs. Sometimes it boils up under pressure, producing hot fountains called geysers. Along ocean ridges, hot springs bring up minerals that form fantastic shapes and structures on the ocean bed. The springs also support weird forms of animal life.

▼ When hot water boils underground the expanding steam pushes the water up until it forms a geyser. With the pressure released, the water falls back, is heated again, and bursts out minutes later.

FACTS

Santorini
Location: Mediterranean Sea
Eruption: 1550 BC
Result: destroyed Minoan civilization on nearby Crete

Krakatau
Location: Sunda Strait (East Indies)
Eruption: 1883
Result: sent giant sea waves half-way round the world

Tambora
Location: Jumbawa, Indonesia
Eruption: 1815
Result: killed 90,000 people

Mount Saint Helens
Location: Washington State, USA
Eruption: 1980
Result: ash flows traveled 17 miles and killed 60 people

Rocks and Minerals

W HAT ARE ROCKS AND MINERALS? When we think of minerals we usually think of precious stones made into jewelry or works of art, or the ores (such as iron ore) used by our industries. But the whole world is made of minerals. Minerals are the building blocks from which all rocks are made. If you look at a rock through a microscope, you will see that it consists of tiny fragments or crystals. Each of these tiny crystals is made of a mineral.

► Igneous rock, such as this granite, often has visible crystals in it.

WHICH ROCKS CAME FROM FIRE?

There are three basic types of rock. Each type is formed in a different way. One group are the igneous rocks – those born in fire. Hot molten material from inside the Earth forms a liquid called magma. This can some-times burst out onto the surface of the Earth as a hot lava, or it may solidify below the Earth's surface. Either way, the once fiery material cools and solidifies into mineral crystals, and these eventually bind together to form rock. Extrusive igneous rocks form when hot lava cools quickly on the surface of the Earth. Intrusive igneous rocks form when it cools slowly underground.

MOLTEN MATERIAL ON THE SURFACE HARDENS INTO IGNEOUS ROCK

HEAT FROM IGNEOUS ROCK COOKS THE SURROUNDING ROCKS TO FORM METAMORPHIC ROCK

HOT MOLTEN MATERIAL RISES TO THE SURFACE

WHAT ARE METAMORPHIC ROCKS?

Sometimes rocks that already exist are changed by great heat or pressure. The rocks they become are called metamorphic rocks. They usually form in mountains where heat and pressure are so great they force new minerals to grow. There are two kinds of metamorphic rock. Heat forms thermal metamorphic rock, and pressure forms regional metamorphic rock. During any 'metamorphism' the rock never actually melts.

SEDIMENTS TURN INTO SEDIMENTARY ROCK

◄ Metamorphic rock, such as this banded gneiss, often shows by the twists in its bands that it was formed under great pressure.

DO ROCKS CHANGE?

Rocks do not remain the same forever. They are being worn away all the time and the loose fragments become part of new rocks. The weather gradually erodes (wears away) the rocks that are at the Earth's surface. The fragments are washed down to the sea where they fall in layers on the sea bed and very gradually turn into sedimentary rocks. These may be buried so deeply that they become metamorphic rocks, or they may melt to become igneous rocks. At any stage they may turn up at the Earth's surface and be broken down again. This constant turnover of the Earth's minerals and rocks is called the rock cycle.

▶ Crystals may be square and chunky, or flat and plate-like, or even long and needle-like, as in this piece of scolecite.

◀ A section of any landscape at any time would reveal the turnover of mineral material that makes up the rock cycle.

WHAT GIVES CRYSTALS THEIR SHAPE?

As a mineral forms, its atoms arrange themselves into a particular pattern. When its atoms have a regular, ordered pattern the mineral grows as a crystal. Crystals have geometric, three-dimensional shapes, with clearly defined and smooth 'faces'. Crystals are usually jammed in against one another within a rock and do not form clear shapes. Sometimes, however, if the mineral is growing in a cavity or in a liquid, it has space to grow and a beautiful crystal shape develops. Crystals can vary in size from microscopic to several feet long.

ERODED MATERIAL WASHES DOWN TO THE SEA

◀ Many sedimentary rocks are made up of the remains of organisms. In the rock shown, the shells of sea creatures are clearly visible.

HOW DO SEDIMENTARY ROCKS FORM?

Sedimentary rocks are formed from particles laid down in layers, usually at the bottom of the sea. As the layers build up, the particles become cemented into a solid mass, or rock. Most sedimentary rocks are formed from particles of broken rocks that already existed. Some are formed from particles that were once part of living things, such as ancient forests. Others are formed from minerals, such as salts that crystallize out of seawater.

WHEN IS A MINERAL A GEM?

Some minerals are really beautiful, because of their color, clearness, or crystal shape. Such minerals are valuable because they can be cut and polished and used in works of art or turned into jewelry. They may also be very rare. These minerals are called gemstones.

Fossils

W HAT ARE FOSSILS? Fossils are the remains and traces of ancient plants and animals that have been preserved. Fossils tell us about the vast number of species that existed millions of years ago. They also tell us about the development of various species.

▲ A fossil can form in a variety of ways. The following is a typical process.
(1) A fish dies and falls to the bottom of the sea, where it is buried in sediment.

▲ (2) The soft flesh rots away and the skeleton is preserved in the sediment as it forms sedimentary rock. The bony material breaks down and is replaced by minerals.

HOW DO FOSSILS TELL US ABOUT EVOLUTION?

Fossils can be very useful in helping us to trace the history of life on Earth. By the process called evolution, animals and plants change through many generations as they respond to a changing environment. As a result, new species are always appearing. At the same time, older species that are not well equipped for the new conditions are dying out. Fossils often reveal these changes to species. We know that birds evolved from dinosaurs because birds' skeletons are similar in many ways to those of dinosaurs. Fossils of the *Archaeopteryx*, an animal which has the features of dinosaurs and birds, show it came at a half-way stage between the two groups of animals.

▼ This baby mammoth was discovered in the 1970s in Siberia. It had been preserved for 12,000 years, buried deep in the frozen ground since the Ice Age.

► Archaeopteryx had the body and wings of a bird and was covered with feathers, but it had the jaws and fingers of a dinosaur.

ARE WHOLE ANIMALS FOUND IN FOSSILS?

Usually only an animal's hard parts, such as the bone and shell, are fossilized. The soft parts, such as the muscle, organs, and skin, are eaten by other animals or rot away. Under some conditions, however, whole animals are fossilized. Entire mammoths are often found preserved in frozen mud in northern Siberia and Canada.

Fossils

▶ This spider is preserved in amber. It died more than 10,000 years ago.

ARE FOSSILS ALWAYS FOUND IN ROCK?

Fossils are valuable in telling us about the history of life on Earth, but some are also very beautiful. When resin oozes from the bark of a tree, insects and spiders may be caught and preserved in the sticky liquid. If this resin is buried it may eventually harden into the mineral amber, with the creatures still inside.

▲ (3) Earth movements change the position of the rocks and lift this sedimentary rock above sea level.

▲ (4) The uplifted rocks are worn away. The mineralized skeleton is exposed at the surface. The fossil will be worn away unless it is collected by a geologist.

HOW IS COAL A FOSSIL?

During the fossilization process some of the original dead material can remain. The original carbon in a fossil fern leaf remains when it is flattened in shale (rock made from clay). Whole forests from prehistoric times have been reduced to carbon like this, and today's coal is the result.

▶ Archaeopteryx fossils are so clear that even the shape of the feathers have been preserved.

WHAT ELSE CAN FOSSILS TELL US?

As well as giving us glimpses of life that has vanished, fossils can be very useful. For example, they can help us date rocks across the globe. Some animals evolved very quickly, existing for only a few million years before dying out. If their fossils are found in rocks at different places, then these rocks must be the same age. Some animals lived only in particular conditions. When we find their fossils we know that the rocks were formed under those conditions. This is useful for identifying different rock types in the search for oil.

Weathering and Erosion

HOW DO WEATHERING AND EROSION AFFECT THE EARTH? Rocks at the Earth's surface are always being broken down by weathering and erosion. They crumble away and grind down to dust, as part of the rock cycle. This can happen through the sheer physical force of the weather and of gravity, or through more subtle chemical changes in the rocks themselves.

▼ Chemical changes in these rocks break them down, and the wind carries the particles away. Sand dunes move as sand is continually swept up one side and deposited on the other (inset).

WHAT IS PHYSICAL EROSION?

The Earth's landscape is affected by various physical processes. Tree roots find their way into rock cracks, splitting rocks apart. Chunks of rock are cracked off as water in their pores freezes and expands. Rocks shrink in the desert sun. Rainwater washes loose soil away. Rivers wear away hillsides. These and other forms of physical erosion, together with chemical erosion, gradually change the shape of the landscape.

HOW DOES A SAND DUNE FORM?

The desert is an ideal environment in which to watch physical erosion at work. There is no moisture to hold the soil together, so it exists as sand, which acts as a powerful erosion agent. The wind blasts it against exposed rocks, polishing them into bizarre mushroom shapes and arches. The constant breakdown of the rocks in turn produces more sand. Most erosion takes place close to the ground, where the sand is bouncing. Vast heaps of sand called dunes move across the landscape, pushed by the wind.

▼ Coastal land is eroded and shaped by the sea.

WHAT DO WAVES DO?

Along the edge of the sea, waves pound the shoreline, gradually wearing away the land. Headlands are attacked from each side as the waves curve in. They become narrow, and caves are cut into each side. The caves eventually enlarge into natural arches, and finally collapse, leaving worn-off fragments of headland called sea-stacks. These eventually wash away, forming beaches elsewhere.

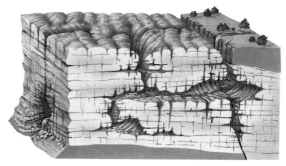

▲ (1) On the surface limestone scenery is often marked by pavements of bare rock and little water, as streams disappear below the surface to flow underground.

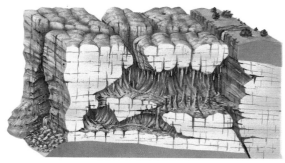

▲ (2) The weak acid in the underground streams often dissolves limestone rock away to form spectacular systems of caves. Beautiful formations, such as stalagmites and stalactites, also appear.

▲ (3) As the caves become larger, the roofs may collapse to reveal steep-sided gorges, waterfalls, and small streams.

WHAT IS CHEMICAL EROSION?

Some minerals break down when they are exposed to the weather. Granite – a coarse igneous rock – consists mainly of the three minerals quartz, mica, and feldspar. These are quite tough, except for the feldspar, which breaks down into clay when it is continually washed by the rain. Once the feldspar breaks down, the rest of the minerals fall loose and the granite disintegrates. Clay mines and industries are common in granite areas. The beaches there will also be sparkling with quartz and mica sand.

HOW DO CAVES FORM?

Caves form in limestone areas as a result of chemical erosion. Carbon dioxide from the soil and air dissolves in streams and rainwater, producing a weak acid that dissolves some of the limestone rock away. When a stream flows onto limestone ground it dissolves a vertical channel through the rock, called a swallow hole. This usually goes down as far as the water table – the level that groundwater, seeping up from below, has reached. At this level horizontal caves begin to form. If the water table drops, the caves are left dry and new caves are dissolved deeper down. As the groundwater seeps through the limestone it dissolves the weak areas, enlarging the natural spaces and cracks in the rock into caves. The dissolved material is deposited on the ceilings and floors of the caves, forming icicle-like stalactites (growing down from the roof) and stalagmites (growing up from the floor). These may meet to form pillars.

▶ These cavers are exploring a vertical cave in Georgia, USA. The cave has a depth of more than 443 feet.

The Power of Ice

How IS ICE POWERFUL? The moving masses of ice that we call glaciers start life as gentle snowfalls. In cold regions or high in the mountains, every snowfall builds on the ones before it, and the snow at the bottom is gradually pressed into ice. Eventually the ice stops being the fragile, splintery substance we know and becomes a solid, heavy glacier that flows slowly down the valley.

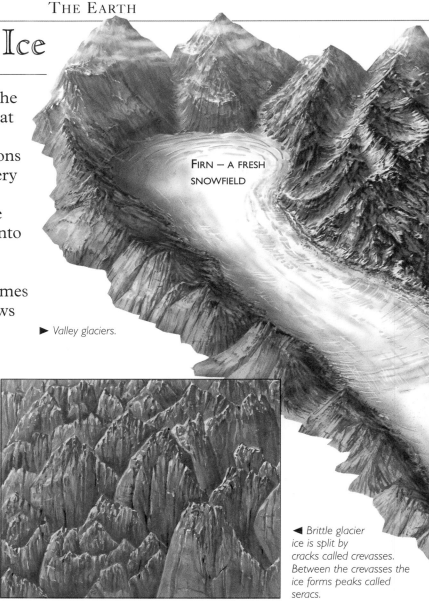

FIRN – A FRESH SNOWFIELD

▶ Valley glaciers.

WHAT IS A VALLEY GLACIER?

A valley glacier is smooth and covered by fresh snow near its source. Farther downhill it becomes broken and split by cracks. The packed ice at the base moves quite fluidly, but the exposed ice at the surface remains light and brittle. Rocky fragments carried along by the movement become more and more visible at the glacier's snout (lower end), as the ice melts away.

◀ Brittle glacier ice is split by cracks called crevasses. Between the crevasses the ice forms peaks called seracs.

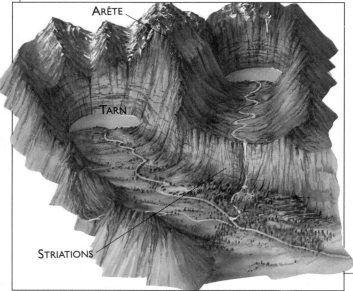

ARÊTE

TARN

STRIATIONS

HOW DOES ICE SHAPE LAND?

The great weight of a moving glacier scoops out the rocks beneath and grinds back the valley sides as it moves. A deep hollow left at the head of the U-shaped glaciated valley is called a corrie, and it may have a lake called a tarn. Arêtes are narrow steep ridges left between two valleys, and peaks are worn back to a pyramidal shape. Beneath the glacier the rocks are gouged into deep scratches called striations.

◀ A landscape of U-shaped valleys and steep shattered peaks remains once the glaciers have melted.

► *Fjords are found along mountainous coastlines near the poles, as in Norway and Greenland (Northern Hemisphere), and Chile and New Zealand (Southern Hemisphere).*

WHAT HAPPENS WHEN GLACIERS MELT?

Valley glaciers often travel all the way to the sea. When glaciers melt at the end of an ice age, the U-shaped valleys they have carved will be very close to sea level. This is because the sea level rises at the end of an ice age. The valleys may then flood. The result is a long narrow sea inlet called a fjord. The build-up of moraine (rocky fragments) at the glacier's snout also produces a shallow region at the mouth of the fjord.

During the Great Ice Age, glaciers ▼ covered much of northern Europe and northern Asia, and most of Canada.

MELTWATER STREAMS

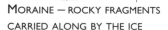

MORAINE — ROCKY FRAGMENTS
CARRIED ALONG BY THE ICE

▼ *Masses of drumlins together produce a very lumpy landscape that is often described as having 'a basket of eggs' shape.*

WHEN WAS THE LAST ICE AGE?

Several times in Earth's history, climates have been very much colder than they are now. Glaciers crept down from the mountains and spread across polar plains, and animals that could withstand cold evolved. The last ice age, often called the Great Ice Age, started two million years ago and ended as recently as 10,000 years ago.

WHAT IS AN ICE SHEET?

Sometimes a glacier is not confined to a valley, but spreads over a wide flat area. These glaciers are also known as ice sheets. There is one floating on the Arctic Ocean, covering the North Pole, another covering the continent of Antarctica, and another over Greenland. Unlike valley glaciers, they grow outward rather than downhill, and the snow builds up in their centers.

WHERE DO ICE-CARRIED ROCKS END UP?

As an ice sheet melts and retreats, as they did at the end of the Great Ice Age, all the rock fragments it carries along are dumped. The last ice sheets left a mixture of fine and coarse material, called boulder clay, over much of northern Europe. It is usually deposited in small, rounded hills called drumlins. Some boulders can be traced to the areas from where they were carried, hundreds of miles up mountains.

Soils

How is soil made? Usually the only part of the Earth's makeup that we can see directly is the loose covering we find on the surface. This is a complex substance we call soil. Soil is formed from the breakdown of rocks through physical and chemical erosion. Dead plant matter adds to the mixture. Chemical reactions with groundwater and oxygen from the atmosphere develop the soil further. Finally, the many millions of animals living in the soil mix it all up.

DOES SOIL CHANGE AS IT GETS DEEPER?

Soil has several layers. The order of these layers is called the soil profile. A typical soil profile has a layer of humus (decaying plant material) at the top. Below this is topsoil, also called the A Horizon by soil scientists. Here humus is mixed with minerals, though some of the useful chemicals have been washed out by groundwater. The next layer is the subsoil, or B Horizon. This layer has less humus but is enriched by the chemicals washed down from above. Below this is a layer of broken rock, the C Horizon, and finally the D Horizon of solid rock from which the landscape is built.

HOW DOES SOLID ROCK BECOME SOIL?

A bottom layer of solid rock is the raw material from which soil is made. This is broken down by physical erosion, such as tree roots cracking rocks apart and water freezing and expanding. Chemical erosion also plays a part by dissolving some of the minerals in the rock.

WHAT IS HUMUS?

Plants that live in the soil usually die there too. Their substance is then broken down by micro-organisms in the soil, such as bacteria and fungi. What remains is called humus. Humus restores valuable minerals and chemicals to the soil so plants can continue to grow in it. Its quality and quantity varies from one soil type to another.

▲ Most animal life in the soil consists of microscopic creatures, like these mites.

◄ Tropical soil is 'old' and deep (1). Desert soil is 'young' and shallow (2). Temperate soil is 'middle-aged' and ideal for agriculture (3).

HOW MANY TYPES OF SOIL ARE THERE?

There are many hundreds of different types of soil, and many ways of classifying (grouping) them. The classifications are usually based on the chemical content, color, texture, and amount of organic material the soil contains. Soil types vary from sand, which is just broken-down rock, to peat, which is mostly humus. The first important studies of soil took place in Russia, so soil types often have Russian names.

▼ Rainwater moves down between the soil particles. As water dries on the surface of the soil, water is drawn upwards.

IS WATER IMPORTANT IN SOIL?

The most healthy, productive soils are those that can hold water and release it to plant roots. Some soils, like clay, are full of water but it is trapped and plants cannot draw on it. In other soils, such as sand, the water flows quickly through it, not staying long enough to be of use to plants.

WHAT ANIMALS LIVE IN SOIL?

Animal life is vital to soil. Micro-organisms like bacteria can speed up necessary chemical changes. Worms burrow through the layers, bringing down humus and carrying up mineral material. As they do this they let oxygen in and mix up the soil.

HOW DOES CLIMATE AFFECT SOIL?

The climate of a region has a huge effect on its soil. In hot, humid climates the deepest layer of solid rock breaks down quickly, so the soil is deep. In cold damp climates, the rock weathers slowly, so the soil is thin.

▼ In hot climates, clay soils can dry up and crack.

Rivers

WHERE DO RIVERS COME FROM? Water evaporates from the ocean surface and blows inland. There it condenses as clouds and falls as rain. The rainwater seeps underground and re-emerges in springs. Streams flow from the springs, combine with one another, and eventually form rivers that return the water to the oceans. The world's greatest rivers are found in tropical areas, where the rainfall is frequent and very heavy.

HOW DOES A RIVER CHANGE?

A river has quite different features in different parts of its course. Close to its source it tumbles about in mountain gorges, forming waterfalls and rapids. Here the river is very powerful and it erodes away the land. It carries rocks along, widening and deepening the valley as it goes.

In lower ground the river slows down as it meanders across the broad, flat-bottomed valley. The flat bottom consists of material washed down from the earlier stage.

In the final stage the river is broad and sluggish as it reaches the sea. It does not erode its bed any more but drops the rest of the material it is carrying. It forms a broad flat floodplain, and sometimes mud banks.

▼ *A waterfall appears when a river falls over a shelf of hard rock. The soft rock beneath is eroded, forming a plunge pool.*

HOW DO WATERFALLS FORM?

In their upper reaches rivers erode the riverbed as they go. When they hit a bed of hard rock they flow over it, eroding the softer rock above and below. As the water drops over the edge of the hard rock it forms a waterfall. Eventually the hard rock is worn down and back so there is not such a steep drop any more. The river then tumbles across the rock, forming a rapid.

► The Grand Canyon has eroded layers of rock, cutting through 600 million years of the Earth's history.

WHY DO RIVERS MEANDER?

A river flowing across a flat surface naturally weaves from side to side. It flows faster around the outside of a curve and the fast current erodes the outer bank. At the same time sediment is deposited on the inside of the curve, where the current is weak. In this way the curve becomes more and more pronounced, forming a loop-like bend called a meander.

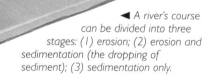

◄ A river's course can be divided into three stages: (1) erosion; (2) erosion and sedimentation (the dropping of sediment); (3) sedimentation only.

HOW DID THE GRAND CANYON FORM?

Meanders develop when a river flows over low-lying flat land. Sometimes low-lying areas are forced up as mountains begin to rise. Any river flowing across such a region then becomes young and active again and begins to erode downward as it did before, cutting into the land. If the river is flowing in a meander then it cuts into the meander, creating a narrow channel called a gorge. The gorge, which swings from side to side along the original river course, is called an incised meander. Probably the most famous incised meander is at the Grand Canyon of the Colorado River, in the United States.

WHAT IS A DELTA?

A river carries sediment all the way to the river mouth, where the river meets the sea. If the sea has a strong current the sediment is washed away, but if there are no currents the sediment is dropped at the mouth. The sediment forms a broad sweep of mud and sand-banks, and the river splits up between the banks to reach the sea. This fan of deposited sediments is called a delta.

FACTS

River Nile
Length: 1,142 mi
Drainage area: 1.4 million mi²

River Amazon
Length: 4,040 mi
Drainage area: 2.7 million mi²

Mississippi–Missouri
Length: 3,733 mi
Drainage area: 1.2 million mi²

River Yenisei
Length: 3,435 mi
Drainage area: 1 million mi²

Oceans, Seas, Islands

WHAT LIES UNDER THE OCEAN? More than two-thirds of our planet is covered by water. Despite this fact, the oceans are largely unknown – certainly not nearly as well-known as the continents are. It is only during the last few decades that we have had the technology that allows us to investigate ocean floors. Amazing new discoveries are being made here all the time.

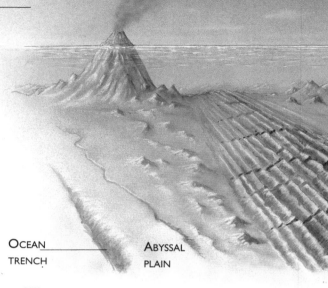

OCEAN_____
TRENCH   ABYSSAL
          PLAIN

WHAT IS ON THE OCEAN FLOOR?

The largest area of the ocean floor is called the abyssal plain. It is a plain – broad and flat – covered with ooze (sediment that has built up from the remains of living creatures). In every ocean there is an ocean ridge. This is a volcanic feature, producing molten material which makes up the Earth's crust.

DO WE SWIM IN THE OCEAN?

Around every coast there is an area of shallow sea. This is not true ocean but merely the flooded edge of the continent. Here the sea floor is called the continental shelf.

▲ *Warm and cold ocean currents are driven along by a pattern of world wind circulation.*

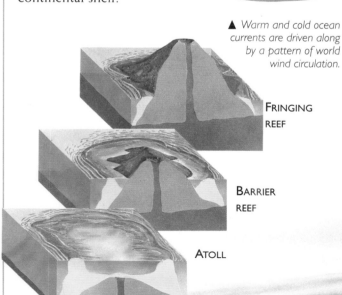

FRINGING
REEF

BARRIER
REEF

ATOLL

WHERE ARE THE OCEANS DEEPEST?

All around the Pacific Ocean, and along parts of the Atlantic and Indian oceans, there are lengthy regions of very deep water. These are ocean trenches, the deepest places on the planet. They occur where the Earth's plates meet, turn down, and slide beneath or over each other.

WHAT GIVES AN OCEAN ITS CURRENT?

In the North Atlantic and North Pacific oceans the water moves in a vast clockwise motion. This movement is called a 'gyre' and it is driven by the prevailing winds. In the South Atlantic, South Pacific, and Indian oceans the prevailing winds drive anticlockwise gyres. The different parts of these gyres are the individual ocean currents.

HOW DO CORAL REEFS FORM?

Corals are sea animals that grow rooted to the spot in the clear shallow waters of tropical regions. They grow near islands and form what is called a fringing reef, a shelf-like ridge surrounding the island.

The movement of the Earth's plates can cause the island to sink. The reef builds upward, keeping just below the surface of the sea. Eventually the sinking island is separated from the reef by a ring of shallow sea called a lagoon. These are called barrier reefs. Finally the island may disappear. The reef continues to grow, eventually appearing as a ring of coral around an empty lagoon. It is then called an atoll.

CONTINENTAL
SHELF

CONTINENT

OCEAN
RIDGE

WHAT MAKES WAVES?

When the wind passes over the
surface of the water it pushes the
water particles along causing a
rolling circular motion, which
is passed along the water
surface. The water itself just
goes round in circles, but the
movement is passed on from
one water particle to the
next, crossing vast areas of
ocean. Eventually the movement
disturbs the water close to shore causing
it to build up and fall as plunging breakers.

► *Surfers ride on coastal waves. Waves travel
thousands of miles on the open oceans before
reaching the shallower coastal waters. Here they are
closer together and so tall that their tops spill over.*

HOW DO TSUNAMIS BEGIN?

A great underwater disturbance, like
an earthquake or a volcanic eruption,
will set off a shock wave that passes
through the ocean water. The ocean
wave (called a tsunami), which is
barely visible on the ocean's surface,
travels at great speed. When it reaches
shallow water it slows down and builds
up to mountainous proportions,
sometimes sweeping up onto land and
destroying coastal towns. People used
to call tsunamis 'tidal waves'.

The Atmosphere

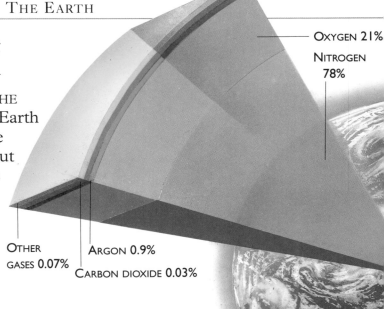

OXYGEN 21%

NITROGEN 78%

OTHER GASES 0.07%

ARGON 0.9%

CARBON DIOXIDE 0.03%

Is THE ATMOSPHERE A PART OF THE EARTH? We usually think of the Earth as layers of solid material, from the core outward. We often forget about the outermost layer, the one that is most important to life on Earth – the atmosphere. It is the lightest layer of all, consisting of a thin envelope of gases.

WHAT IS THE ATMOSPHERE MADE OF?

If you sampled the atmosphere anywhere near the Earth's surface you would find a similar mix of gases. The amounts of each gas only vary a little with height. Nitrogen is the most plentiful gas, taking up about 78 percent of the atmosphere. Next comes oxygen, which takes up about 21 percent . Carbon dioxide takes up only about 0.03 percent. Apart from these there are traces of a few other, much less important, gases. There is one other vital ingredient in the atmosphere – water vapor. The amount varies from place to place and time to time.

▲ *The Earth's outer covering – the atmosphere – is made up of a mix of different gases.*

HAS THE ATMOSPHERE ALWAYS BEEN THE SAME?

When the Earth first formed, 4,500 million years ago, the atmosphere was mainly made up of hydrogen and carbon dioxide. Most of the hydrogen, being light, then spread out into space and the carbon dioxide became locked up in rocks. Oxygen was not a feature of the atmosphere until about 2,000 million years ago, when plants evolved.

DOES THE ATMOSPHERE HAVE LAYERS?

The Earth's atmosphere forms several well-defined layers. The outermost layer is the exosphere. Here gases are so thin they fade off into the vacuum of space. Further in is the thermosphere. Its thin gases trap radiation from the sun, making it extremely hot. Also in this layer sun particles sometimes strike atoms and molecules, producing beautiful colored lights called auroras. Beneath this is the mesosphere, where the atmosphere is thick enough to slow down and burn up any falling meteors. The next layer is the stratosphere. It contains a layer of ozone gas, which absorbs the Sun's harmful rays. The final layer, the troposphere, is the one we live in. All the weather we experience is formed within it.

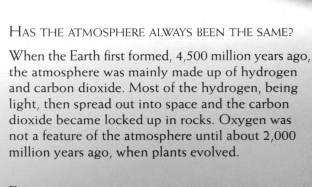

430 MI

EXOSPHERE

310 MI

THERMOSPHERE

AURORAS

60 MI

MESOSPHERE

METEORS

30 MI

STRATOSPHERE

OZONE LAYER

6 MI

TROPOSPHERE

0

WHAT IS DIFFERENT ABOUT THE TROPOSPHERE?

The troposphere is only about 7 miles thick and so it only takes up about 1.5 percent of the atmosphere's total space. However, it is so dense, compressed by the other layers lying on top of it, that it contains over 80 percent of the atmosphere's mass, and keeps the Earth's surface warm.

WHAT ARE TRADE WINDS?

The sun is directly overhead in the tropics. The atmosphere here heats up and rises. Cooler air rushes in from north and south to take its place. This produces winds that blow towards the equator, called trade winds. If they blow from the sea then the winds bring rain, if they blow from inland then they are dry winds. Trade winds are diverted to the west by the turning of the Earth.

HOW DO OTHER WINDS CIRCULATE?

Over the north and south poles the air is extremely cold and dense. It creeps outward, producing cold winds that blow from the poles. Meanwhile the hot air that rose around the equator descends in the region of the tropics of Cancer and Capricorn, north and south of the equator. There it moves back toward the equator again, or it moves toward the poles. At the poles it runs head-on into icy polar winds, causing very unstable climates in the regions between the tropics and the poles.

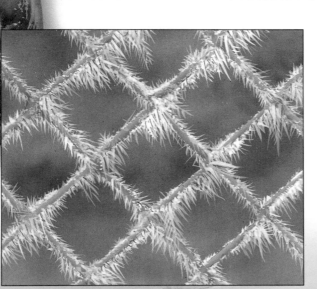

► *When conditions are very cold, water vapor in the atmosphere solidifies as ice crystals called hoar frost.*

WHAT COLORS THE SKY?

The sky appears to be blue most of the time. This is because the different colors of white sunlight are scattered by gases in the atmosphere and the blue part is reflected back to Earth. In good weather, when the air is still, the setting of the sun may appear red as the sunlight bounces off dust particles that hang steadily in the air.

A red sky at dawn is caused by sunlight reflected from water droplets, telling us it is going to be rainy that day.

Weather

WHAT IS THE WEATHER LIKE TODAY? That is a question we hear people ask daily. It is a common question because the atmospheric conditions change everywhere from day to day. For example, warm temperatures can follow cold weather and heavy rain can follow drought. These changeable conditions are what we call the weather.

HOW DOES WATER MOVE?

Water evaporates from the ocean surface into the atmosphere as water vapor. When the temperature or pressure of the atmosphere changes, the vapor may condense once more into water droplets and fall as rain or snow. On land this water sinks into the soil, becoming ground-water, or forms lakes and swamps, and eventually flows back to the ocean as rivers. This whole circulation is called the water cycle.

▲ *The water cycle produces a constant circulation of water from the ocean, into the atmosphere, and over the land. This movement of moisture is one of the most important influences on the weather.*

HOW DO RAIN, HAIL, AND SNOW FORM?

Water vapor is an invisible gas. When it condenses in the atmosphere it forms tiny water droplets that hang in the air. Clouds are formed by masses of these water droplets. If the condensation process continues the droplets accumulate to form larger drops, and fall as rain. Sometimes the air is so cold that the raindrops freeze to lumps of ice, forming hailstones. Sometimes the water vapor turns directly into crystals of ice, forming snowflakes.

WHAT ARE CLOUDS MADE OF?

The very highest clouds are actually made of ice crystals. These clouds have a wispy feathery look about them. Most clouds, however, are made of water droplets. They can be layer clouds, which weather forecasters call 'stratus' clouds, or heaped clouds, which they call 'cumulus' clouds. Clouds are usually white, but when they are thick they are gray and dull.

CIRRUS

CIRROCUMULUS

CUMULUS

NIMBOSTRATUS

What is a weather front?

Different weather conditions in different places produce different masses of air. A front is a moving line along which different air masses meet, and cold air replaces warm and warm air replaces cold. Fronts always cause a change of weather.

▼ In a thundercloud a difference in electrical charges causes lightning.

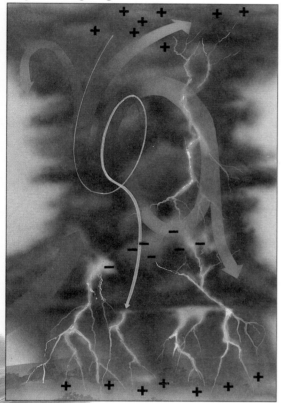

◄ 'Stratus' clouds are layered, and 'cumulus' clouds are heaped. Different types of cloud are found at different heights.

What is meant by a 'twister'?

'Twister' is the name that is sometimes given to a tornado, a violent wind. A tornado is a swirling tube of air, produced by turbulence in a severe thunderstorm, which marches across the countryside, sucking everything up as it goes. Tornadoes are common in central North America, where dry cold air from the Rocky mountains meets warm damp air from the ocean.

Where does thunder come from?

Inside a thundercloud there is always warm air rising and cold air descending. Raindrops caught up in this are flung about and split apart into smaller drops. This movement produces a difference in electrical charges, which creates a huge spark across the sky, called lightning. As lightning streaks through the air it causes a loud bang, called thunder.

Can weather be predicted?

Over the centuries scientists have come to recognize various weather patterns and these are useful in weather forecasting. Observation stations all over the world can check these patterns from day to day. Nowadays we can watch the approach of fronts or thunderstorms by satellite photography, giving us a good overall view of the weather patterns that are building up.

FACTS

Hailstones can be as big as tennis balls.

Winds can reach 186 miles per hour in a typical storm called a hurricane.

Weather is most unstable in the latitude of Europe. Here there are constant frontal systems between cold air from the North Pole and warm air from the tropics.

Climate

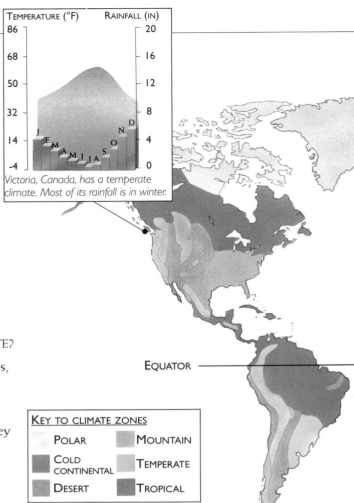

TEMPERATURE (°F)   RAINFALL (IN)

Victoria, Canada, has a temperate climate. Most of its rainfall is in winter.

WHAT IS THE DIFFERENCE BETWEEN CLIMATE AND WEATHER? The funny answer is that climate is what we are supposed to get, while weather is what we actually get. Climate is the total of all the varying atmospheric conditions – temperature, rainfall, pressure, and so on – of an area, averaged over a number of decades. Weather is the day-to-day variation within this.

HOW DOES THE EARTH'S SHAPE AFFECT CLIMATE?

The Earth is shaped like a sphere. Because of this, places on and near the equator get more of the Sun's heat. Near the poles the Sun's rays have to travel through more of the Earth's atmosphere before they reach the surface, by which time they have lost some of their heat.

NORTH POLE

SOUTH POLE

▲ *The Sun's rays are more spread out and weaker north of the equator than they are in equatorial regions.*

EQUATOR

KEY TO CLIMATE ZONES

POLAR	MOUNTAIN
COLD CONTINENTAL	TEMPERATE
DESERT	TROPICAL

WHERE ARE THE WORLD'S CLIMATIC ZONES?

The Earth is divided into a number of climatic zones, depending mostly on the temperature and moisture of the region. The zones are generally parallel to one another and to the equator. The equatorial zone is hot and moist. To the north and south of this lie tropical desert zones, which are hot and dry. Further towards the poles lie cooler, temperate zones, while cold polar zones exist near the extreme north and south. On all continents, inland regions are drier than coastal regions.

WHAT IS CLIMATE LIKE IN THE MOUNTAINS?

The change in climate and vegetation that you meet as you go up a mountain matches the changing conditions you would meet if you traveled toward the North Pole. After passing through zones of plentiful lowland vegetation you come to zones where plants have adapted to colder, dryer conditions, followed by the sparse tundra vegetation of an even colder climate, finally reaching barren, icy regions.

◄ *In a mountain region the snow line is clearly visible. Above it there is snow all the year round.*

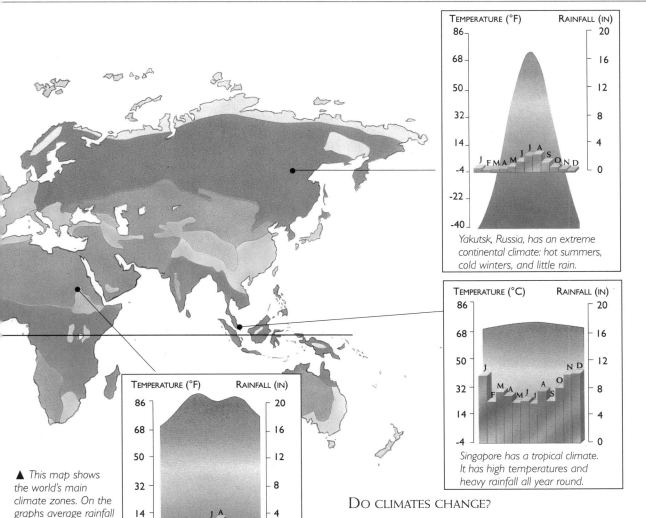

TEMPERATURE (°F)   RAINFALL (IN)

86
68
50
32
14
-4
-22
-40

20
16
12
8
4
0

J F M A M J J A S O N D

Yakutsk, Russia, has an extreme continental climate: hot summers, cold winters, and little rain.

TEMPERATURE (°C)   RAINFALL (IN)

86
68
50
32
14
-4

20
16
12
8
4
0

J F M A M J J A S O N D

Singapore has a tropical climate. It has high temperatures and heavy rainfall all year round.

▲ *This map shows the world's main climate zones. On the graphs average rainfall and temperatures are shown for places in four different climate zones.*

TEMPERATURE (°F)   RAINFALL (IN)

86
68
50
32
14
-4

20
16
12
8
4
0

M J J A S O

Khartoum, Sudan, has a desert climate. It is hot and dry all year round.

WHAT DO WE MEAN BY A TEMPERATE CLIMATE?

When a climate is neither very hot nor very cold, we call it temperate. People in temperate regions spend less time and effort avoiding the effects of extreme heat and cold than people elsewhere. Europe and most of North America lie in temperate regions.

WHAT IS A MONSOON?

Coastal areas of Southeast Asia have heavy rain in the hot season, as rising hot air over the continent pulls in moist air from the surrounding oceans. In winter, cold dry winds spread from the inland regions of the continent. This wind system, which produces a hot rainy season followed by a dry winter, is called a monsoon.

DO CLIMATES CHANGE?

Over the last two million years the Earth has slipped in and out of ice ages. During the ice ages, glaciers covered much of the northern hemisphere. During warmer periods, the sub-tropical vegetation spread as far north as London. These changes took place within a few thousand years and they continue to happen. Human civilization has also been changing the atmosphere, with smoke and waste gases, which adds to climate change.

▲ *Floods are common in India when monsoon winds bring torrential rain in summer.*

People and the Planet

HOW HAVE HUMANS AFFECTED THE PLANET? We have looked at how rocks and landscapes change through erosion and the rock cycle. We have also looked at how climates change during ice ages. Now even greater changes are being brought about by human civilization. Since our species has spread across the Earth's surface there is hardly a corner of the planet that has not been altered in one way or another by our activities, whether it be clearing natural forest for agriculture, digging away mountainsides for raw materials, or spreading cities and fields across the countryside.

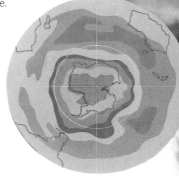

▼ A satellite photograph – with different parts of the atmosphere in different colors – shows the ozone 'hole' above the North Pole.

WHAT IS 'THE GREENHOUSE EFFECT'?

Most of our energy comes from fossil fuels – coal, oil, and gas. These were formed millions of years ago, as living things – which absorb carbon dioxide from the atmosphere – died and left carbon deposits in the rocks. Nowadays we burn up the carbon that is in these fossil fuels to release its energy. Unfortunately this means we also release vast quantities of carbon dioxide gas. In the last few decades we have released millions upon millions of years' worth of the gas. The increased level of carbon dioxide in the atmosphere traps the sun's rays, and this leads to an increase in the temperature on Earth. This is known as 'global warming' or 'the greenhouse effect'.

ARE SEA LEVELS RISING?

One of the possible effects of global warming could be the melting of glaciers and ice sheets. It would be like an ice age in reverse. The water now locked up as ice would fill the oceans, raising the sea level worldwide, possibly by as much as 225 feet. Many low-lying areas of the world, such as Bangladesh or Florida, or the island nations of the Pacific, such as Kiribati and Tuvalu, would be almost completely submerged under water.

WHAT IS THE 'OZONE HOLE'?

In the stratosphere is a layer that is rich in the gas ozone. It is crucial to life on Earth because it filters out harmful ultraviolet rays from the sun. We now know that the ozone layer is thinning, especially near the poles, because waste gases – from factory chimneys, for example – break ozone down. We call this thinning the 'ozone hole', and the thinner the layer becomes, the more the sun's harmful rays will get through.

◄ Flooded towns will become more common if the polar ice caps continue to melt and the sea level rises.

1960

1971

1987

◄ *The Aral Sea in central Asia has been drying up since 1960. The rivers flowing into it have been diverted to water cotton plantations.*

ARE WE CHANGING THE WORLD?

Our world is dirty. This is one result of human civilization. We grow our own food in farms, but this changes the landscape and leaves waste products. We manufacture our clothing and other essentials, but this means digging out vast quantities of raw materials, and there is always rubbish left over that must be disposed of. These activities, and many others we do, change the surface of our planet in some way. The Earth's surface environment has always been changing, but never so rapidly as it is now.

◄ *Smoke and chemical fumes, belching from factory chimneys, change the composition of the atmosphere.*

► *Waste products are becoming a big problem. Even if we recycle materials we need to find recycling methods that are less destructive to the environment.*

SHOULD WE CHANGE THE LANDSCAPE?

Big schemes to benefit the people of an area often backfire. Rivers, for example, are dammed so the trapped water can be used to water desert areas. However, much of the reserved water is often then lost as it evaporates from the surface, and the rest of the supply can become clogged up with silt.

WHAT SHOULD WE DO WITH WASTE?

Our civilization uses up lots of raw material, and produces lots of waste. There are many ways to dispose of the waste, but none is problem-free. We can put it in holes in the ground, such as old quarries – this can make new land to build on, but poisons in the soil will remain there. We can burn it – this reduces its volume but may produce poisonous smoke. We could dump it in the sea – this could poison the sea life.

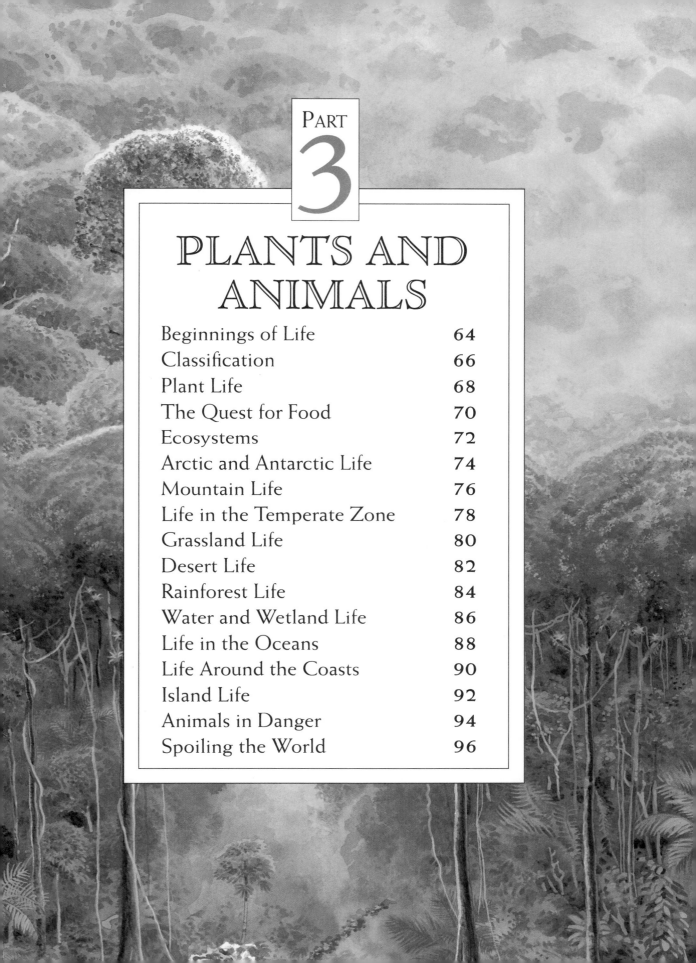

PLANTS AND ANIMALS

Beginnings of Life

WHEN DID LIFE BEGIN ON EARTH? About four billion years ago, violent thunderstorms, exploding volcanoes, and a choking mix of gases in the atmosphere created just the right conditions for the first organisms (living things) to evolve in the waters of the ocean. Each was made up of just a single simple cell.

WHAT WAS EARLY OCEAN-LIFE LIKE?

For two billion years, single-celled organisms in the oceans were the only form of life. Then, as the Earth became less stormy, more complicated ocean plants and animals gradually began to evolve and compete with each other for food and living space. Trilobites, like this, lived on the seabed 500 million years ago, sifting the sand for food.

▼ In the Carboniferous swamp forests, dragonflies hunted other insects and were themselves hunted by early amphibians and reptiles.

WHEN DID PLANTS AND ANIMALS MOVE ONTO LAND?

About 520 million years ago, mats of green algae and bacteria began to appear on the land. Eighty million years later, tiny millipede-like creatures crawled ashore to feed on them. By the Carboniferous period, 365 million years ago, forests had evolved on land and the first amphibians (like fish with legs) left their swamps to live among the trees.

▼ Dinosaurs came in many shapes and sizes. Triceratops (below left) was a peaceful plant-eater. The horns and the bony plate on its head helped protect it from Tyrannosaurus (right), the largest hunting animal ever.

WHEN DID DINOSAURS RULE THE WORLD?

About 290 million years ago, one type of amphibian developed a shelled egg that no longer had to be laid in water. The conquest of the land, and the age of the dinosaurs, had begun. For 150 million years, dinosaurs and other reptiles were the only large animals – even in the skies, where giant pterosaurs (flying reptiles) flew.

◀ Like other pterosaurs, Rhamphorhynchus had long, narrow wings. The paddle on its tail helped it steer through the air.

WHY DID THE DINOSAURS DIE OUT?

The fossil record shows that the dinosaurs and giant sea reptiles all died, quite suddenly, 65 million years ago. It is thought the climate got colder, perhaps because a giant meteorite collided with the Earth, throwing up clouds of dust that blocked out the sunlight. Furry, warm-blooded mammals were better at coping with the cold and soon replaced the dinosaurs. Only a few feathered pterosaurs survived. In a sense, modern birds are just feathered, flying dinosaurs.

WHEN DID MAMMALS APPEAR ON THE SCENE?

Even as the dinosaurs were evolving 200 million years ago, the first mammals were living among them. They were small insect-eaters, rather like modern shrews, and probably laid eggs, like the platypus and echidna still do. They could not compete with the giant reptiles, so they remained small, but mammals evolved as quick movers and thinkers. That gave them a huge advantage when the dinosaurs died out.

▲ The earliest mammals probably looked rather like this modern tree shrew, a primitive relative of monkeys and apes (primates).

HOW DID HUMANS EVOLVE?

After the death of the dinosaurs, mammals developed into many forms. Some mammals moved back into the sea and the first bats took to flight. One group of tree-living mammals developed long tails and arms to swing through the branches, and sensitive fingers to grasp fruit. These were the primates – relatives of monkeys and apes. Three million years ago, a few apes in Africa began to walk on their hind legs. The fossil skeleton on the left, nicknamed Lucy, belongs to one of the first human-like apes. True humans did not appear until about a million years ago in Africa.

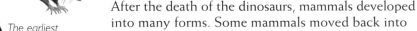

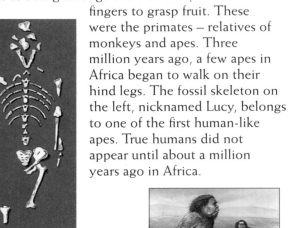

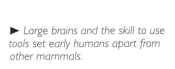
▶ Large brains and the skill to use tools set early humans apart from other mammals.

Classification

W HAT IS CLASSIFICATION? We share Earth with vast numbers of different plants and animals. To describe this life, we need to give each sort a name, and to help us understand the variety, we gather these names into groups, just like similar books are gathered on a library shelf. This system of grouping is called classification.

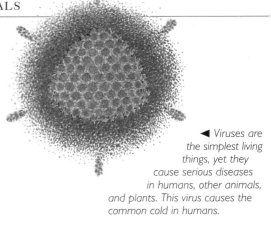

◀ *Viruses are the simplest living things, yet they cause serious diseases in humans, other animals, and plants. This virus causes the common cold in humans.*

WHAT DO WE CALL DIFFERENT TYPES OF PLANTS OR ANIMALS?

Each different type of plant or animal is called a species. Generally speaking, a plant or animal will only breed with its own species. The way animals behave helps stop them inter-breeding (breeding with other species), while in plants, chemical and physical barriers prevent the pollen from one flower pollinating the flower of another species. Scientists give each species a scientific name, usually in the international language of Latin. For example, the human species is called *Homo sapiens*.

WHAT IS THE SIMPLEST FORM OF LIFE?

Viruses are the simplest form of life. They are too small to be seen under ordinary microscopes. They are made up of a small amount of chemicals surrounded by a protective coat. When a virus invades an animal or plant, its chemicals take over the workings of the host cell, like aliens in a spaceship. Viruses cause many illnesses, such as colds, measles, and mumps, and deadly diseases like polio, rabies, and AIDS.

HOW DOES CLASSIFICATION WORK?

To help us find books in a library, all the books on a subject are gathered on one shelf, and all the books by the same author are kept together on that shelf. Classification works by grouping plants and animals in the same way. The biggest division in the animal kingdom is between animals with backbones, called vertebrates, and those without backbones, called invertebrates. Amongst the vertebrates, the ones with feathers are classed as birds, and the ones with fur as mammals. Mammals that share characteristics are put together into smaller groups. For example, the flying mammals belong to the bat group called the Chiroptera, and the true hunters are in the group Carnivora. These groups, in turn, are divided again into even smaller groups. They contain many species, such as dogs and cats within the Carnivora group. Like the library, this arrangement is mostly for our convenience, but it may also tell us which animals are related to each other by a common ancestor.

▶ *The human species belongs in a group called the primates, which are a type of mammal. Primates are placed in an even larger group, called the vertebrates.*

▶ *Primates, including chimpanzees, are mammals that evolved to live in the trees, with grasping hands and fingernails instead of claws. Their teeth show they eat many different foods.*

WHICH ANIMAL GROUP HAS THE MOST SPECIES?

The truthful answer is that scientists do not know for sure. Just over one million species of animals have been cataloged by scientists. More than half of these are insects, including 290,000 species of beetles, 112,000 species of butterflies and moths, and 103,000 species of bees, wasps, and ants. But the latest research suggests there could be 100 million species of tiny worms called nematodes, although only a few of these have been studied and most are less than a sixteenth of an inch long. Scientists recently found 325 different nematodes species within a deep sea trench west of Scotland, in a volume of mud smaller than the inside of a car!

▲ Animals without backbones (invertebrates) come in a huge variety of shapes and forms, but all have evolved to find food and escape enemies. For example, there are at least 300,000 species of spider including this Mexican tarantula.

▼ This single-celled, microscopic amoeba is one of the simplest living things. It moves by flowing like jelly.

WHY SHOULD WE LOOK AFTER THIS VARIETY OF ANIMALS AND PLANTS?

Only a fraction of living things have been studied, and we cannot tell which of the rest might be useful to us. Many people also believe that all living things have a right to exist. That is why in the 1990s the world's governments made a promise to protect what is called 'biodiversity' – the total variety of living things, including their ways of life and the places where they live.

DO SCIENTISTS KNOW HOW MANY SPECIES EXIST?

In truth, nobody knows with any certainty, because new species are always being found. In 1982, an American scientist did a calculation. He used a poisonous gas to kill all the insects in a single rain forest tree. Among the dead insects that rained to the ground, he identified 163 species of beetles that lived only in that sort of tree. But there are 50,000 tropical tree species, and, if each had as many beetles, that makes over 8 million beetles. Allowing for all the other sorts of insects in the trees and on the forest floor, he estimated that there must be at least 30 million insect species in total. More cautious scientists say there are at least 13.6 million species of living things.

▼ Mammals, like this elephant shrew, are vertebrates covered in hair, which feed their young on milk.

◄ Lemurs are primitive primates from the forests of Madagascar. They use their long tails to help them balance in the branches and also to signal to each other.

▼ Vertebrates are advanced animals with backbones and complex brains. They include fish – such as this shark – amphibians, reptiles, birds, and mammals.

Plant Life

HOW ARE PLANTS AND ANIMALS DIFFER- ENT? Unlike animals, plants generally do not move from place to place. Also, unlike animals, they either make their own food, using sunlight, or absorb it from their surroundings. However, some microscopic organisms (living things) show characteristics of both plants and animals, and are placed in their own kingdom, called the Protistans.

CHLOROPLAST NUCLEUS MITOCHONDRION

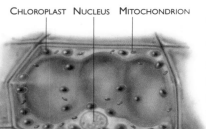

WHAT MAKES UP PLANT TISSUE?

The bodies of all plants and animals are made up of units called cells. The nucleus controls the workings of the cell, and the mitochondria provide energy. Unlike animal cells, plant cells are surrounded by a rigid cell wall, and they contain green chloroplasts, which make the plant's food from sunlight.

HOW DO PLANTS MAKE THEIR OWN FOOD?

Plants draw water from the soil through their roots to their stem and leaves. Their leaves also take in carbon dioxide, a gas from the atmosphere, through special surface pores. In the chloroplasts of the leaf cells, energy from sunlight is used to fuel a chemical reaction called photosynthesis, which transforms the water and carbon dioxide into energy-rich sugars. In the process, oxygen is released back into the atmosphere. The sugars are stored in the form of complex chemicals called starches, and are broken down again as the plant needs energy to live and grow.

DO PLANTS ONLY TAKE WATER FROM THE SOIL?

No. They also absorb minerals and nutrients, which they need to grow and which are used to build up the various parts of the plant cell.

SUN'S ENERGY

OXYGEN

CARBON DIOXIDE

SUGAR SOLUTIONS

WATER AND NUTRIENTS

RAIN- FALL

▼ *The leaf of the Venus flytrap snaps shut, trapping any insect that touches its hairy edge. The victim is dissolved and provides nutrients for the plant's growth.*

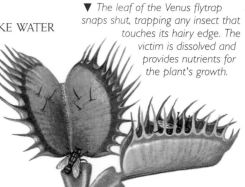

ARE THERE MEAT-EATING PLANTS?

Some plants live partly as carnivores (meat-eaters). They usually grow in boggy areas where the soil is poor. They use sticky hairs or spring-loaded traps on their leaves to catch insects, which are dissolved to provide the extra nutrients the plant needs for healthy growth.

Evaporation of water
from the leaves draws
water up the tree's trunk,
and makes its roots suck in
more water and nutrients
from the surrounding soil.
Sugar solutions, made in the
leaves, are pumped around
the tree to supply energy.

EVAPORATION

Carbon dioxide passes through pores
into the leaf, where sunlight is used to
manufacture sugars in chloroplasts in the
cells (photosynthesis).

WHAT IS THE JOB OF A FLOWER?

The main purpose of a flower is to produce
seeds, by which the plant can reproduce and
spread. However, if the seeds were produced
only by a single plant, all the resulting young
plants would be exact copies of the parent. To
ensure a bit of healthy variety
many plants need to
exchange material with another
plant of their own kind before they
can produce seeds. In this process – called
pollination – pollen grains (male sex cells) from
one flower are transferred to the ovules (female
sex cells) in the center of another flower, and
these then blend to form the seeds. The pollen
can be carried from flower to flower by wind or
water, or transferred unknowingly by a bee, a butterfly, a bat, or a bird that feeds from the flower. A
sugary juice, called nectar, attracts pollinating
animals to the flower.

WHAT IS THE SMALLEST FLOWERING PLANT?

Although many plants are
microscopic in size, they
reproduce not by
pollination but by simply
splitting in two. The smallest flowering plant is
a type of duckweed, called wolffia, that floats on
pond surfaces. It consists of a single leaf, less than a
sixteenth of an inch across, with minute flowers
hidden in a pocket on its underside.

▼ Wolffia is the
smallest flowering
plant.

► The giant sequoia
tree is the biggest
plant in the world.

WHAT IS THE BIGGEST PLANT?

The tallest trees in the world are coastal redwoods in
the USA, which reach 360 feet in height. But the
biggest plant in the world is a giant sequoia tree.
Although only 272 feet tall, it has a massive trunk,
more than 79 feet round, and is estimated to weigh
about 2,000 tons.

HOW ARE SEEDS SPREAD?

If seeds fell straight to the ground, the sprouting
seedlings would soon be competing with the parent
plant for light and space. To avoid this, some seeds
have wings, or parachutes of hairs, to carry them off in the wind.
Others are designed to be spread by rivers or the sea. Many rely on
animals to spread them. They either become hooked in the animal's fur
or feathers, or they are eaten and pass unharmed through the animal's
gut, emerging in a nourishing pile of natural fertilizer!

► When squirrels eat
a nut, they often drop
the seed inside it.

The Quest for Food

WHY DON'T ALL ANIMALS EAT PLANTS? In one sense, all animals rely on plants for food. The starches in plants are the main source of food for all animals, but the tough plant cell walls are difficult to digest. Herbivores, animals that only eat plants, are able to digest grass and leaves to produce the energy they need. Other animals get their energy second-hand by eating herbivores, which store the goodness of plants in their flesh. They are called carnivores (meat-eaters) or scavengers (animals that eat dead remains of other animals).

► This ground squirrel is food for a small python, which might be eaten by a banded mongoose.

WHAT HUNTS THE HUNTERS?

All herbivores, like the ground squirrel, are hunted by predators, like the python. But predators themselves may be hunted. Mongooses hunt pythons, and mongooses, in turn, may be killed by an eagle (called a top predator, because nothing hunts it). So there is a chain of feeding: from grass to squirrel, to python, to mongoose, to eagle. But the python eats many other small animals, and the eagle will kill anything it can find. So food chains link together, forming a complex food web.

◄ Hyenas and vultures are scavengers, feeding on dead animals.

▼ Predators, like this lion, need to creep up quietly to avoid being seen by their prey. Once they have been noticed, they need to move very quickly to catch their prey, and be very strong to kill it.

HOW DO HUNTERS HELP THEIR PREY?

Although no herbivore 'wants' to be killed by a predator (a hunting animal), predators have an important role in controlling their numbers. Without predators, there would soon be too many herbivores, which would eat all the plants and finally end up starving.

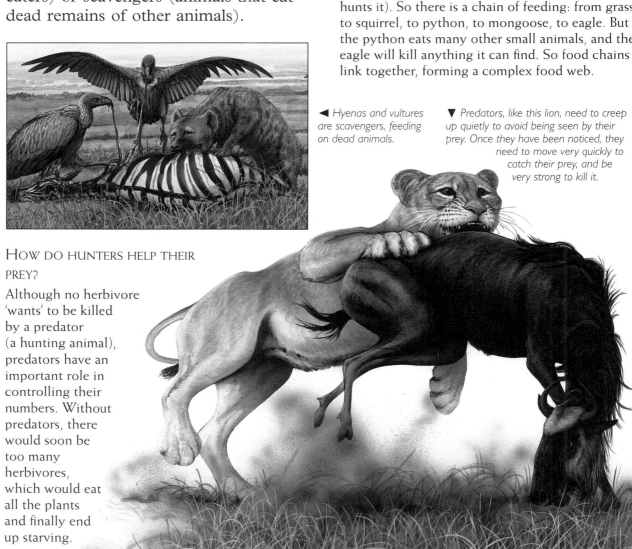

WHY DO SOME ANIMALS HAVE A DOUBLE STOMACH?

Most leaves and fruits are easy for herbivores to eat. But grass, the most plentiful green plant, is tough and difficult to digest. To help them cope, many grass-eaters have a double stomach system. When they graze, the grass is held in the front chamber of their stomach, called the rumen. Later, they 'cough up' the partly-digested grass and chew it more thoroughly before finally swallowing it. This is known as 'chewing the cud'.

ARE ALL ANIMALS PLANT-EATERS OR HUNTERS?

Not all carnivores (meat-eaters) are predators. Some, like the hyena and vulture, are scavengers, searching for dead animals to eat. Other, much smaller scavengers help to break up the bits of bone and fur that the large scavengers leave behind. And fungi and bacteria also help to break up (decompose) the remains of dead animals. Some animals, such as dung beetles, feed on undigested food that has passed through the gut of other animals and been dumped in their droppings.

▼ *Impalas graze quickly on the open plain. The grass stays in their front stomach chamber until later, when in safety, they cough it up to chew it more thoroughly.*

▶ *Some micro-organisms 'make' nitrates, a vital nutrient, from nitrogen in the atmosphere. Decomposers recycle nitrates in dead plant and animal matter back into the soil.*

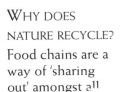

ANIMALS

MICRO-ORGANISMS

PLANTS
SOIL

DECOMPOSERS

WHY DOES NATURE RECYCLE?

Food chains are a way of 'sharing out' amongst all living things the energy that plants capture from sunlight. The nutrients plants need in order to continue growing would soon be used up unless these were recycled back into the soil for plants to use again.

Decomposers – tiny animals, fungi, and bacteria – have a vital role in breaking-up dead plant and animal material and releasing their locked-up nutrients back into the soil. Among the most important nutrients for plant growth are nitrates. Although nitrogen gas makes up four-fifths of the atmosphere, only a few microscopic plants and animals (micro-organisms) are able to make nitrates from nitrogen, so they have a very important role as soil enrichers. Otherwise, plants rely on decomposers to recycle the nitrates needed for their continued growth.

HOW DO FUNGI HELP?

Fungi (mushrooms, toadstools, and their relatives) look like plants but have no green chloroplasts, so they cannot photosynthesize. Instead, they rely on a network of root-like threads running through the soil, which dissolve dead leaves and other plant material, providing nutrients and energy. Many fungi live partly on or in the roots of trees and other plants. In return for protection, they provide their 'host' plant with extra nutrients.

▼ *The vital part of this toadstool is a tangle of root-like threads in the soil or the roots of a tree.*

Ecosystems

WHAT IS AN ECOSYSTEM? The world can be divided up into a series of natural zones of life, in which all the animals and plants share roughly the same problems and advantages. These zones are called ecosystems. The animals and plants are also part of the ecosystem. The trees of a forest ecosystem, for example, provide shelter and food for other plants and animals, and the leafy 'roof' they create makes the forest floor shady and damp.

Ice cap

Although there is no land at the North Pole a vast sheet of ice floats on the Arctic Ocean throughout the year. The huge continent of Antarctica in the south (not shown on the map below) is covered by a dome of ice up to 2.8 miles thick that hides almost all the land beneath. No plants can live on these ice caps, and only a few animals occasionally wander here in search of food. Some hardy birds use the Antarctic ice as a breeding ground.

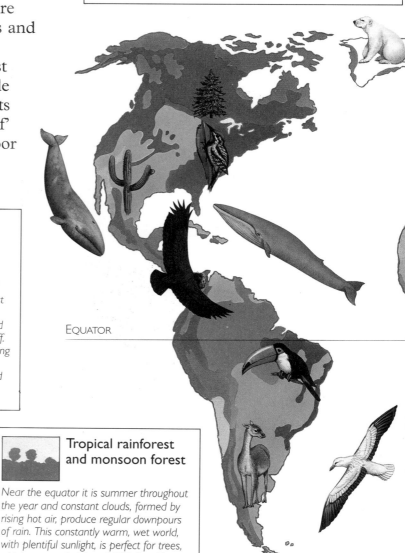

EQUATOR

Coniferous forest

The trees that grow farthest north are generally conifers, recognized by their needle-like leaves and seed-bearing cones. They form a vast zone of forest called the taiga. Their tough, narrow leaves allow them to cope with the snow that falls in winter, and their 'Christmas-tree' shape helps the snow slide off. Their cones provide food for squirrels and seed-eating birds such as crossbills and nutcrackers, while wild boar, bison, and deer live beneath the trees, hunted by wolves.

WHY ARE DESERTS DRY AND RAIN FORESTS WET?

All the world's hot deserts lie in two bands north and south of the equator. At the equator, constant high temperatures heat the air, which then rises into the atmosphere. This makes it shed its moisture as rain, creating the rainforests. The resulting hot, dry air moves away from the equator at high level. It drops closer to the ground and is drawn back toward the equator, creating hot winds in the desert that suck the remaining moisture from the ground.

Tropical rainforest and monsoon forest

Near the equator it is summer throughout the year and constant clouds, formed by rising hot air, produce regular downpours of rain. This constantly warm, wet world, with plentiful sunlight, is perfect for trees, which grow to heights of 197 feet. This forms the tropical rainforest and the even wetter monsoon forest.

ARE THERE ANY OTHER ECOSYSTEMS?

Yes, there is another ecosystem – perhaps the most important ecosystem of all. It is the sea. Because humans live on land, we often forget the sea, but it is full of hidden life and is the main influence on the world's weather.

Broad-leaved and mixed forest

South of the coniferous forest zone, the world was once shrouded in a forest of trees with large, flat leaves, called broad-leaves. These need at least three times as many warm days as conifers to grow well, so they only grow in the milder south, although many shed their leaves in autumn to protect them from the winter ice. In summer, many birds and mammals feed on their berries and nuts. Today, humans have cleared much of this forest to make way for farmland.

Arctic and mountains

South of the northern ice-cap is a rim of land that is free from ice and snow for just a few, short weeks each summer. Then, flowers burst briefly into bloom, insects hatch and fly, and birds and mammals arrive from farther south to breed. High in the mountains, the weather is just as cold and windy as it is near the Arctic, and similar plants and animals survive.

Grassland, dry grassland, and scrub

Between the desert and the broad-leaved forest is a zone that is too dry and too thin-soiled for trees to grow. Here, the shallow roots of grasses spread beneath the surface to soak up moisture. Some of these grasslands are little more than grassy deserts, but, in slightly wetter areas, vast plains of grass develop, variously called savannah, prairie, pampas, or steppe. Huge herds of grazing animals feed here, closely followed by their hunters. A few scrubby bushes may also grow here, with roots that reach deep to find water.

Desert

As the rising hot air over the equator sheds its moisture as rain, dry air is drawn in from the north and south. This creates a zone where dry winds bring less than 10 inches of rainfall a year – the desert zone. Without clouds, the sun beats down endlessly here, so daytime temperatures rise to 136°F, but temperatures drop swiftly at night, sometimes to below freezing. A fifth of the Earth's land surface is desert, most of it bare and rocky although some is sandy. Life is desperately difficult here, but a few plants and animals are adapted to survive the heat and drought.

WHAT ARE VEGETATION ZONES?

If you flew from the equator to the Arctic on a clear day, you would notice the appearance of the land change beneath you. Vegetation grows in zones. Plants grow higher and more densely where the air is warmer and more humid – near the equator. Few plants grow in the cool, dry air of the Arctic.

Arctic and Antarctic Life

HOW IS LIFE DIFFICULT AT THE POLES? Although it can be extremely cold in the Arctic and Antarctic, the animals and plants there have adapted to cope. Their biggest problems are that the water they need is locked up as ice, and that the snow smothers plants and makes it difficult for animals to search for food.

▲ Arctic animals include (clockwise from top) the polar bear, snow bunting, skua, walrus, musk ox, arctic hare, reindeer, and arctic tern.

WHAT IS IT LIKE LIVING IN THE ARCTIC?

There is no land at the North Pole. Most of the Arctic is a vast ice sheet, up to 13 feet thick, floating on the sea. No plants grow on the ice, where temperatures drop to −89°F, and the only animals are wanderers searching for food. Most life is in the rich ocean around the ice sheet and on the slightly warmer land further south.

► Snowy owls hunt voles and lemmings in the tundra.

WHAT IS THE TUNDRA?

The rim of land around the Arctic Ocean is a vast, icy wilderness called the tundra, where no trees can grow and the land is free of snow for only a few summer months. Voles, lemmings, and hares feed on plants that blossom in summer and survive beneath the winter snow. Musk oxen and reindeer also live here, pawing beneath the snow to find food. These animals are food for hunters like the arctic fox, wolf, polar bear, and snowy owl. These predators also hunt the visitors that come to the tundra in summer to breed, such as geese, shorebirds, and seabirds.

► The arctic tern escapes the Arctic winter by flying south to the Antarctic summer.

WHAT ARRIVES ON THE TUNDRA IN THE SUMMER?

In summer, bumblebees and butterflies emerge to feed on the tundra's summer flowers, and mosquitoes hatch from lakes and ponds. These provide more than enough food for the animals that live in the region all year. Geese and shorebirds, which spend the winter further south, fly here to lay their eggs and feed their young, and the sea-cliffs are covered with breeding seabirds.

HOW DO PLANTS SURVIVE IN THE TUNDRA?

Most arctic plants flower together in a mass to attract the pollinating insects that emerge in the brief summer warmth. Their low-growing cushions of leaves barely survive the winter, protected beneath a blanket of snow.

► The leaves of many arctic plants form tight cushions, hugging the ground to avoid icy winds.

▲ Antarctic animals include the orca, weddell seal, elephant seal, emperor penguin, skua, blue whale, sheathbill, krill, and albatross.

WHY IS THE ANTARCTIC OCEAN FULL OF LIFE?

Around the huge Antarctic continent, deep-sea currents well up, carrying with them rich supplies of the nutrients plants need. Although the sea temperature rarely rises above 32°F, microscopic floating plants, called phytoplankton, use the nutrients and the long hours of summer daylight, and quickly multiply. Tiny animals feed on them, and they in turn are eaten by shrimp-like creatures called krill. The krill provide plentiful food for whales and for fish, which then become the prey of seals, penguins, and other seabirds.

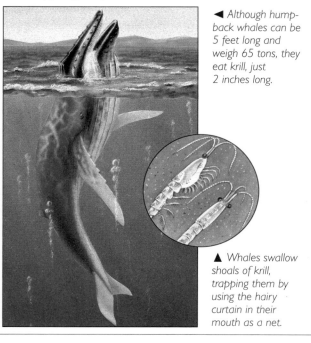

◄ Although hump-back whales can be 5 feet long and weigh 65 tons, they eat krill, just 2 inches long.

▲ Whales swallow shoals of krill, trapping them by using the hairy curtain in their mouth as a net.

WHAT LIVES ON ANTARCTICA?

Antarctica is a vast, mountainous continent, where temperatures drop to −128°F and only tiny areas near the coast are ever free of snow and ice. Just two species of flowering plants are found in Antarctica, so there are no grazing animals, although a few insects feed among the banks of moss and lichen that briefly thaw in summer. Most life depends on the rich food available in the ocean, but fish-eating animals, such as seals and penguins, must come ashore to breed, sometimes in huge numbers. Seabirds called petrels scavenge dead seals and penguins, while skuas wait around penguin colonies to grab sick birds or unprotected chicks.

HOW DO PENGUINS KEEP WARM?

Penguins have a thick layer of oily fat called blubber and a double coat of feathers to keep them warm. Their cylindrical shape and small ears also help to reduce heat loss. Protected in this way, the largest penguins (emperor penguins) spend the entire winter living on the ice, huddled together in colonies of up to 50,000 birds, while they rear their young.

▼ King penguins stand 35 inches tall. They breed in huge colonies on the less snowy islands north of Antarctica, such as South Georgia. They make no nest, incubating their single egg balanced on their feet, protecting it by a fold of skin.

Mountain Life

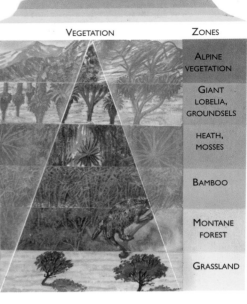

HOW ARE MOUNTAINS AND THE ARCTIC ALIKE? Because there is only a thin blanket of atmosphere above mountains, heat is lost rapidly at night and in winter, and conditions on the mountain tops can be as cold and windswept as in the Arctic. Even in Africa, the highest mountain tops are covered in snow all year, and plants and animals have to cope with the same problems as those living near the poles.

VEGETATION	ZONES
	ALPINE VEGETATION
	GIANT LOBELIA, GROUNDSELS
	HEATH, MOSSES
	BAMBOO
	MONTANE FOREST
	GRASSLAND

▲ *The Mountains of the Moon have many zones of life, from the African grasslands to the snowy peaks.*

WHAT IS IT LIKE LIVING IN THE MOUNTAINS?

Although the weather can be very arctic on the mountain tops, lower down the slopes it can be much warmer and more sheltered. This depends on the part of the world the mountains are in. In the Mountains of the Moon in East Africa, for example, the foot of the mountains are hot savannah and there is dense rainforest on the lower slopes, while the tops are always snow-covered. This series of zones, getting gradually colder up the mountain, means that animals can escape the cold of the high tops by moving downhill in winter. Few animals live high up all year round, although many move up in summer, when grazers find lots of plants free from snow and predators hunt the grazers.

▼ *The warm coats of snow leopards are grayish and spotted to help them hide among the mountain rocks as they hunt sheep and goats.*

▲ *Mountain snowbells open their flowers beneath the snow to get a quick start when the snow melts.*

HOW DO PLANTS SURVIVE THE MOUNTAIN FREEZE?

Similar plants grow on mountains and in the Arctic because in both areas they need to cope with winter snow, freezing winds, and a very short season in which to grow, flower, and set seed. Many grow in low cushion shapes to protect them from the wind and help them survive beneath the winter blanket of snow. Also, because rain drains quickly from the rocky slopes, many have small, leathery leaves which reduce water loss, and are less likely to freeze.

WHICH BIRDS SCAVENGE IN MOUNTAINS?

Vultures are the most famous mountain scavengers, circling high in the sky looking for dead animals on which to feed. In other countries, buzzards and eagles fill the same role. The lammergeier, or bearded vulture, which lives in mountains from the European Alps to the Himalayas, is famous for its trick of carrying bones to heights of up to 200 feet in the sky, then dropping them, so the bones smash on rocks and the bird can feed on the rich marrow inside.

Condors, the largest American vultures, can travel more than 20 miles in search of food. Sadly, the Californian condor suffered so badly from colliding with electricity cables and from eating poisoned baits left by farmers that all the wild birds had died out by 1987. But about 50 birds survive in zoos, and these are being bred so that some can be released back into safer areas in the wild.

▼ *A wingspan of 10 feet allows Andean condors to soar effortlessly in search of prey.*

▲ *Dotterels winter in hot grasslands farther south, but in summer they breed in European mountains and the Arctic.*

WHICH MALE BIRDS REAR THEIR YOUNG?

Dotterels are related to the wading birds that feed on seashores, but they breed in the mountains of Europe and the Arctic, where there are plenty of insects when their chicks hatch in summer. Until then, food is so scarce that the female uses up all her energy reserves just laying her eggs. Afterwards she flies off and the male hatches the eggs and rears the young.

WHAT MAKES MOUNTAIN GOATS 'SURE-FOOTED'?

From bighorn sheep in North America to chamois in the Alps, sheep and goats are the main grazers in mountains. They are incredibly 'sure-footed', able to nimbly pick their way across almost sheer rock-faces. Chamois have flexible hooves with dimpled soles that grip the rock as well as mountaineers' boots do. They can leap 23 feet between rocks or 13 feet up a vertical rock-face, with 'shock absorbers' in their legs to cushion the impact of landing. They also have sharp eyes and ears, warning them of approaching predators.

▶ *Chamois are agile goat-antelopes. They live mostly in woodland high in the Alps, but move farther up the mountains in summer.*

Life in the Temperate Zone

WHAT DOES 'TEMPERATE' MEAN? Temperate means 'moderate in climate'. The temperate zone is the zone that best suits humans because it is neither too hot nor too cold, and there is enough rainfall throughout the year to grow crops. This is the natural zone of broad-leaved woodland, now mostly cleared to make farmland.

WHERE DO MOOSE LIVE?

Moose, the largest living deer, live in the temperate forests of North America, trampling the winter snow to find leaves and bark to eat. In summer they often wade into rivers to eat water weeds and escape the plagues of mosquitoes.

▲ *The moose of North America is known as an 'elk' in the forests of northern Europe and Asia.*

DOES ANYTHING LIVE BENEATH TREE BARK?

If you peel back the bark of an old or dead tree, you may find galleries of tunnels in the wood. These are made by the young (larvae) of wood-boring beetles, like the longhorn beetle above. The adult beetles lay their eggs in the wood, and the larvae, when they hatch, munch their way through the wood, making a tunnel that gradually widens as they grow. Then they change (metamorphose) into adult beetles and chew their way out of the tree, leaving a neat hole at the tunnel's mouth. The adults fly off to find mates, so they can lay their eggs and start the process again. The fat 'grubs' are safe beneath the bark from most hunters except woodpeckers, which drill through the bark to find them.

HOW DO SOME ANIMALS LIVE WITH HUMANS?

Over the last 5,000 years, humans have made huge changes to the planet, destroying large areas of wild ecosystems and replacing them with landscapes of fields, buildings, and planted forests. Some animals and plants, unable to cope with these changes, are now rare, but others have adapted to live alongside humans. The house mouse and rat have traveled around the world with human farmers and sailors. Rabbits have been introduced to many countries, originally for food, but have since become a major pest on crops. Plants adapted to grow on open ground have become 'weeds' in fields and gardens, while many animals have learnt to take advantage of the feast of food in field crops. Insects have found new homes in the warmth of houses. Some wood-boring beetles, for example, have moved from dead trees into the timber of roof beams, floors, and furniture, where their highly damaging larvae are called 'woodworm'.

▼ *From grasslands, harvest mice have moved into wheat fields. The grain provides plentiful food but weasels and harvesting machines are a danger to them.*

▶ Two backward-pointing toes, sharp claws, and stiff tail feathers help woodpeckers climb tree trunks.

◀ Wood-boring beetle larvae live beneath the bark of trees, making tunnels as they eat their way through the tough wood. When they are ready to turn into flying adults, they drill their way out through the bark.

WHY DO WOODPECKERS DRUM?

The drumming of a woodpecker in summer is a display noise – like the song of other birds – to attract a mate and warn other woodpeckers off its home patch. The noise is made by hammering a tree trunk up to 25 times in a second, and the woodpecker's skull is strengthened to cope with this pounding. The chisel-like bill is also used, more quietly, to dig beneath bark for insects, which are scooped up by its long tongue, or to drill nest holes in old trees.

▼ Although racoons normally live in woods and bushy places in America, some have moved into cities, where they live in sheds and attics. They raid garbage cans at night for food, and can even untie ropes knotted around them.

WHAT DRIVES ANIMALS TO MIGRATE?

Even in the temperate zone, winter can be cold, and most insects pass the winter in hibernation or as eggs or larvae. So insect-eating birds, like swallows, swifts, and warblers, fly south to spend the winter where insects are still plentiful. But, even here, there would not be enough insects to feed all the hungry young born in springtime, so the migrants move back north to raise their families as the insects hatch there. Other migrants, like geese and shorebirds, nest in the Arctic in summer, but move south for a more temperate winter.

▼ After spending the winter in California and Mexico, monarch butterflies migrate 1,800 miles north to breed.

WHICH ANIMALS HAVE MOVED TO CITIES?

Surprisingly many animals have adapted to city life. Urban pigeons live in cities from Rome to New York, a long way from where their ancestors once nested on sea-cliffs. Huge flocks of starlings roost on the warmth of city buildings in London and Paris, and kestrels and peregrine falcons have followed them, nesting on the highest ledges of skyscrapers, churches, and towers. Sparrowhawks swoop on songbirds feeding at garden bird tables in a new kind of city food chain. Foxes are common in parks and railway embankments in the middle of towns, and badgers raid garbage cans at night for food. In America, racoons and skunks have invaded cities in the same way.

FACTS

Long-distance migrants
The arctic tern flies farthest on migration: one was recorded covering 13,969 miles from Russia to Australia.

Adult eels may swim 3,000 miles from rivers around Europe and North America to the Sargasso Sea off the Caribbean to lay their eggs.

High-flying migrants
Migrating whooper swans have been recorded flying 26,995 feet above sea level.

Grassland Life

WHERE ARE THE GRASSLANDS? Around the world, there are vast plains of grass, known by various names: savannah in Africa; steppes in Europe; prairie in North America; and pampas in South America. Grassland occurs where the weather is too dry and the soil is too poor or shallow for trees to grow well, although sometimes heavy grazing by farm animals turns wooded areas into grassland, or dry grassland into desert.

▲ Emus are relatives of ostriches and can run at up to 30 miles per hour across the dry grasslands of Australia to escape enemies.

DOES GRAZING DESTROY GRASSLAND?

The shoots of grasses grow so close to the ground that the mouths of grazing animals leave them untouched, and grass leaves keep growing even if their tips are nibbled. So grass continues to grow even when it is grazed, providing a non-stop supply of food. In the African savannah there is enough for the large herds of antelopes, wildebeest, and zebras, and the smaller numbers of buffalo, rhinoceroses, and elephants. These animals in turn provide plentiful food for lions, leopards, cheetahs, hyenas, and hunting dogs.

WHAT GRAZES ON THE PRAIRIE, STEPPES, AND PAMPAS?

Each grassland area has its own wildlife. Once there were 50 million buffalo roaming the American prairie, although hunting almost made them extinct and today most of the prairie has been converted to farmland. Semi-wild horses and cattle are the main grazers on the steppes, and the ostrich-like rhea is the largest grazer of the pampas.

► On the African savannah, giraffes eat leaves from the few trees with roots that can reach water. Impalas mainly eat grass and are hunted by cheetahs.

▼ Prairie dogs have litters of up to ten pups, which are born in warm chambers in underground burrows. Pups come to the surface to graze after about seven weeks.

▲ Locusts are tropical grasshoppers, up to 2.5 inches in length.

WHICH ANIMALS BUILD THEIR OWN CITIES?

Prairie dogs bark like dogs but they are actually ground-dwelling squirrels, living in networks of burrows beneath the American prairie. When they leave their burrows to graze, some individuals stand on mounds like soldiers on guard, watching out for hunters such as ferrets, foxes, buzzards, and snakes. Individual colonies are grouped together into 'cities', and in 1901 one prairie dog city in Texas was estimated to cover 23,000 square miles and hold 400 million prairie dogs. Because these ate as much grass as one and a half million cows, farmers poisoned and shot them in huge numbers. Despite this, several million still survive on the prairie today.

HOW MANY LOCUSTS MAKE A PLAGUE?

After years of drought, autumn rains in north Africa trigger female locusts to lay up to 1,000 eggs. The wingless locusts that hatch soon eat up all the green food locally. They then molt, emerging with wings, and are carried off by the wind in 'plagues' of up to 50 thousand million. They strip vegetation wherever they land, until the drought returns and they starve.

WHY DO ANIMALS GATHER AT WATERHOLES?

The rainfall in the savannah is so low and seasonal that some areas shift between grassland and desert with just a slight change in climate. At the end of the dry season, when the grass is brown and parched, waterholes become vital for the thirsty grazing animals.

◀ Animals, like these zebra, visit waterholes in large herds. They drink quickly, while some animals watch for predators, including crocodiles. If they are attacked, most of the herd escape in the panic that follows. The marabou storks are waiting for any victims.

Desert Life

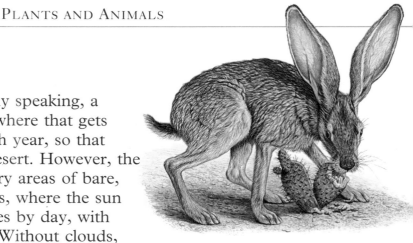

W HAT IS A DESERT? Strictly speaking, a desert is defined as anywhere that gets less than 10 inches of rain each year, so that even parts of Antarctica are desert. However, the term is usually used for hot, dry areas of bare, shattered rock or shifting sands, where the sun beats down from cloudless skies by day, with temperatures reaching 136˚F. Without clouds, night-time temperatures drop rapidly, sometimes to below freezing.

▲ *The jack-rabbit's huge ears help to keep it cool.*

HOW DO ANIMALS COPE WITH THE EXTREME HEAT?

Most desert animals survive the day in burrows, under stones, or in nests in cacti (like this elf owl), coming out to feed in the cool of night. Many have light coats that reflect heat to keep them cooler. All desert animals save water carefully. The night-time dew provides some moisture but most water comes from the animal's food.

HOW DO PLANTS SURVIVE IN THE DESERT?

Most desert plants survive the long, dry periods as seeds in the soil, sprouting as soon as the rare desert rains arrive. They flower rapidly in a mass of color, quickly releasing their seeds before the drought returns. A cactus has a mass of roots, just beneath the sand, which rapidly absorb rain-water. This is stored in its barrel-like stem, which is pleated so it can swell up quickly.

WHY DO JACK-RABBITS HAVE BIG EARS?

Jack-rabbits (above) live in the deserts of America and are actually hares, not rabbits. In the hottest weather they spend much of the time in shade, but when they do come out, their huge ears, which are full of blood vessels, act like car radiators to help cool them down. When it gets cold at night, they fold their ears back along their body to save heat. Jack-rabbits get all the moisture they need by nibbling cactuses, chewing round the spines and eating the moist, fleshy pulp inside.

◄ *The lesser long-nosed bat drinks nectar from the flower of the saguaro cactus, pollinating it as it crosses the desert.*

HOW DOES THE SIDEWINDER GET ITS NAME?

The sidewinder snake of southern African deserts does not push its way forwards through the soft, shifting sand. Instead it slithers sideways in a rapid series of S-bends, which is less tiring, allows it to move much faster, and means that only two parts of its body touch the scorching sand at any time.

WHICH ANIMALS CAN LIVE FOR THREE YEARS WITHOUT A DRINK?

Jerboas survive the desert heat by living underground in burrows, blocked by a plug of sand to keep out hot air and predators. They come out to feed at night, and are so good at conserving moisture that they can live for three years in a laboratory eating only dry seeds, without water to drink. Although only 6 inches long, they can hop up to 10 feet using their strong hind legs.

HOW DO CAMELS SURVIVE THE DESERT HEAT?

Since camels cannot escape desert heat down burrows or find anything big enough to shade them, their bodies must be adapted to cope with heat. Their body temperature can vary between 93°F and 106°F without ill effects (unlike humans, who soon die if they overheat). Camels do not store fat beneath their skin like most mammals because this blocks heat loss. Instead the fat is stored in their humps. (Bactrian camels have two humps, and Arabian camels, or dromedaries, have one.) The hump can be broken down to provide energy and about 13 gallons of water. It is soon restored when the camel drinks again.

◀ An Arabian camel.

▲ The sidewinder can travel at almost 3 miles per hour – much faster and using much less energy than a human moving across the desert sand.

◀ Jerboas reach speeds of 15 miles per hour hopping across the desert, using their long tail for balance, but return to their burrows when danger threatens.

Rainforest Life

Is the rainforest a jungle? Tropical rainforests are sometimes called 'jungles', but they are rarely as dense as that name suggests, except along the banks of rivers. They grow near the equator, where it is always warm. In the steamy heat, clouds bring at least 100 inches of rain a year, producing perfect conditions for plant growth. Trees grow 130–160 feet tall, their tops forming a dense green canopy.

How is a rainforest like an apartment block?

The sunny canopy is very different from the forest floor, and different animals live in each layer of the trees, like people in an apartment block. The 'basement' is the dark, damp jungle floor, where termites, worms, and land crabs feed on plant material falling from above. On the 'ground floor' pigs and antelopes eat fallen fruit, and are hunted by jungle cats, while leeches suck their blood.

What lives in the forest 'attic'?

Many animals feed on leaves and fruits in the canopy. Spider monkeys (1) use their grasping tails to swing through the trees, while 'flying' squirrels glide between branches using flaps of skin between their legs. Other monkeys, squirrels, bats, and birds also feed in the canopy, hunted by pythons and by eagles circling above. Some plants, called epiphytes (2), grow closer to sunlight by perching on branches high above the ground.

Which insects are farmers?

Leaf-cutter ants (3) farm their own food. First they snip off portions of leaves with their scissor-like jaws. Then they carry the leaf segments to their underground nests, where they chew them into a pulp. At this stage they lay the pulp aside until a fungus grows on it. Then they harvest and eat the fungus, which provides much better food than a tough leaf.

▶ *The tops of rainforest trees form a continuous green canopy (C), broken only by occasional taller trees called emergents (B). Some of these are flowering emergents (A), which flower at any time of year. The jungle floor (H) is mostly dark, except where fallen trees make clearings (F). Giant ferns (E) often grow in these. The tallest trees have buttress roots (G) to prop them up, and lianas (D) hang down from their tops.*

HOW DO SOME INSECTS AVOID BEING EATEN?

With so many predators in the rainforest, animals have adopted all sorts of tricks to avoid being eaten. Many are colored and shaped to camouflage (disguise) them from hunters. This insect (left), called a katydid, is the exact shape and color of a leaf, complete with vein-like markings.

◀ *To improve their camouflage among the leaves, katydids shake as they move, like leaves in the wind.*

WHY DO BRIGHT COLORS WARN OF DANGER?

Instead of camouflage, some rainforest creatures rely on bright colors for protection. The skin of the poison-arrow frog contains a poison so strong that one drop can kill a large bird. Human hunters have also used it to tip their poisoned arrows. But the poison is of no use to the frog if the frog is eaten first. Its bright colors are there to warn hunters that it is dangerous and should be left alone.

WHAT MAKES HOWLER MONKEYS HOWL?

The deep howls of male howler monkeys echo round the South American rainforest at dawn and dusk. They make the noise to warn other howler monkeys to keep out of the family group's patch of forest, so they can keep the food supplies there for themselves.

◀ *A bony box in the thick neck of the howler monkey amplifies its howling calls.*

Water and Wetland Life

WHY DOES WATER MAKE A GOOD HOME? Three quarters of a living cell is water. Most organisms struggle to maintain this water level in their bodies, but it is not a problem for plants and animals living in water. Water is slow to heat or cool, so it generally stays at a perfect temperature for life.

▼ Herons wade in lakes to catch fish. Water lilies grow up from the mud to flower on the surface.

WHAT LIVES IN RIVERS AND PONDS?

The larvae (young forms) of many insects live among stones on the beds of rivers and ponds. These are food for fish, which are then eaten by birds and otters. Some water plants float below the water, while others, like water lilies, grow up from roots in the mud, so their leaves float on the surface. Dense reed beds around the water's edge provide a nesting place for birds. They are also a platform for insect larvae to rest on when they leave the water and turn into flying adults.

WHY DO SALMON BREED IN RIVERS?

Salmon spend most of their lives at sea, where they find plentiful food. But when it is time to breed they return to the river, struggling upstream to lay their eggs in shallow gravel beds. Then they go back to the sea, although many die of exhaustion on the way. Newly-hatched salmon find plenty of small insects as food and they meet fewer dangerous fish in the rivers. They only head to sea after several years, when they are big enough to be relatively safe from sea predators.

WHAT HAPPENS TO PONDS IN WINTER?

Water expands when it freezes. This makes ice lighter than water, so it floats on the surface of ponds, forming a protective blanket that stops deeper water freezing. The air gap beneath the ice provides oxygen for air-breathing water creatures.

WHY ARE PONDS DISAPPEARING?

Sometimes people fill in ponds, but shallow ponds also disappear naturally. Water plants around the edge trap mud amongst their roots, raising the pond bed until willow trees can grow there. These dry the pond out, and woodland takes over. Only regular trampling by animals or clearance by humans stops this natural change. Many ponds are disappearing from neglect because they are no longer needed to water horses and cattle.

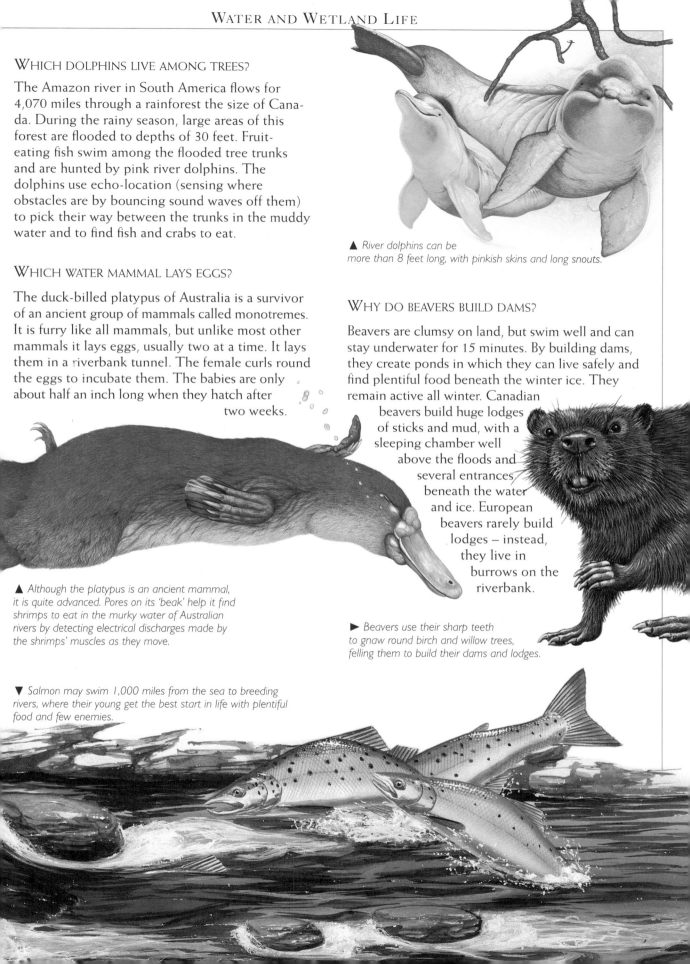

WHICH DOLPHINS LIVE AMONG TREES?

The Amazon river in South America flows for 4,070 miles through a rainforest the size of Canada. During the rainy season, large areas of this forest are flooded to depths of 30 feet. Fruit-eating fish swim among the flooded tree trunks and are hunted by pink river dolphins. The dolphins use echo-location (sensing where obstacles are by bouncing sound waves off them) to pick their way between the trunks in the muddy water and to find fish and crabs to eat.

▲ River dolphins can be more than 8 feet long, with pinkish skins and long snouts.

WHICH WATER MAMMAL LAYS EGGS?

The duck-billed platypus of Australia is a survivor of an ancient group of mammals called monotremes. It is furry like all mammals, but unlike most other mammals it lays eggs, usually two at a time. It lays them in a riverbank tunnel. The female curls round the eggs to incubate them. The babies are only about half an inch long when they hatch after two weeks.

WHY DO BEAVERS BUILD DAMS?

Beavers are clumsy on land, but swim well and can stay underwater for 15 minutes. By building dams, they create ponds in which they can live safely and find plentiful food beneath the winter ice. They remain active all winter. Canadian beavers build huge lodges of sticks and mud, with a sleeping chamber well above the floods and several entrances beneath the water and ice. European beavers rarely build lodges – instead, they live in burrows on the riverbank.

▲ Although the platypus is an ancient mammal, it is quite advanced. Pores on its 'beak' help it find shrimps to eat in the murky water of Australian rivers by detecting electrical discharges made by the shrimps' muscles as they move.

► Beavers use their sharp teeth to gnaw round birch and willow trees, felling them to build their dams and lodges.

▼ Salmon may swim 1,000 miles from the sea to breeding rivers, where their young get the best start in life with plentiful food and few enemies.

Life in the Oceans

DOES THE SEA MAKE A GOOD HOME? Seawater provides a perfect life-support system for plants and animals. This is true for large animals as well as small fragile ones floating freely in the water. Their bodies are supported by the water, so they don't need strong skeletons. The water contains plenty of minerals and nutrients for healthy growth, which are constantly mixed by the ocean currents, and water temperatures stay steady throughout the year.

IS IT DARK IN THE DEEP SEA?

In murky seawater near coasts, all sunlight disappears about 300 feet beneath the surface. But in clear, tropical waters some light reaches down to 1,900 feet. Near the surface there is plenty of light for photosynthesis to occur and huge numbers of tiny plants (phytoplankton) float here, forming the first link of all animal food chains. No plants can live in the colder, totally dark water lower down, and the relatively few animals there rely mostly on food that drifts down from above. Because of the different conditions at different ocean depths, there are zones of life, just as there are at different heights on a mountainside (page 76).

WHICH IS THE LARGEST FISH THAT HUNTS?

The great white shark is the largest hunting fish, reaching 21 feet long and weighing up to 1.5 tons. Although there is a larger shark – the whale shark – it does not hunt but feeds by filtering tiny animals from the water. Great whites live mainly in tropical and subtropical seas. They hunt near the surface where there are most fish and may catch seals.

HOW FAR DO WHALES MIGRATE?

Many species of whale spend the summer in oceans near the Poles, were there is abundant fish or krill to eat. Then, before the seas freeze over, they migrate up to 12,500 miles to warmer, sheltered waters near the equator, where they give birth to their calves.

▼ Different creatures live at different levels in the sea, from jellyfish near the surface to deep-sea eels and anglerfish. Near the surface phytoplankton are the first link in the food chain.

SEAL

PHYTOPLANKTON

JELLYFISH

KILLER WHALE

OCTOPUS

SQUID

DEEP-SEA EELS

ANGLERFISH

WHY DO JELLYFISH STING?

Jellyfish use their sting as a weapon to catch prey. The stinging cells on their tentacles paralyze small fish, which are then brushed to the jellyfish's mouth by beating hairs before being eaten. The jellyfish's sting also protects it from hunting animals.

▼ A jellyfish swims by jetting water out of its 'bell'.

FACTS

Deep holes
Mount Everest could be sunk in the deepest ocean trenches and still have 6,500 feet of water above it!

Ocean depths
The average depth of the sea is 12,500 feet, but some ocean trenches are more than 36,000 feet deep.

Water world
Sea covers 71 percent of the surface of the Earth. Perhaps we should call it Planet Sea instead.

Dark waters
300 feet down there is only 1 percent of the sunlight that is falling on the water's surface, but no red light reaches beneath 100 feet.

HOW DO ANGLERFISH GO FISHING?

Anglerfish have a thread-like feature on their heads, with a fleshy, quivering tip, which acts like a fly on a fishing rod to attract small fish. The anglerfish then opens its large mouth, and its prey is sucked in with the in-rushing water. On some deep-sea anglerfish this lure glows in the dark to attract prey.

HOW DOES A SCALLOP ESCAPE TROUBLE?

The soft bodies of scallops are protected by two hinged shells. They feed by opening their shells a little, then sucking in water and filtering food particles from it. They escape enemies, such as starfish or octopuses, by clapping their shells shut and jetting out water, which propels them forward.

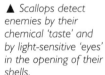

▲ Scallops detect enemies by their chemical 'taste' and by light-sensitive 'eyes' in the opening of their shells.

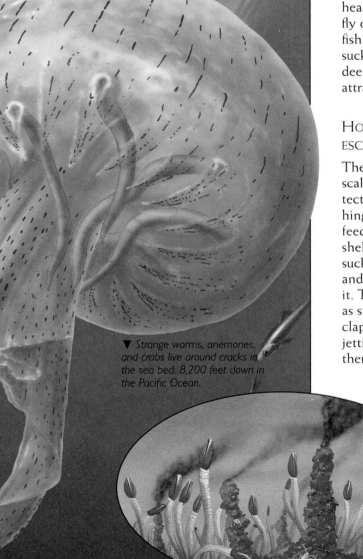

▼ Strange worms, anemones, and crabs live around cracks in the sea bed, 8,200 feet down in the Pacific Ocean.

WHERE IS THERE LIFE WITHOUT SUNLIGHT?

Although most life relies directly or indirectly on the energy that plants capture from sunshine, animals around a few deep-sea vents can live without any input from the Sun's energy. Here, bacteria feed on sulfur-rich chemicals emerging from the Earth's crust. Strange clams and worms eat the bacteria, and crabs eat them.

Life around the Coasts

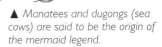

WHY ARE COASTS SO FULL OF LIFE? Coastal seas are especially rich in wildlife, which is why we see so many seabirds feeding around their shores. In shallow water there is plenty of light for seaweed to grow. Small animals feed on the seaweeds and shelter among them. Others hide in rock cracks, or burrow and feed in the rich mud. Many fish come into the safety of shallow sea inlets to breed, and these are food for fishing birds and seals.

▲ Manatees and dugongs (sea cows) are said to be the origin of the mermaid legend.

HOW ARE CORAL REEFS MADE?

In tropical seas, many coasts are fringed by shallow reefs built by remarkable animals called corals, living in huge colonies. They are like small sea anemones, with sticky tentacles for catching minute animal food from the seawater. Tiny plants inside the corals make food by photosynthesis in sunlight, and this extra nourishment helps the corals grow. As corals die, new ones grow on top of their remains. The rock-like mass of coral skeletons, cemented together by a crusty pink seaweed, forms the crumbly reef.

WHAT MAKES CORAL REEFS SO SPECTACULAR?

Corals, and the seaweed growing on them, provide rich feeding and shelter for many animals including shellfish, starfish, sea urchins, and fish, and these form the basis of complex food chains. Many fish want to protect a patch of reef for themselves, so they are brightly colored to warn others to keep out, as well as to attract a mate. The colors of other coral reef fish help them keep together in shoals (large groups), so they can all share in the richest feeding.

► A cross-section of a coral animal. Groups of coral animals build tropical coral reefs, homes to many colorful fish.

WHICH STARFISH DESTROYS REEFS?

Coral reefs are easily damaged by thoughtless divers, pollution, and silt from land erosion. Humans have caused another problem by collecting triton shellfish for their beautiful shells. The tritons hunted crown-of-thorns starfish, but with the triton gone, the starfish has become very common on some reefs. Each one can eat 54 square feet of coral a year, and in large numbers the starfish destroy whole reefs.

DO SEA COWS EAT SEA GRASS?

Surprisingly enough, they do! The name 'sea cow' is given to manatees and dugongs, a group of air-breathing sea mammals that live in shallow seas and salty river mouths. They can dive for up to eight minutes to feed on seaweed and sea grasses, distant relatives of land grasses, which form huge underwater meadows on shallow sandbanks. Sea cows give birth in the water, and mothers feed their young on milk for up to 18 months.

▼ Crown-of-thorns starfish are damaging some coral reefs since humans have removed their natural enemies.

▲ Guillemots breed crowded together on sea-cliff ledges, laying their eggs on the bare rock without nests.

WHY DO SO MANY BIRDS LIVE ON THE COAST?

Many seabirds spend most of the year far out to sea, feeding on fish near the ocean surface. But they must come back to land to nest. Steep cliffs provide perfect nesting sites, safe from predators but with easy access to the sea to find fish for their chicks. Other shore birds wade in shallow water, using their long bills to dig worms and shellfish from the mud.

WHAT LIVES BETWEEN THE TIDES?

The shore between the highest and lowest reach of the tide is a remarkable world. Low on the shore, large brown seaweeds called kelps are exposed only briefly at the lowest tides. Many animals live on their tough stalks anchored to the rocks. Higher up the shore, other seaweeds cling to the rocks and sea snails shelter among their moist tangles until the sea returns and they can emerge to feed. At the top of the shore, some seaweeds survive long, dry periods and animals retreat to damp rock cracks while the tide is out. Rock pools on the shore provide a refuge for crabs, sea anemones, and small fish which cannot survive out of the water.

► Hermit crabs live in empty snail shells, sometimes crowned by a sea anemone.

Island Life

WHY DO ISLANDS HAVE SPECIAL WILDLIFE? Many islands are home to animals (and plants) that are found nowhere else. Ancient ancestors of these animals were perhaps swept there by the tide on a floating branch or blown off course during flight. On the island, they found plentiful food and few enemies, and, left alone over thousands of years, they gradually developed into unique island species.

▲ The Galápagos Islands, 600 miles west of the South American coast, are a nature reserve for their many unique animals.

◄ Marine iguanas dive beneath the sea of the Galápagos Islands to feed on seaweed. They can stay underwater for 20 minutes but must surface to breathe.

WHAT MAKES THE GALÁPAGOS ISLANDS FAMOUS?

In 1835, a naturalist called Charles Darwin visited the Galápagos Islands in the Pacific. He discovered animals there that resembled animals on the mainland but differed in many ways. This led him to work out the theory of how animals change, or evolve, over many thousands of years.

WHERE DO LIZARDS SWIM FOR FOOD?

Marine iguanas live only on the Galápagos Islands. Their ancestors were land iguanas, like those that still live on the islands. However, long ago, some iguanas discovered that seaweeds offered abundant food. Over thousands of years, they evolved into marine iguanas, which dive beneath the sea for food and even slow their heartbeat to save oxygen underwater.

HOW ANCIENT ARE MARSUPIALS?

Australia, South America, and Africa were once joined up in a huge landmass called Gondwanaland. About 150 million years ago, as the continents moved like floating plates on the Earth's crust, Australia split away, becoming the world's biggest island. By then the first mammals, called marsupials, had appeared on Gondwanaland. These gave birth to tiny young, which lived in a pouch on their mother's front until they grew big enough to leave. On other continents, the later mammals that evolved wiped out the marsupials, but, because these later mammals never reached Australia, marsupials like kangaroos and koalas still survive there. A few marsupials also live in South America, another fragment of Gondwanaland.

WHY DO TURTLES NEST ON BEACHES?

Marine turtles live in tropical seas, feeding on sea grass and coming to the surface to breathe. To breed, the turtles must return to land. Female turtles swim up to 1,250 miles in seven weeks to reach their breeding beaches. Here they dig a hole in the sand, lay about 100 eggs, and cover the nest with sand. Once the eggs are safely hidden beneath the sand, warmed by the tropical sun, the mother turtles leave. The baby turtles hatch after ten weeks, dig their way to the surface, and dash for the sea, chased by hungry gulls and crabs.

▲ Newly-hatched turtles run for the sea, guided by the bright reflection and noise of waves.

WHICH OTHER ISLANDS ARE SPECIAL?

Most remote island groups have their own special wildlife. Giant tortoises, for example, live on several islands in the Indian Ocean. Forests on the island of Madagascar, off the east coast of Africa, are the home for lemurs. These are ancient relatives of monkeys, but some look like squirrels.

◀ Kangaroo babies live in their mother's pouch for up to 16 months. They get a bumpy ride as their mother bounds along with 6-foot hops.

▼ The baobab tree of Africa and Australia can live 2,000 years and has a trunk of up to 59 feet in circumference.

WAS THE DODO A DEAD LOSS?

The ancient ancestors of dodos were pigeons that reached the island of Mauritius in the Indian Ocean and settled there. With abundant food and no enemies to fly away from, they evolved, over many thousands of years, to the size of a turkey, with small, useless wings. When humans reached Mauritius in 1507 they found dodos easy to hunt, and dogs and rats from their ships stole their eggs and chicks. Within 170 years the dodo was extinct.

▲ The last dodo died on the island of Mauritius in about 1681.

HOW DID BAOBABS REACH AUSTRALIA

Baobabs are massive trees of dry grasslands, with barrel-shaped trunks that store water. In Africa, elephants strip baobabs' fibrous trunks for moisture and nourishment when food is short. Baobabs also grow in tropical areas of Australia but it is not known how they got there. Perhaps their large, woody fruits were washed to its shores by the sea, or perhaps they are an ancient remnant of the time when Africa and Australia were joined in the great continent of Gondwanaland.

Animals in Danger

◄ Although once very common, the last passenger pigeon died in a zoo in 1914.

HOW BIG IS THE PROBLEM? Scientists think that there are over 13 million species on Earth, but a quarter of these are in serious danger of extinction (dying out) within 30 years. At least 1,000 species of birds and mammals may soon disappear for ever. Some animals and plants are in danger as a result of hunting or collection, but the most serious problem is the way people are destroying their habitats (the places where they live).

WHY DID THE PASSENGER PIGEON BECOME EXTINCT?

Passenger pigeons were once so common in North America that a naturalist estimated that a huge flock flying past him contained 2,230 million birds. Such vast numbers tempted people to shoot them for money, and by 1914 the species was extinct.

HOW IS THE GORILLA A VICTIM OF WAR?

Mountain gorillas are gentle plant-eaters that live in a small area of rain forest on the borderlands of Rwanda, in Central Africa. Many people also live there, and clear the forest to make way for crops. Some also shoot gorillas to sell to wealthy tourists. By 1980, only about 400 mountain gorillas remained. Then, in 1994, a civil war broke out in Rwanda. In the chaos, gorillas could not be protected and at least seven were found murdered in 1995.

► Male mountain gorillas weigh up to 450 pounds and can eat 65 pounds of plants a day.

WHY ARE ELEPHANTS IN TROUBLE?

African elephants once roamed large areas of Africa (shown in yellow above). Unfortunately for them, humans value the ivory of their tusks. These are extra-long teeth, weighing 100 pounds or more each, which they use to fight, to strip bark, and to dig at salt licks. In 1976, estimates suggest as many as 400,000 elephants were shot for ivory, which sold at around $25 a pound. By 1989 only about 600,000 African elephants were left in scattered areas (shown in orange).

WHAT IS CONSERVATION?

Conservation is the name given to the work of helping endangered animals and places. For example, turtles are still hunted in many countries for their meat to make soup. Also, in many of the hot countries where they live, tourist hotels and cafes are filling the beaches where the turtles once bred. To give turtles the best chance on beaches where they do still breed, eggs are taken to protected nest sites. When the young hatch, they are guarded as they run down the beach, so that as many as possible reach the sea safely.

▼ Protecting turtle nests gives them the best chance of survival.

ARE WHALES STILL HUNTED?

People have hunted whales for centuries for their meat, oily blubber, and whalebone. As the numbers of some species fell, other species were hunted, and bigger ships, equipped with radar and rocket-powered harpoons, meant that more were killed. Between 1925 and 1975, 1.5 million whales were slaughtered. By 1989 most large whales were close to extinction. The whaling countries at last agreed that all whaling for profit should stop. But as whale numbers slowly recovered, Norway and Japan wanted to start whaling again.

IS THERE A BETTER WAY?

People are beginning to realize that we must start valuing plants and animals while they are still alive. Wise farmers do not sell all their wheat each year; they keep back some grain to plant next year's crops. In the same way, when we catch fish or hunt animals, we must learn to leave enough so that people in the future will also be able to use these animals. And we must find other ways of benefiting from wildlife. For example, many boats now make more money by taking people whale-watching than they ever did from hunting whales.

▼ In 1985 a French bomb blew up the Greenpeace protest ship Rainbow Warrior.

WHO ARE THE CONSERVATION WARRIORS?

Conservationists work in many ways. Some look after animals in the wild and protect the places where they live. Some gather scientific evidence to persuade governments to protect wildlife. Others try to encourage ordinary people to help look after the world. A few use dramatic ways to bring the damage caused to the attention of newspapers and television. The most famous of these conservation organizations is Greenpeace. Its members put themselves in small boats between whaling ships and whales to stop the whale slaughter. They climb to the top of chimneys that are polluting the air, or collect samples of poisons leaking from pipes. Their actions are not always welcomed. In 1985 French government spies planted a bomb to blow up a Greenpeace protest ship.

▲ By 1989, whaling had reduced the numbers of blue whales – the largest animal that ever lived – to around 500.

Spoiling the World

▼ Poor farmers fell the rain forests to make fields.

WHICH IS THE MOST DESTRUCTIVE ANIMAL? Only one species has the power and knowledge to destroy the world: the human species. With our knowledge we could use the world wisely, but that rarely happens because of greed and thoughtlessness.

WHY IS THIS DESTRUCTION HAPPENING?

Perhaps the biggest problem is that there are too many people, all needing space to live. As a result, wild places are destroyed for farmland, houses, and roads. To make money, animals and plants are hunted or gathered, and natural resources like oil, coal, and water are used wastefully and carelessly.

WHY ARE RAINFORESTS DISAPPEARING?

Rainforests are felled for their valuable timber like mahogany or to make farmland. In 1991 it was estimated that an area almost as big as Great Britain was being destroyed each year.

▲ The dark green on this map shows the area of South American rainforest damaged or destroyed since the 1940s. The pale green is all that was left in the 1980s.

▼ Tiny algae like these form choking 'blooms' in ponds and rivers.

HOW DO OIL SPILLS SMOTHER THE SEAS?

Over millions of years, oil was created underground from the bodies of tiny sea plants. It is used as a fuel and to manufacture plastics, but, because it is rarely found where it is needed, it is transported all round the world in vast tankers. Sometimes tankers run aground and break up in the waves. The thick black oil smothers any animals which get caught up in it, although the detergents used to clean up the spill often do more damage than the oil itself.

WHAT ARE ALGAL BLOOMS?

Sometimes ponds and rivers get choked with a green sludge (a 'bloom') of tiny plants called algae. In large quantities their waste products can poison people and animals. Excess farm fertilizers washed off fields by rain caused the rapid growth of algae.

▼ In 1989 18 million gallons of oil escaped from a tanker called Exxon Valdez, wrecked off Alaska. The spilt oil killed 36,000 birds and 3,000 sea otters.

FACTS

People pressure
There are estimated to be 5.5 billion people in the world today, but every day there are 250,000 more people than the day before.

Global warming
Gases produced by human activity are trapping heat beneath the atmosphere, making 1995 the warmest year ever recorded, worldwide.

Overfishing
In 1989 fishermen around the world caught a record 100 million tons of fish. But since then fish stocks have run out in many areas, and catches have fallen.

Rainforests
In 1991 the United Nations estimated that 35–50 million acres of rainforest are destroyed each year.

► Over half the forests in Germany, Norway, and parts of eastern Europe have been badly damaged by pollution caused by factories and cars.

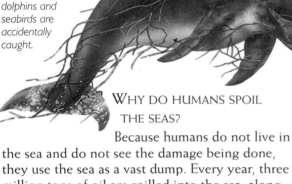

► Fine nets stretch for 60 miles behind some fishing boats, creating 'walls of death' in which dolphins and seabirds are accidentally caught.

WHY DO HUMANS SPOIL THE SEAS?

Because humans do not live in the sea and do not see the damage being done, they use the sea as a vast dump. Every year, three million tons of oil are spilled into the sea, along with millions of tons of sewage, rubbish, and waste chemicals. This destroys ocean food chains and can even threaten human health.

WHAT IS THE OZONE HOLE?

High in the atmosphere, a layer of ozone gas shields Earth from harmful ultraviolet rays from the Sun. In 1982 scientists discovered that this layer was getting thinner. The ozone was being destroyed by chemicals called CFCs, used in spray cans and refrigerators, which release them when they are dumped. CFC-use has now been much reduced so the ozone layer should gradually recover.

WHERE DOES ACID RAIN COME FROM?

Early this century, smoke from factory chimneys produced choking smogs that caused dangerous lung diseases in humans. To reduce this problem, taller chimneys were built, but these moved the pollution higher into the sky, where it reacted with the moisture of clouds, turning them acid. The acid clouds and mists hanging over trees kills their leafy crowns, and when acidic rain gets into the soil it releases aluminum into streams and lakes, where it kills fish. Yet humans go on polluting the skies.

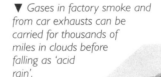

▼ Gases in factory smoke and from car exhausts can be carried for thousands of miles in clouds before falling as 'acid rain'.

THE HUMAN BODY

The Human Cell

WHAT ARE OUR BODIES MADE OF? Although we look and feel solid, we are actually made of billions of separate building-blocks called cells. Cells are so tiny that they are invisible to the naked eye. By looking at them through powerful microscopes we can see that each cell is a living world of its own, designed to make energy, grow, and carry out all kinds of jobs. To do these things, the cell needs a steady supply of food and oxygen. Each cell has its own job to do, but cells work together to keep your body healthy.

WHAT ARE CELLS LIKE INSIDE?

A cell's control center is called its nucleus. It contains a set of instructions telling the different parts what to do. In some parts of the cell, chemicals are made for particular jobs and these are moved around through special branching tubes. In other parts, food is burned to make energy for the cell. The whole cell is covered with a thin sheet, called a membrane, controlling what enters and leaves. The membrane lets oxygen and food into the cell, and lets waste out.

▼ Cells come in many different shapes and sizes.

▼ An egg cell makes a blood cell look tiny – but the egg cell itself is smaller than a pin head! Despite their differences in size, most cells contain the same basic parts.

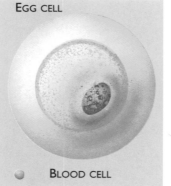

EGG CELL

BLOOD CELL

HOW SMALL ARE CELLS?

Your smallest cells are in part of your brain. If you lined these cells up, 2000 of them would reach less than half an inch! The largest cells are women's egg cells. They can just about be seen – but are still much less than a sixteenth of an inch wide.

DO ALL CELLS LOOK THE SAME?

All cells contain the same important parts that keep them alive. But they come in many different shapes and sizes because they have different jobs to do. Nerve cells have long, thin branches to carry messages around the body. Men's sperm cells are shaped rather like tadpoles so that they can swim towards an egg. Some white cells in the blood can put out finger-like projections to trap and eat germs. Many cells in your lungs have tiny hairs so they can catch dust before you breathe it in.

▼ Each tiny cell is a world of its own. If one was enlarged billions of times and sliced open, you would see a nucleus at the center surrounded by strange-looking parts, each doing a different job.

FACTS

There is only one kind of cell without a nucleus – the red blood cell. This is because its only job is to carry oxygen, which isn't too complicated. Each person has about 30 billion red blood cells!

A piece of skin the size of a small coin has over 3 million cells in it!

Bones have cells too – they look like spiders and live for up to 30 years.

The longest cells in the body are some of the nerve cells carrying messages from the toes to the brain. They are almost as long as the body itself!

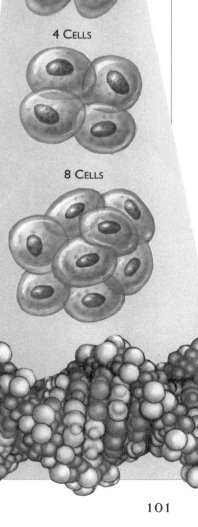

HOW MANY CELLS DOES THE BODY HAVE?

By the time we are adults, we have about 50 billion cells! And yet we start life as a single cell. That cell goes on to divide millions of times as we grow. As cells divide, they pass on their information to new cells. This means that all of the cells in the body have the same instructions for life and can work together.

Some cells continue to divide after we have stopped growing. Skin has to keep on making new cells to replace ones that are worn away. If you break a bone or cut yourself, new cells are quickly made to repair the damage. Sometimes cells carry on dividing when they don't need to. This happens in some illnesses such as cancer and leukemia.

I CELL

2 CELLS

4 CELLS

8 CELLS

▶ We all start as one tiny cell that then divides millions of times.

DO CELLS LIVE AS LONG AS WE DO?

Cells do not always live as long as we do. Many cells die during our lifetime and are continually replaced by new ones. The cells in our intestine and on our skin only live for a few days because they are always being rubbed off. But some cells, like those in our brain, are as old as we are, and can't be replaced if they are damaged.

HOW DOES A CELL KNOW WHAT ITS JOB IS?

Inside each cell's nucleus are packages of information telling the cell how to grow and what to do. The chemical that stores this information is called DNA, and it stores it in a kind of code that the cell has to translate. Each tiny cell contains a complete set of information for the whole body! However, it only needs to read the part of the code that tells it about its own particular jobs.

▼ DNA is shaped like a twisting ladder, and contains the cell's instructions for life.

The Digestive System

How DOES FOOD BECOME FUEL? The food we eat contains carbohydrates, proteins, and fats. Food is changed into nutrients by a complicated process known as digestion. Food cannot pass into the blood system and be used as fuel until the digestion process has broken it down. The entire process takes many hours to complete. Once it is finished, all that is left of the food is waste, which is released from the body and flushed down the toilet!

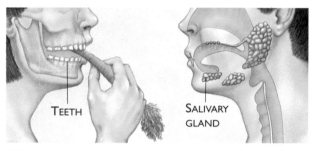

TEETH   SALIVARY GLAND

WHY DOES YOUR MOUTH SOMETIMES 'WATER'?

Watery fluid called saliva pours out of salivary glands in your mouth when you feel hungry. The saliva makes it easier for you to chew food. It also contains chemicals called enzymes that start to break food down into one of the three types of nutrients your body needs – carbohydrates, proteins, and fats. So, digestion actually begins in your mouth.

HOW LONG IS THE DIGESTIVE SYSTEM?

The digestive system is over 26 feet long but it is neatly packed inside your body. It begins at the mouth and ends at the rectum in your bottom. It consists of a tube from the back of the mouth going into the stomach, the stomach itself, and then a very long length of tube called the intestine, which leads to the rectum.

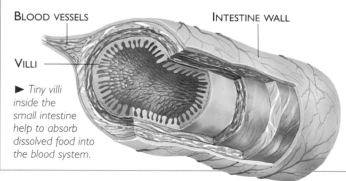

BLOOD VESSELS   INTESTINE WALL

VILLI

▶ Tiny villi inside the small intestine help to absorb dissolved food into the blood system.

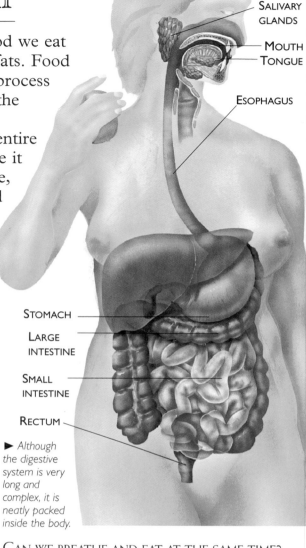

SALIVARY GLANDS

MOUTH
TONGUE

ESOPHAGUS

STOMACH

LARGE INTESTINE

SMALL INTESTINE

RECTUM

▶ Although the digestive system is very long and complex, it is neatly packed inside the body.

CAN WE BREATHE AND EAT AT THE SAME TIME?

When you swallow food, a protective flap of tissue falls into place over your trachea (windpipe) – so you don't breathe in or out for a moment. This prevents food going down into your lungs. If a tiny piece of food sticks in the back of the throat, you dislodge it by coughing.

WHAT DO THE INTESTINES LOOK LIKE?

The intestines are divided into two parts: the small intestine and the large intestine. They are both hollow tubes. The small intestine is lined with tiny finger-like projections called villi, which help to absorb dissolved food. Once the food has been digested, it passes into the blood vessels as fuel. The large intestine removes water from the undigested food that is left before it passes out of the body.

HOW IS FOOD BROKEN DOWN?

Enzymes in the stomach's fluids and a special acid in the stomach walls help to break food down into very small pieces. The muscular walls of the stomach also squeeze and squash the food until it becomes a mushy liquid. At this stage the liquid moves into the small intestine. More digestion takes place here as the mushy liquid is broken down further by enzymes, and the dissolved food is absorbed by the villi into the bloodstream.

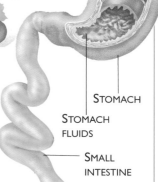

VILLI BLOOD SUPPLY ENZYME

DISSOLVED FOOD FOOD

MUSCLE LAYERS

STOMACH
STOMACH FLUIDS
SMALL INTESTINE

▲ *Different enzymes in the stomach fluids and in the intestine attack various parts of the food, so that it will dissolve into the bloodstream.*

CAN FOOD GET STUCK ON THE WAY DOWN?

Food does not usually get stuck in the intestine because it is pushed through by muscles all along the intestine wall. When you get hungry you can sometimes feel these muscles pushing – it can feel uncomfortable because the muscles have no food to work on. A good amount of fiber from vegetables and fruit also helps food to move more easily through the intestines.

RELAXED MUSCLE WALL

MUSCLE WALL SQUEEZING IN

FOOD PUSHED ALONG

▼ *Digestion doesn't use gravity – the food is pushed down by muscles. This means you can eat food anywhere – even in space!*

HOW LONG DOES IT TAKE FOR FOOD TO TURN INTO FUEL?

Some foods, such as sweets, drinks, and medicines, are easily digested and can be in the blood after about half an hour. Other foods can take three to four hours to leave the stomach and get into the small intestine and then another hour before the food is ready as fuel.

▼ *Food takes at least eight hours to be digested. It can take up to 24 hours!*

FOOD IS EATEN
1 PM

ALL FOOD IN STOMACH
1.30 PM

FOOD REACHES SMALL INTESTINE
4.30 PM

FOOD ABSORBED BY SMALL INTESTINE
6.30 PM

FOOD REACHES RECTUM
9.30 PM

WHY ARE WE SOMETIMES SICK?

Muscles in the stomach wall will force partly digested food back up when there is something wrong with the food or with the stomach itself. 'Sick', or vomit, contains mushy food, enzymes, and acid, which gives it a bitter taste.

The Food We Eat

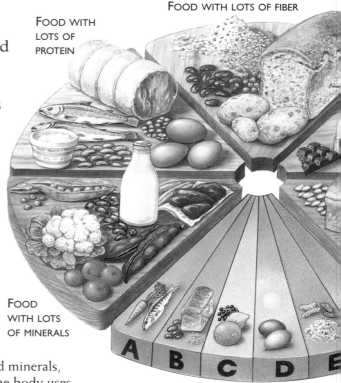

FOOD WITH LOTS OF FIBER

FOOD WITH LOTS OF PROTEIN

FOOD WITH LOTS OF MINERALS

A B C D E

▲ *A healthy balanced diet involves a variety of food and includes vitamins and minerals.*

WHERE DO WE GET FOOD FROM? Food appears in an endless variety of forms, but it all comes from plants or animals. Most people eat food that comes from both plants and animals, but some people, called vegetarians, choose not to eat food that comes from animals. Food often needs to be prepared and cooked before we enjoy eating it. Some people like to grow their own vegetables and fruit. They believe it tastes better and is more healthy because it is fresh and may be produced without chemicals.

WHY DOES THE BODY NEED FOOD?

Food contains essential ingredients called nutrients. These are proteins, carbohydrates, fats, vitamins, and minerals, and they are released from food during digestion. The body uses them to keep healthy. Protein – from fish, meat, or dairy products – is used to help the body grow and repair. Carbohydrates are used as fuel to give the body energy for everything it has to do. Carbohydrates are plentiful in bread, potatoes, rice, and pasta. Fats, from fatty food, are also a source of energy, though the fuel they provide is not as useful as the fuel from carbohydrates. The body also needs to have fruit and vegetables for the fiber, vitamins, and minerals they contain.

▼ *The body is similar to a car. It uses calories as energy just as a car uses gasoline.*

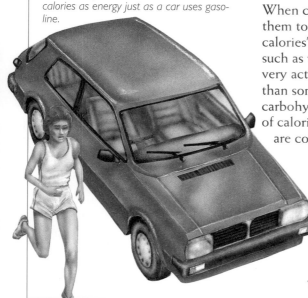

WHERE DOES THE BODY GET ITS ENERGY FROM?

When carbohydrates and fats have been digested, the body burns them to produce energy. We measure this energy in units called 'kilocalories', or just 'calories'. The body uses calories for all its activities, such as walking, running, working, and even sleeping. Someone who is very active – an athlete, for example – will use up many more calories than someone who is less active, and so would need to eat more carbohydrates and fats. Babies and growing children also need a lot of calories. When calories are taken into the body and not used, they are converted into fat and stored as fatty tissue.

DO WE HAVE TO EAT PROTEIN?

Meat and other foods, such as nuts, cheese, and pulses (edible seeds), provide the body with protein, which is essential for its growth and for its tissues to be repaired. Without protein, cuts and sores would not heal properly, the muscle tissue would start to shrink, and the body would lose weight. If weight loss becomes severe it is known as malnutrition.

FOOD WITH LOTS OF ANIMAL
OR VEGETABLE FAT

FOOD WITH LOTS
OF CARBOHYDRATES

HOW DOES FOOD AFFECT WEIGHT?

If we eat the right amount of food for the type of life we lead, and the food itself has enough nutrients, our body usually stays healthy and our weight remains about the same. Some people eat too much food or become less active, which causes them to put on weight. Others eat too little or become too active, causing them to lose weight. It is not healthy to weigh much more or much less than average for your height and build.

FACTS

On average, people need about 1,200–3,000 calories per day. Children usually need more calories than adults because they are still growing.

Your body needs 13 vitamins to keep it healthy. Those like vitamin A and C are found in fruit and vegetables.

After you finish eating and leave the table the food you have eaten stays in your stomach for a further 3 to 4 hours.

▲ Some people like to rest after eating a meal as they believe it helps the process of digestion.

HOW DOES FOOD AFFECT THE BLOOD?

The stomach and intestines need a good supply of oxygenated blood to help digest food. Usually the blood system can cope very well with this job and the rest of the body can continue with its usual activities. Sometimes, a large or rich meal will need extra blood to help the digestive system digest all the food. This means there is less oxygenated blood flowing around the body. Areas like the brain and muscles are affected, which can make you feel sleepy. This usually lasts for 1 to 2 hours until digestion is well underway.

WHAT IS 'JUNK FOOD'?

'Junk food' is food that has been produced for its appealing taste rather than for its health value. It is great fun to eat and it can look very appealing, but it is not good for the body. It often con-tains added chemicals that make it taste nice but are unhealthy. It usually also contains a lot of animal fat or sugar. Foods like chips, burgers, crisps, cakes, and biscuits are high in animal fats. Sweets and fizzy drinks like cola and lemonade are high in sugar. When we eat large amounts of fat, our bodies turn them into fatty tissue, and large amounts of sugar can damage our teeth and skin. Junk food generally lacks the vitamins and minerals we need. Although it is all right to eat junk food occasionally, the body does best when it is given a healthy balance of nutri-ents from freshly prepared foods.

HOW MUCH SHOULD YOU EAT?

Everyone's size and build is different, so the amount of food we need varies from person to person. There are guides to the amount of calories girls and boys should eat. Many books on nutrition have tables which give these figures. Between the ages of 10 and 12, girls usually need about 2,500 calories a day. Boys need 3,000–3,500 calories a day. Very active children would probably need even more.

◀ Junk foods like these are poor sources of the energy and protein your body needs.

The Liver and Kidneys

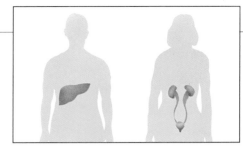

HOW DOES THE BODY GET RID OF THINGS IT DOESN'T NEED? The liver and kidneys do this job in different ways. The liver makes poisons safe by breaking them up. The kidneys filter the blood, taking out any waste and flushing it out of the body in urine. The liver has other important jobs. It sorts out the food that you have digested and stores some of it, ready for when you need it. It also makes some important parts of blood, and destroys old or damaged blood cells.

WHERE ARE THE LIVER AND KIDNEYS?

The liver and kidneys are tucked away under the rib cage – the liver at the front and the kidneys at the back. The urine that the kidneys make runs along two tubes called ureters to the bladder, where it is stored before you go to the toilet.

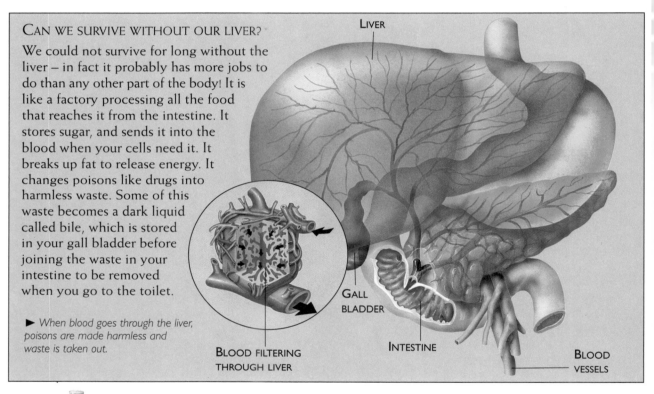

CAN WE SURVIVE WITHOUT OUR LIVER?

We could not survive for long without the liver – in fact it probably has more jobs to do than any other part of the body! It is like a factory processing all the food that reaches it from the intestine. It stores sugar, and sends it into the blood when your cells need it. It breaks up fat to release energy. It changes poisons like drugs into harmless waste. Some of this waste becomes a dark liquid called bile, which is stored in your gall bladder before joining the waste in your intestine to be removed when you go to the toilet.

▶ When blood goes through the liver, poisons are made harmless and waste is taken out.

LIVER

GALL BLADDER

BLOOD FILTERING THROUGH LIVER

INTESTINE

BLOOD VESSELS

IS ALCOHOL DANGEROUS?

Although most adults like to drink alcohol, the body treats it as a poison. The liver breaks down small amounts into harmless waste, but too much can damage the liver, so that it no longer works properly. This is why people should limit how much alcohol they drink.

◀ It is all right for adults to drink alcohol – but they must be careful not to drink too much.

WHAT MAKES URINE YELLOW?

Urine is usually yellow in color because of the particular waste that it contains, called urea. Urea also gives urine its sharp smell. The less you drink, the darker and smellier it is, as there is less water to dilute it. Urine can also become dark and cloudy if you have an infection. Some foods can turn urine strange colors – too much beetroot, for example, can turn it pink!

HOW CAN KIDNEYS GO WRONG?

Kidneys usually work perfectly for a lifetime. You can help to keep them healthy by drinking plenty to flush them out. Sometimes people get infections in the bladder that can spread up to the kidneys. This makes them go to the toilet more often than usual, and it may hurt when they do. Infections like these are cured by medicines called antibiotics. Sometimes, if urine is not as watery as it should be, stones can form in the kidneys. These can be of different shapes and colors – and are sometimes almost as large as the kidney itself! They are often painful, but can be removed without an operation. Special lasers are used to bombard the stones so they break up and come out in the urine.

WHY DOES HEAT MAKE YOU THIRSTY?

When you are hot, you sweat to cool yourself down. Sweating makes you lose water, so you need to drink more liquids to make up for it. You also go to the toilet less. This is because your kidneys are trying to stop water leaving your body in urine. Heat also makes you flushed, as blood passes closer to the skin surface to be cooled down.

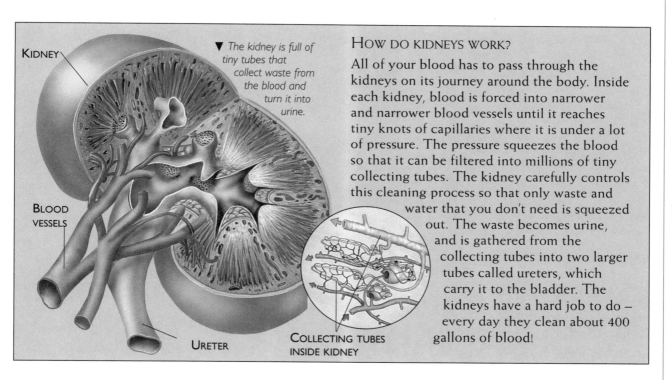

KIDNEY

▼ The kidney is full of tiny tubes that collect waste from the blood and turn it into urine.

BLOOD VESSELS

URETER

COLLECTING TUBES INSIDE KIDNEY

HOW DO KIDNEYS WORK?

All of your blood has to pass through the kidneys on its journey around the body. Inside each kidney, blood is forced into narrower and narrower blood vessels until it reaches tiny knots of capillaries where it is under a lot of pressure. The pressure squeezes the blood so that it can be filtered into millions of tiny collecting tubes. The kidney carefully controls this cleaning process so that only waste and water that you don't need is squeezed out. The waste becomes urine, and is gathered from the collecting tubes into two larger tubes called ureters, which carry it to the bladder. The kidneys have a hard job to do – every day they clean about 400 gallons of blood!

WHAT HAPPENS WHEN KIDNEYS DO NOT WORK?

Some people have kidneys that do not work properly. They may be able to use special machines that do the kidney's job. The person's blood passes through a tube into the machine, where it is filtered and cleaned before being returned to the body. This treatment is called dialysis. It has to be done three or four times a week, and takes several hours. Many people having dialysis treatment are waiting to be given a new kidney by a healthy person. The person who gives a kidney is called a donor. Kidney donors help to save lives, and can live perfectly well with the one kidney they have left.

▼ When the kidneys do not work, a dialysis machine will clean the blood for them.

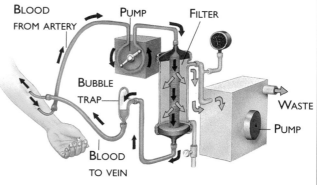

BLOOD FROM ARTERY

PUMP

FILTER

BUBBLE TRAP

BLOOD TO VEIN

WASTE

PUMP

The Blood System

HOW DOES BLOOD MOVE AROUND THE BODY? It is the heart's job to pump blood around the body, sending it through many small tubes, called blood vessels. The blood carries oxygen and dissolved food to your cells, and takes waste away. When you run around, your cells need more oxygen than usual for energy. This is why you can feel your heart beating faster, as it pumps the blood around more quickly.

WHY IS BLOOD RED?

If you looked at blood under a micro-scope, you would see thousands of tiny cells. Most of these are bright red because they contain iron, which helps them to carry oxygen. Blood also contains white 'fighter' cells, which attack germs entering the body. Finally, blood contains floating parti-cles called platelets. When you cut yourself, these make the blood near the wound sticky, which eventually stops the bleeding.

▼ *The left side of your heart pumps blood with oxygen along the arteries. Veins return the blood to the right side of the heart, which then pumps it to the lungs to pick up more oxygen. Then the journey starts again.*

VEIN

CAPILLARIES

ARTERY

ARE ALL BLOOD VESSELS THE SAME?

No, there are three kinds of blood vessels. Arteries have thick, strong walls. They carry blood with oxygen away from the heart and lungs. Veins have thinner walls, and carry used blood back to the heart and lungs. Capillaries are tiny blood vessels that surround the cells like nets.

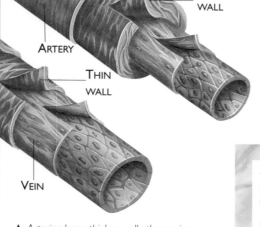

THICK WALL

ARTERY

THIN WALL

VEIN

▲ *Arteries have thicker walls than veins. Veins have a number of flaps inside them, to stop the blood falling downwards as it is pumped back up to the heart.*

WHERE IS BLOOD MADE?

Blood is made inside some of your bones, in the soft, spongy area called the bone marrow. Worn-out parts of blood are continually being destroyed by the body, so the bone marrow has to keep replacing them throughout your life. But although blood is always being created and destroyed, the total amount stays the same – about 1.5 gallons in an adult.

FACTS

There are 200 million red cells in one drop of blood, and you make 2.5 million new ones every second!

If you laid all your blood vessels end-to-end, they would stretch 60,000 miles – that's 2.5 times round the world!

Your heart beats 100,000 times every day, and a mouse's heart beats 7 times faster than this!

Your blood system is like a central heating system. It moves heat from warm body parts to cooler parts.

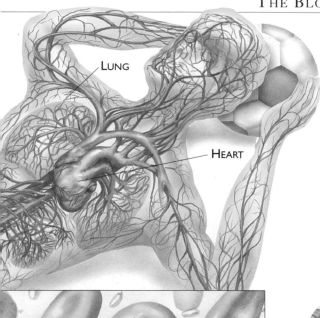

Lung

Heart

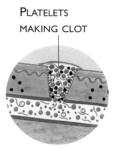

Cut skin

WHAT ARE SCABS MADE OF?

If you cut yourself, platelets quickly make your blood sticky so that the cut in the skin is soon plugged up and the bleeding stops. The sticky blood is called a clot. As the clot dries it becomes a scab, which protects the cut underneath. The scab eventually drops off when the cut has healed and new skin has grown over it.

BLOOD VESSEL BLEEDING

PLATELETS MAKING CLOT

SCAB FORMING

▲ White cells rush to the area of a cut, so that they can eat any germs that get in, and clear away damaged cells.

▲ Red cells are shaped like saucers, and can bend easily to squeeze through blood vessels. White cells are larger, and patrol the body for germs. The tiny particles, called platelets, help to make your blood sticky and stop a cut from bleeding.

▼ Lymph travels around in a network of vessels, just as blood does.

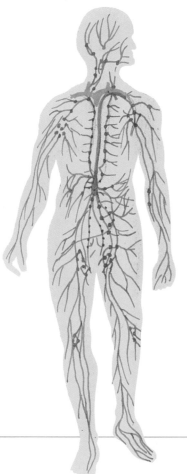

WHAT IS HEMOPHILIA?

Hemophilia is a disease that a small number of boys are born with. Most people have blood that becomes sticky when they are cut or bruised, and this stops them from bleeding too much. The blood of a hemophiliac, however, does not become sticky and so he bleeds very easily. Hemophiliacs also gets bruised very easily, since bruises are areas where blood vessels have broken under the skin. There are medicines that help the blood of a hemophiliac to work as it should, but it is still a very serious disease.

WHY DOES NO ONE GET MEASLES TWICE?

When germs enter your body, they are attacked by thousands of white cells, which may eat the germs or destroy them with poisons. In certain illnesses, like measles, the white cells cannot stop you from getting sick the first time the germs enter your body. However, they remember what the germs were like and are able to make a much quicker and stronger attack if they ever attack again. This stops you from getting the illness a second time.

WHAT ARE SWOLLEN 'GLANDS'?

One of the fluids in the body is called lymph. It contains white blood cells, among other things. Lymph drains into parts of the body that are known as 'glands', where the lymph is cleaned up. These areas become swollen and painful when germs enter your body because the white cells are busily attacking the germs.

The Heart

HOW FAST DOES THE HEART BEAT? The heart of an adult usually beats about seventy to eighty times a minute. The heart of a child usually beats about one hundred times a minute and babies' hearts can beat even faster. The heart is mainly made of special muscle tissue and it works as a pump, pushing blood around the body. It is controlled by special nerves, which means it beats without you having to think about it. The heart carries on beating all of your life – in the end it will have beaten about three billion times!

▲ Used blood from the body enters the upper right chamber and oxygenated blood from the lungs enters the left chamber.

IS THE HEART HEART-SHAPED?

The heart does not have the classic heart-shape we draw. It is shaped more like a pear and is about the size of a clenched fist. It sits in the chest, slightly left of center. You can find where it is by putting your ear on someone's chest and listening for their heartbeat. Or you can try to find your own heart by putting your hand on the left side of your chest to feel your heart beating. The heart is divided into a right and left side. Each side has an upper and lower chamber. Between these there are flaps called valves that open to let blood through from one chamber to the other and close to stop blood flowing backwards. The heartbeat you detect is actually the sound of the valves opening and closing.

WHERE DOES BLOOD GO AFTER LEAVING THE HEART?

Blood leaves the left side of the heart and goes into a system of blood vessels called arteries. Arteries carry blood that is full of oxygen to the body's tissues. Another set of vessels called veins carry the used blood back to the right side of the heart, and then to the lungs for the blood to be refilled with oxygen.

◄ The heart pumps blood around the body through a system of blood vessels. The system follows the shape of a figure of eight.

► Regular exercise is good for your heart. It will grow stronger and you won't feel so out of breath!

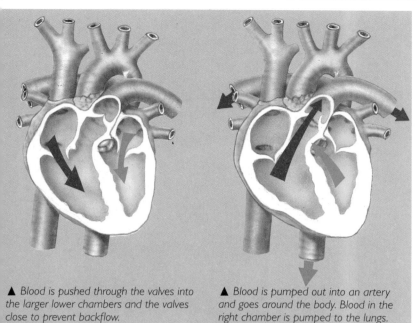

▲ Blood is pushed through the valves into the larger lower chambers and the valves close to prevent backflow.

▲ Blood is pumped out into an artery and goes around the body. Blood in the right chamber is pumped to the lungs.

WHAT IS A PULSE?

A doctor may feel a patient's pulse to check how their heart is beating. You can easily find your own pulse, either on the inside of your wrist or on your neck. These are places where a blood vessel is very near to the surface of the skin. Your pulse shows how your heart is beating because as the heart pumps it sends shock waves along the blood vessel.

▲ There are many pulse points on the body. The easiest to find are on the inside of your wrist or the side of your neck.

HOW DOES EXERCISE AFFECT THE HEART?

When you run around or ride a bike, cells in your body burn more fuel and oxygen. This means that the heart has to pump more blood, bringing more oxygen and fuel to the cells. It also causes you to breathe more quickly. Your heart, lungs, and blood vessels all work together to pump fuel and oxygen around the body. If you exercise regularly your heart and lungs grow stronger, and do not need to work as hard. This is why people who exercise regularly do not get so breathless.

HOW DOES THE HEART WORK?

The heart's action is triggered by electrical messages from the brain to the nerves in the heart. One message makes the two upper chambers squeeze blood through the valves and into the larger lower chambers. Another message makes these two chambers squeeze the blood out into the blood vessels.

CAN WHAT YOU EAT AFFECT YOUR HEART?

Some types of animal fat in our food can find their way into the arteries that surround the heart. Over many years this fat may block an artery so that blood cannot get through. If this happens it can lead to a heart attack.

WHAT HAPPENS IF THE HEART STOPS BEATING?

If your heart is healthy it will not stop beating during your lifetime. Sometimes older and less healthy people have heart attacks, and their heart stops beating. If this happens, emergency treatment can sometimes be given to try and start the heart again. A special machine gives the heart an electrical shock to make the chambers work again. If a blocked artery causes a heart attack, it is possible to replace it with a vein taken from the leg. This involves a complex operation.

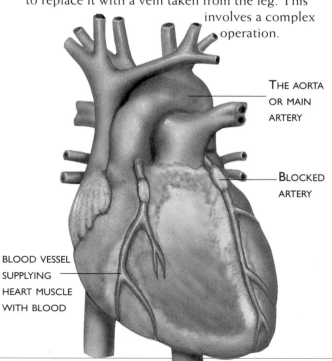

THE AORTA OR MAIN ARTERY

BLOCKED ARTERY

BLOOD VESSEL SUPPLYING HEART MUSCLE WITH BLOOD

Breathing

WHY DO WE BREATHE? Every time we breathe, our lungs remove the gas oxygen from the air and pass it into our blood. Every cell in the body needs the oxygen to make energy for life. If you run a race, you breathe much faster. This is because your muscle cells burn much more oxygen than usual when they work harder.

WHAT IS ASTHMA?

When you breathe in, air rushes through your nose and mouth and down your trachea (wind pipe). It travels down to the lungs through two tubes called the bronchi, which branch into thinner tubes called the bronchioles. Finally the air reaches tiny pockets called alveoli. People with asthma have bronchi and bronchioles that can become narrower than normal, making it hard for them to breathe. They may use inhalers. These contain medicines that make the bronchi and bronchioles wider again.

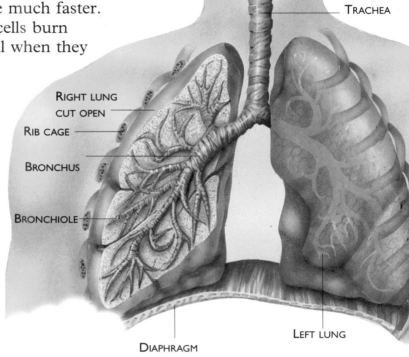

TRACHEA

RIGHT LUNG
CUT OPEN

RIB CAGE

BRONCHUS

BRONCHIOLE

DIAPHRAGM

LEFT LUNG

▲ You have two lungs, which are on either side of your heart. They are protected by your rib cage.

WHAT CONTROLS OUR BREATHING?

Although you can affect your breathing pattern if you want to – by taking longer, slower breaths, for example – most of the time your brain controls your breathing without you having to think. When you breathe in, your brain tells the chest muscles to pull your ribs outwards and tells the diaphragm, a large muscle at the bottom of your chest, to move downwards. This creates room in your chest for your lungs to fill up with air. When you breathe out, your ribs move back in and your diaphragm moves back up, pushing the air out again.

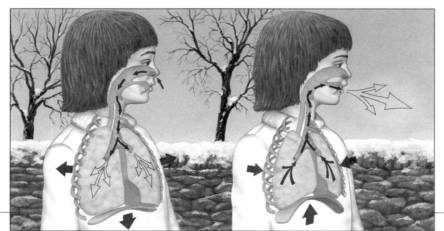

◄ When you breathe in (far left) your ribs move outwards. When you breathe out, they move back in (left). In winter you can see your breath as tiny drops of water.

WHAT DO LUNGS LOOK LIKE INSIDE?

From the inside, lungs look like two red sponges. This is because they are full of millions of air pockets called alveoli. The alveoli are covered with a network of tiny blood vessels, giving the lungs their red color. As air travels down the bronchi, it is cleaned by tiny hairs that trap dust and germs. This makes it safer by the time it reaches the alveoli. Oxygen from the air passes through the very thin alveoli walls into the surrounding blood. The blood, in turn, passes waste gas (carbon dioxide) from the cells to the alveoli, so it can be breathed out.

Smoking cigarettes can damage the lungs in many different ways. It may destroy alveoli so oxygen does not pass across as easily. It may also make the tubes so narrow that it becomes difficult to breathe.

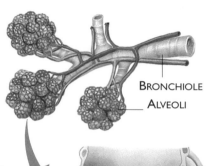

BRONCHIOLE
ALVEOLI

CAPILLARIES

▼ As this diver holds his breath, his heart will beat faster to try and pump as much oxygen to his cells as possible.

ALVEOLUS
WALL

CARBON
DIOXIDE

OXYGEN

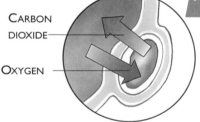

WHY DO WE YAWN?

When we are tired or bored, our breathing sometimes becomes shallow, and so our blood receives less oxygen. Yawning gives us a very deep breath, which fills our lungs and provides us with extra oxygen again. The effect of opening our mouth widely also allows more blood to pump through blood vessels in our neck to the brain, making us more alert. Yawning is an example of a reflex – something we can't usually help doing – though it is possible to stop yourself yawning by taking deep breaths.

◄ The waste which passes from the body into the lungs and is then breathed out is a gas called carbon dioxide.

FACTS

If all the alveoli in your lungs were laid out flat, they would cover a quarter of a tennis court!

You normally breathe about 12 times every minute, but you can breathe up to 75 times a minute!

An adult's lungs hold 1.3 gallons of air – that's like 20 glasses of milk!

HOW LONG CAN A PERSON HOLD THEIR BREATH?

People who have trained themselves can hold their breath for at least two minutes! Most of us can only hold it for about 30 seconds, and we soon feel dizzy because our brain needs more oxygen. Some divers in tropical countries train themselves so they can hold their breath for as long as possible while they dive for coral or pearls. Divers who study underwater life use special breathing equipment. They usually carry air tanks strapped onto their backs. The air is compressed so that it takes up less space.

WHAT MAKES US COUGH AND SNEEZE?

The tubes in your lungs clean themselves by making a sticky liquid called mucus. Sometimes they make more than usual to trap germs or pieces of dust. When you cough, your chest muscles give a quick push to get rid of this extra mucus. Sneezes get rid of any germs and dust caught in your nose. The muscles give a very strong push, and air rushes out at over 100 miles an hour!

The Skeleton and Muscles

HOW MANY SEPARATE BONES ARE THERE IN A
SKELETON? The skeleton is made up of about
206 bones – 106 of these are
just in the hands and feet!
The main job of your bones
is to support you, so you
don't collapse under the weight
of your body. Bones connect with each
other at joints, which allow the body to move with the
help of muscles. Bones also protect some important
parts of the body, such as the brain and lungs.

ARE ALL MUSCLES THE SAME?

Muscles are all made of the same material, but they come in many
shapes and sizes. Your largest muscle is in your thigh, and it enables
you to straighten your leg. A very small muscle is in your eyelid, allowing you to blink more than 100,000 times every day. Your strongest
muscles are on either side of your mouth. You use them to chew.
 Muscles work together. You use 200 muscles with every step, and
15 muscles just to smile! They are attached to bones by strong cords
called tendons. You can feel your Achilles tendon,
which connects your leg muscle to your heel bone,
on the back of your ankle.

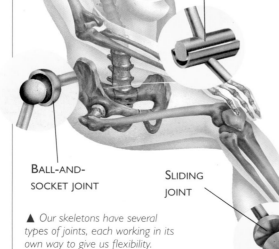

SWIVEL
JOINT

HINGE
JOINT

JOINT
FLUID

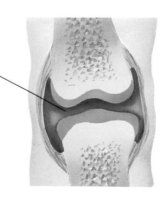

BALL-AND-
SOCKET JOINT

SLIDING
JOINT

▲ *Our skeletons have several
types of joints, each working in its
own way to give us flexibility.*

WHAT IS THE SPINE LIKE?

Your spine is made
up of 26 bones.
Because they
are all hinged
together, your
back is very
flexible –
just watch
a gymnast!

▲ *The spine extends
from the hips to the skull.*

WHAT IS ARTHRITIS?

Bones usually have very smooth
ends so that they can slide over
each other at joints. The joints
are also enclosed in a kind of bag
containing a fluid that makes
movement even easier. In arthritis, the smooth ends of bones
become chipped, and the bag
around the joint may become
thicker. This makes joints
swollen, painful, and difficult
to move.

DO ALL JOINTS WORK IN THE SAME WAY?

There are several different kinds of joints, each allowing different kinds of movements. Your hip and shoulder have
ball-and-socket joints. This means that the top of your leg and
arm bones are shaped like balls, and can roll around in any
direction. Your knees and elbows have hinge joints, so they
can only move up or down. Your skull is connected to your
neck by a swivel joint, so you can turn your head from side
to side. Your wrists and ankles have sliding joints, so the
bones can slide over each other.

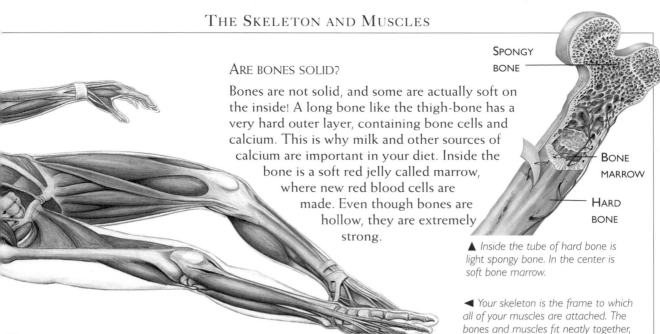

SPONGY
BONE

BONE
MARROW

HARD
BONE

ARE BONES SOLID?

Bones are not solid, and some are actually soft on the inside! A long bone like the thigh-bone has a very hard outer layer, containing bone cells and calcium. This is why milk and other sources of calcium are important in your diet. Inside the bone is a soft red jelly called marrow, where new red blood cells are made. Even though bones are hollow, they are extremely strong.

▲ *Inside the tube of hard bone is light spongy bone. In the center is soft bone marrow.*

◄ *Your skeleton is the frame to which all of your muscles are attached. The bones and muscles fit neatly together, making a great range of movement possible.*

HOW ARE BROKEN BONES REPAIRED?

When a bone breaks, it bleeds in the same way as a cut. Soon the blood clots, white cells clean up the mess, and new bone is formed to join up the broken ends. Special cells ensure that this new bone is the right shape. To heal properly, a broken bone should be kept still. This is why plaster-casts are worn. But when it has healed, the bone is often stronger than ever before!

WHY DO MUSCLES BULGE?

If you lift something, a muscle in your arm called the biceps pulls in order to bend your elbow joint. The muscle pulls by becoming shorter and fatter, making it bulge. As this happens a muscle under your arm, called the triceps, relaxes by getting longer and thinner. When you lower the weight again, it is the biceps turn to relax whilst the triceps get shorter, pulling your arm straight. Muscles pull and never push – so they often work in pairs like this.

WHY DON'T WEIGHTLIFTERS HURT THEMSELVES?

You may have noticed that weightlifters wear special belts. These help to support their backs. When athletes lift weights they need to keep their backs straight, because back muscles can be damaged if the spine is twisted.

HOW DO MUSCLES WORK?

Muscles are made of millions of special cells, joined together in thin threads called fibers. When you clench a muscle, your brain sends signals through your nerves, telling the muscle's cells to shorten. This makes the fibers shorten and slide over each other, causing the whole muscle to become shorter and fatter as it pulls.

▼ *Your biceps and triceps muscles work together to pull your elbow in opposite directions.*

► *Weightlifters use their very strong thigh muscles to straighten up as they lift.*

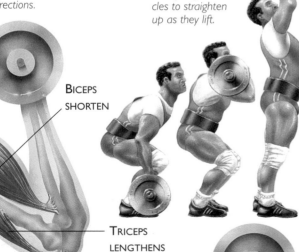

BICEPS
SHORTEN

TRICEPS
LENGTHENS

► *Hair-like fibers in a muscle shorten when the muscle pulls.*

MUSCLE FIBERS SHORTENING

The Nervous System and the Brain

Is THE BRAIN LIKE A COMPUTER? In some ways, the brain is like a computer. It is your own control center. It processes data from your surroundings, makes complex calculations, and tells you what to do. But your brain is far more amazing than any computer! It enables you to speak, play sports, listen to music, imagine, and learn different subjects. Above all, it gives you your own personality. Brains may look similar on the outside, but each works slightly differently, making everyone unique.

WHAT IS THE SPINAL CORD?

Inside your backbone, or spine, is an important bundle of nerves called the spinal cord. It is like a highway for the nerves, since they all pass through it on their journey to or from the brain. A broken spine often paralyzes the body below the break because of the damage done to the nerves.

HOW DOES YOUR BRAIN CONTROL YOUR BODY?

The brain and the rest of the body communicate through the nerves. Some nerves carry messages from the brain to the body. Others carry messages from the body back to the brain. Nerves are made of strangely-shaped nerve cells that have long thin branches called axons. The messages, in the form of tiny electrical signals, pass from one nerve cell to another across a gap called a synapse.

BRAIN

SPINAL CORD

NERVES BRANCHING OUT

◄ *Your nerves are like a complex system of telephone wires. Messages are constantly racing to and from your brain.*

HOW DO NERVES CARRY MESSAGES?

Nerve messages are electrical signals, which race along the nerve cells at 250 miles an hour. If you burn your toe in the bath, a signal runs up the nerves in your leg and up your spinal cord until it reaches your brain. A second or two later, your brain decodes the electric signal as pain.

NERVES BRANCHING INTO ARM

NERVES BRANCHING INTO LEG

SPINE

PROTECTIVE COVERING

SPINAL CORD

SPINAL NERVE

AXON

NUCLEUS

►*Nerve cells release special chemicals to help signals pass from one cell to the next.*

SYNAPSE

L

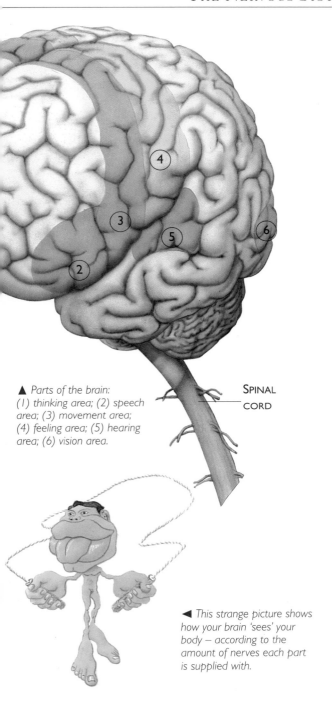

▲ *Parts of the brain:
(1) thinking area; (2) speech
area; (3) movement area;
(4) feeling area; (5) hearing
area; (6) vision area.*

SPINAL
CORD

◄ *This strange picture shows
how your brain 'sees' your
body – according to the
amount of nerves each part
is supplied with.*

WHY DOES A PRICK ON YOUR FINGER HURT MORE THAN A PRICK ON YOUR ARM?

Hands are supplied with more nerves than other
parts of the body, so they feel touch and pain more
easily. We need sensitive hands because we use
them to feel and work with objects around us. The
mouth also has many special nerves for tasting
food. The more nerves a part of the body has, the
more brain space is needed to deal with the signals
that come from it.

WHAT HAPPENS WHEN SOMEONE HAS A STROKE?

Different parts of the brain have different jobs to
do. The front part enables you to think. The middle part enables you to move, speak, and feel. The
back part enables you to understand what you see.
The brain is also divided into right and left halves,
which you use for different kinds of thinking.
When somebody has a stroke, a small part of their
brain dies, because its blood supply stops. The type
of problem they are left with depends on which
part has died. They may not be able to use some of
their muscles, or they may find it difficult to speak.
But the brain can be clever at coping with these
problems! Often other parts of the brain take over
the jobs that the dead part used to do, and the person can gradually recover.

WHY IS THE BRAIN GRAY, WRINKLED, AND SLIMY?

The outside layer of your brain is gray, where
billions of nerve cells are packed together. This is
its 'thinking' part. It is wrinkled because this allows
more cells to be squashed into the space inside
your skull. It is slimy because it is surrounded by
fluid that cushions it as you move your head
around.

▼ *A cross-section (sliced-through) view of the brain. It is
organized into areas that control different parts of the body.*

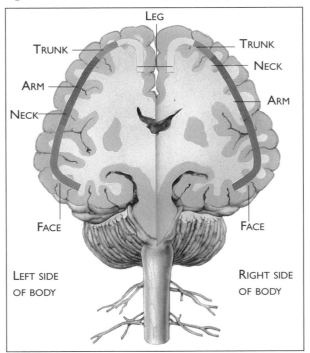

LEG

TRUNK

TRUNK

NECK

ARM

ARM

NECK

FACE

FACE

LEFT SIDE
OF BODY

RIGHT SIDE
OF BODY

Hearing, Seeing, and Tasting

HOW DO WE USE OUR SENSES? Our eyes, ears, nose, and mouth pass information to the brain about sights, sounds, smells, and tastes from the world outside. Usually these senses work together. Some people, however, may lose one of them, such as their sight or hearing. When this happens, the other senses may become even sharper to make up for the loss.

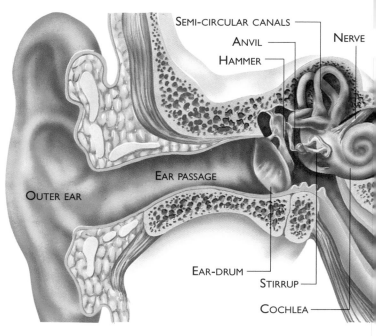

▼ *Inside your ear is a complicated system of bones and passages which turn sounds into nerve signals.*

SEMI-CIRCULAR CANALS

ANVIL

NERVE

HAMMER

OUTER EAR

EAR PASSAGE

EAR-DRUM

STIRRUP

COCHLEA

WHY ARE EARS A STRANGE SHAPE?

Ears are curved and grooved to collect as much sound as possible, and direct it into your ear passage. Sounds are really vibrations in the air. At the end of the ear passage these vibrations hit a thin sheet called the ear-drum. This makes the ear-drum and the three tiny bones next to it vibrate. The bones are called the hammer, anvil and stirrup, and they are the smallest bones in the body.

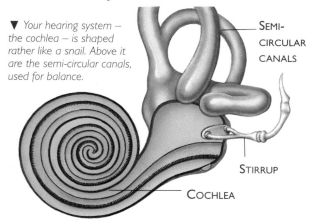

▼ *Your hearing system – the cochlea – is shaped rather like a snail. Above it are the semi-circular canals, used for balance.*

SEMI-CIRCULAR CANALS

STIRRUP

COCHLEA

WHY DOES SPINNING AROUND MAKE YOU DIZZY?

Inside your ear are three semi-circular canals – tubes shaped like half circles – that contain liquid. When you move around, nerves pick up vibrations in the liquid and send signals to your brain about what you are doing. If you spin around, the liquid in the tubes swirls around too, and it carries on swirling for a little while when you stop. This causes your brain to think you are still spinning around – and you feel dizzy.

WHAT IS THE COCHLEA?

The cochlea is a coiled-up tube in the inner ear. It is filled with liquid. When the small bones in your ear vibrate they knock against the cochlea and make the liquid vibrate. This is picked up by nerves that send signals to the brain. High sounds vibrate in the first part of the cochlea, and low sounds vibrate farther along. This is how your brain can tell what sort of sound you are hearing.

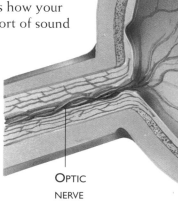

RETINA

OPTIC NERVE

▶ *A cross-section of the eye. The iris, surrounding the pupil, gives the eye its color. A thick liquid within the eyeball helps the eye keep its shape.*

HOW DOES SMELL WORK?

When you smell something like a flower, tiny amounts of chemicals from the flower enter your nose and dissolve in the nostrils' liquid lining. Special cells at the top of your nose detect these chemicals and send nerve signals to your brain. Your sense of smell is also used when you taste things. That is why if you have a cold blocking your nose, food seems to have less taste.

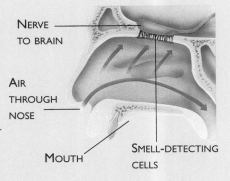

Special cells at the top of your nose detect smells in the air you inhale.

WHY ARE SOME SMELLS BAD?

In the past, humans had to hunt and gather their food, and things that smelt bad may have been a warning that they were poisonous. But we are not sure why some people like smells that others don't. We do know that the nose can detect about 4,000 different kinds of smell!

▼ *The skunk sprays a foul-smelling liquid at its enemies.*

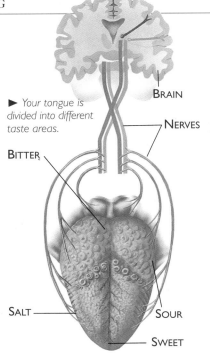

▶ *Your tongue is divided into different taste areas.*

WHAT ARE TASTE BUDS?

The tongue is covered with tiny stalks that contain special cells called taste buds. These detect chemicals in food and send nerve signals to the brain. The different types of taste – sweet, salty, sour, and bitter – are detected in different areas of the tongue.

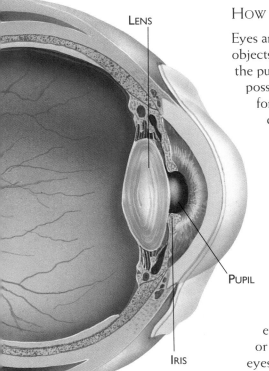

HOW DO OUR EYES SEE?

Eyes are a bit like tiny cameras, but much more complicated! Light from objects around us enters our eyes through a small hole in the eyeball – the pupil. In the dark the pupil becomes larger to let as much light in as possible. The light then passes through a lens that bends it so that it forms a sharp picture on the retina, at the back of the eye. The lens can change shape to ensure the picture is in focus – like focusing a camera. The light on the retina is detected by millions of special cells. Those in the middle are better at detecting color, and those around the edge are better at detecting black and white. This is why you can actually see better from the corner of your eye at night! The cells send signals to the brain through the optic nerve at the back of the eyeball. Finally, the brain de-codes these signals and works out what we are seeing.

HOW DO GLASSES HELP PEOPLE SEE?

Sometimes the lens in the eye cannot focus light properly, and things look blurred. This can happen in young people, or in adults as they age. Glasses contain lenses that work with the eyes' own lenses to focus light properly.

The Skin

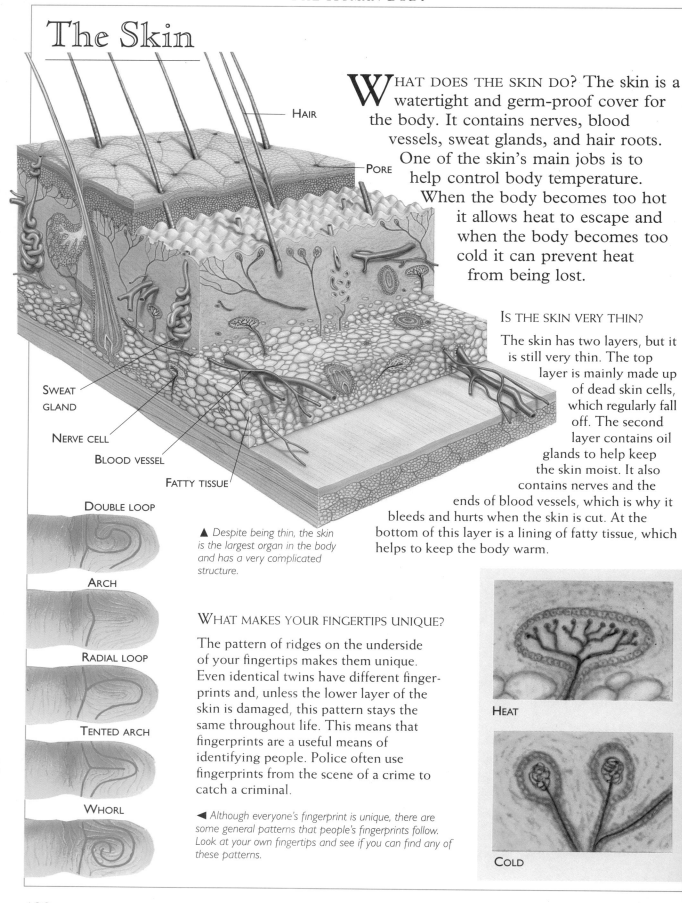

HAIR

PORE

SWEAT GLAND

NERVE CELL

BLOOD VESSEL

FATTY TISSUE

▲ *Despite being thin, the skin is the largest organ in the body and has a very complicated structure.*

DOUBLE LOOP

ARCH

RADIAL LOOP

TENTED ARCH

WHORL

W HAT DOES THE SKIN DO? The skin is a watertight and germ-proof cover for the body. It contains nerves, blood vessels, sweat glands, and hair roots. One of the skin's main jobs is to help control body temperature. When the body becomes too hot it allows heat to escape and when the body becomes too cold it can prevent heat from being lost.

IS THE SKIN VERY THIN?

The skin has two layers, but it is still very thin. The top layer is mainly made up of dead skin cells, which regularly fall off. The second layer contains oil glands to help keep the skin moist. It also contains nerves and the ends of blood vessels, which is why it bleeds and hurts when the skin is cut. At the bottom of this layer is a lining of fatty tissue, which helps to keep the body warm.

WHAT MAKES YOUR FINGERTIPS UNIQUE?

The pattern of ridges on the underside of your fingertips makes them unique. Even identical twins have different fingerprints and, unless the lower layer of the skin is damaged, this pattern stays the same throughout life. This means that fingerprints are a useful means of identifying people. Police often use fingerprints from the scene of a crime to catch a criminal.

◄ *Although everyone's fingerprint is unique, there are some general patterns that people's fingerprints follow. Look at your own fingertips and see if you can find any of these patterns.*

HEAT

COLD

SKIN PORE

BLOCKED PORE

SPOT

INFECTED SPOT

WHERE DO SPOTS COME FROM?

A spot occurs when oil in the skin gets blocked in a pore. It swells slightly and becomes red and hard. If bacteria get in, the spot becomes infected.

◄ *Spots are quite common during teenage years, when hormone changes increase oil content in the skin.*

DOES EVERYONE GET WRINKLES?

Eventually everyone gets wrinkles of some sort. Wrinkles appear as the skin ages, losing its tightness and becoming less elastic. As the skin becomes looser it falls into fine lines and folds. You can often see wrinkles on the hands and faces of older people. Wrinkles around the eyes are often called laughter lines as they appear most clearly when people laugh.

WHAT IS ACUPUNCTURE?

Acupuncture is an ancient Chinese medical treatment. Fine needles are inserted into the skin at certain places, called pressure points. Although most doctors from Western countries do not know how it works, many people find the treatment helpful.

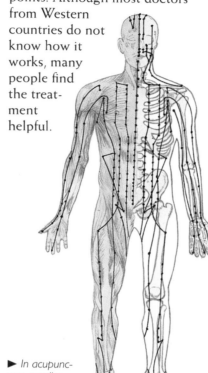

► *In acupuncture, needles are inserted into particular parts of the body.*

WHAT ARE FRECKLES?

Everyone's skin has a different amount of melanin, a substance that colors the skin shades of light pink to dark brown. Melanin helps to protect the skin from being burnt by the sun. People with very light skin often have uneven amounts of melanin, which appear as freckles. New freckles can appear or existing freckles can become darker when the skin is exposed to the sun.

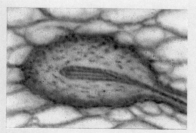
PRESSURE

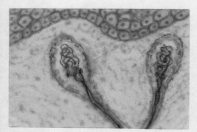
TOUCH

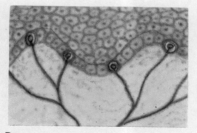
PAIN

HOW DO WE FEEL 'TOUCH'?

Nerve endings in the skin have different shapes according to the kind of sensation they detect (left). Some nerves tell us about pain or if the skin is becoming hot or cold. Others tell us about touch, or pressure on the skin.

IS THE SUN DANGEROUS?

If you wear a sun hat and sun-screen lotion, and keep your body lightly covered, it is usually safe to be out in the sun for a short time. The skin can easily burn if you stay out for too long, and this can be painful or even dangerous if it happens a lot.

Sexual Reproduction

HOW IS A NEW LIFE MADE? Every new-born baby starts life as just one cell! This cell is made when a woman's egg cell and a man's sperm cell join together, which can happen as a result of having sex. Because these cells come from both parents the baby will have something in common with each of its parents. It is also possible to make a baby outside the woman's body and then to put the tiny new life back in the uterus to grow and be born.

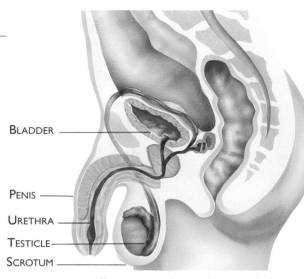

BLADDER

PENIS

URETHRA

TESTICLE

SCROTUM

▲ The male sexual organs hang outside the body. They have to be protected from damage because if they are hurt it can cause terrible pain.

WHAT ARE TESTICLES FOR?

Testicles hang behind the penis, and make male sperm – about 500 million every day! Sperm are stored in a special chamber for up to a week and are released when a man ejaculates. Any unused sperm are absorbed back into the body. If a man ejaculates, the sperm pass along a tube into the penis, and are squirted out in a sticky liquid called semen. Semen travels out through the same tube in the penis as urine from the bladder.

WHERE ARE A WOMAN'S EGGS MADE?

Girls and women have two ovaries, low inside the tummy, which make their eggs. Once a girl has her period, an egg is released every month from an ovary into a tube called the fallopian tube. Each ovary has a fallopian tube leading to the uterus. This is a cavity with thick, spongy walls where a new baby can develop. Leading to the outside is a passageway called the vagina. Girls have a separate tube for urine, leading from the bladder to a hole just in front of the vagina.

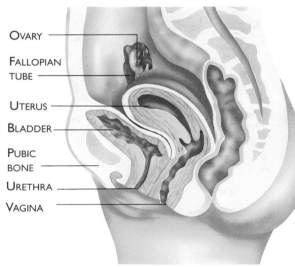

OVARY

FALLOPIAN TUBE

UTERUS

BLADDER

PUBIC BONE

URETHRA

VAGINA

▲ The female sexual organs are inside the pelvis, behind the pubic bone. The pair of ovaries and fallopian tubes are tucked behind the uterus.

WHAT IS 'HAVING SEX'?

Men and women usually like 'having sex', or 'making love'. It often involves a lot of kissing and touching of each other's bodies. The man's penis usually becomes hard, so that he can put it inside the woman's vagina. The move-ments of lovemaking eventually cause a sudden release of sperm, which squirts into the vagina.

HOW IS PREGNANCY PREVENTED?

Products called contraceptives can stop a woman from becoming pregnant. A man can wear a condom on his penis to stop sperm escaping into a woman's uterus or a woman can have a special cap or other device inside her. Women can also take 'the pill' – tablets that change hormone levels and prevent pregnancy.

CONDOM

CAP (DIAPHRAGM)

IUD (INTRA-UTERINE DEVICE)

PILL

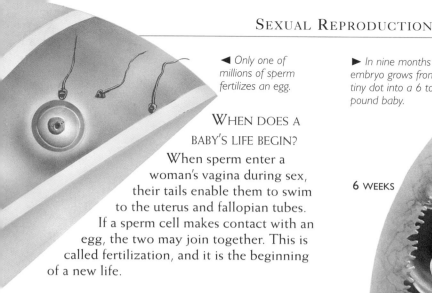

◀ Only one of millions of sperm fertilizes an egg.

▶ In nine months an embryo grows from a tiny dot into a 6 to 9 pound baby.

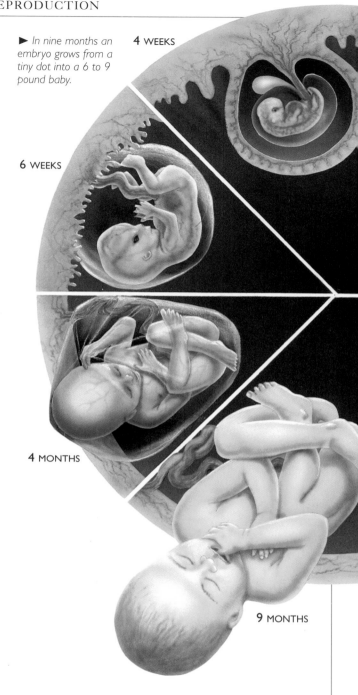

4 WEEKS

6 WEEKS

4 MONTHS

9 MONTHS

WHEN DOES A BABY'S LIFE BEGIN?

When sperm enter a woman's vagina during sex, their tails enable them to swim to the uterus and fallopian tubes. If a sperm cell makes contact with an egg, the two may join together. This is called fertilization, and it is the beginning of a new life.

HOW DOES A BABY GROW?

The fertilized egg cell begins dividing into more cells until it is made up of hundreds of cells. The ball of cells then implants itself into the wall of the womb and continues to grow. By this stage it has all the genetic information needed to develop into a baby. At first the baby, called an embryo, is tiny – about the size of a pea. After about six weeks it starts to grow arms and legs. After eight to nine weeks, the embryo becomes a fetus – it is still tiny but all of its organs and body parts have formed. It takes nine months for the baby to reach the right weight and size to be born. As it grows the woman's uterus stretches. When it is time for the birth, the woman has to work hard to push the baby out through her vagina. Sometimes this can take many hours. Finally the baby comes out, still attached to the mother by a cord, which has to be cut.

HOW DO WOMEN'S BREASTS FEED A BABY?

During pregnancy a woman's breasts grow larger due to special hormones in the blood that help the breasts to produce milk. Breast milk is thinner than milk from a bottle but it has lots more goodness in it to help the baby grow. It also protects the baby from infections. The baby is put to the breast and sucks on the nipple at the end of the breast. The sucking helps to bring the milk out of the mother's breast and into the baby's mouth.

WHAT ARE PERIODS FOR?

Periods are the monthly cycle of bleeding that happens to females during their adult lives. A period takes place when fertilization has not occurred. Each month an egg is prepared in one of the ovaries. It is then released halfway through the monthly cycle and travels along the fallopian tube to the uterus. At the same time, the uterus prepares a lining of blood to receive the fertilized egg. If the egg is not fertilized it dies. The blood lining is then discarded and passes out of the body through the vagina.

Growth

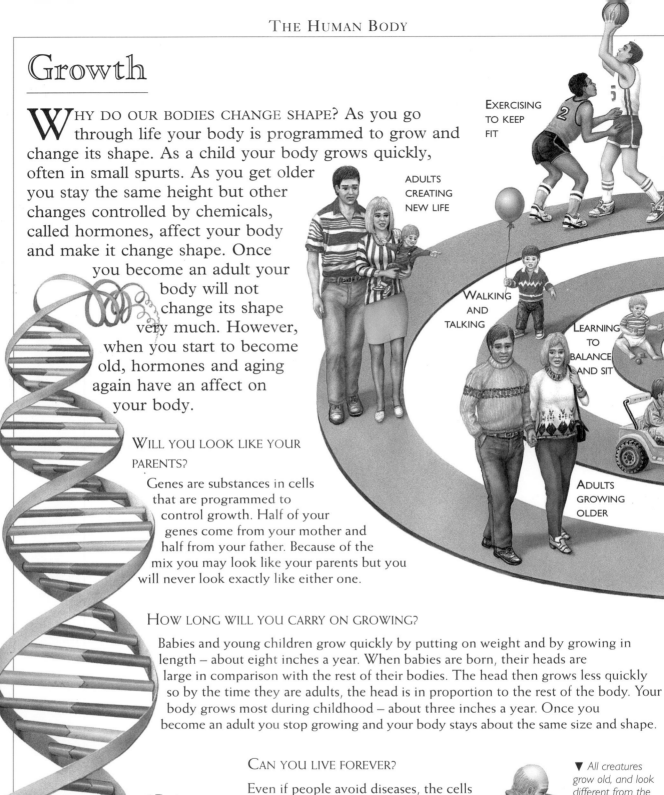

WHY DO OUR BODIES CHANGE SHAPE? As you go through life your body is programmed to grow and change its shape. As a child your body grows quickly, often in small spurts. As you get older you stay the same height but other changes controlled by chemicals, called hormones, affect your body and make it change shape. Once you become an adult your body will not change its shape very much. However, when you start to become old, hormones and aging again have an affect on your body.

EXERCISING TO KEEP FIT

ADULTS CREATING NEW LIFE

WALKING AND TALKING

LEARNING TO BALANCE AND SIT

ADULTS GROWING OLDER

WILL YOU LOOK LIKE YOUR PARENTS?

Genes are substances in cells that are programmed to control growth. Half of your genes come from your mother and half from your father. Because of the mix you may look like your parents but you will never look exactly like either one.

HOW LONG WILL YOU CARRY ON GROWING?

Babies and young children grow quickly by putting on weight and by growing in length – about eight inches a year. When babies are born, their heads are large in comparison with the rest of their bodies. The head then grows less quickly so by the time they are adults, the head is in proportion to the rest of the body. Your body grows most during childhood – about three inches a year. Once you become an adult you stop growing and your body stays about the same size and shape.

CAN YOU LIVE FOREVER?

Even if people avoid diseases, the cells in their bodies begin to wear out with old age. This is because we are programmed to live for a certain number of years. As people grow older they may develop problems, such as difficulty in seeing, hearing, and walking.

◀ The program for growth is written onto a substance in your genes called DNA. Each strand of DNA is very complicated.

▼ All creatures grow old, and look different from the way they once did.

▼ *Growth is divided into stages. The same changes happen to everyone's body as it grows from infancy to adulthood.*

GROWING UP

TRYING TO WALK

GROWING TALLER AND STRONGER

LEARNING TO CRAWL

GROWING INTO OLDER AGE

WHEN WILL YOU BECOME AN ADULT?

It is a slow process but the physical changes begin for both girls and boys around the ages of ten to twelve. The body then begins to produce larger quantities of special chemicals called sex hormones. These hormones are responsible for changing the shape and look of your body. Girls begin to develop rounded hips and breasts. Boys' voices become deeper, and thicker hair begins to grow on their faces. Both girls and boys grow hair under their arms and around the genital areas. Girls also begin to have periods.

CAN THE BODY GROW TOO TALL?

Sometimes programming or hormones that control growth are faulty. The body may carry on growing until it becomes unusually tall or 'giant'. The body may also not grow enough and be very short. Records currently show the tallest person to be 7.5 feet tall and the shortest person to be 1.9 feet in height.

DO ANIMALS LIVE AS LONG AS PEOPLE?

Like people, animals have programmed growth and development. Some animals, like mice, only live for two to three years. Cats and dogs usually live for ten to fifteen years. The length of time an animal lives is related to how many predators (hunting animals) it has. Animals with lots of predators are programmed to grow and reproduce quickly, so they have shorter lives.

► *A cat, elephant, and mouse all live for different lengths of time. An animal's lifespan is programmed into its genes.*

| | | | 80 |
| 70 |
| 60 |
| 50 |
| 40 |
| 30 |
| 20 |
| 10 |

YEARS

MOUSE CAT ELEPHANT HUMAN

CAN YOU MAKE YOURSELF GROW MORE QUICKLY?

Because your growth is programmed you cannot control how your body grows and changes shape. Some people are programmed to be taller or shorter than others. Some people will be bigger or smaller than others. However, the amount and type of food you eat can affect the development of your body. The body is programmed to grow in a certain way but it needs to be looked after properly.

HOW LONG CAN YOU EXPECT TO LIVE?

Humans live for about seventy-five to eighty years. In the past, people lived much shorter lives. We live longer because many of the conditions and diseases that once killed people can now be prevented or cured.

◄ *Hormones control many of the changes that take place in the body once childhood growth has stopped.*

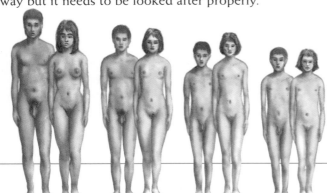

Diseases and Medicines

IS THERE A MEDICINE TO CURE EVERY DISEASE? There are many diseases that can affect the body and there are lots of medicines that help to treat or cure diseases. But there are some diseases that are very difficult to treat or sometimes cannot be cured, such as certain types of cancer and genetic diseases. New medicines are being invented all the time and most diseases are not serious ones.

WHAT IS A BRAIN SCAN?

A brain scan is a special type of photograph of a person's brain. The procedure for having a brain scan does not hurt. It involves lying on a table and being slowly moved into the center of a hollow brain-scanning machine. The pictures that are produced look like blurred photographs. They are used by doctors to find out what is happening inside a patient's brain. The information they provide help doctors to decide on the best treatment and medicine to give the patient.

WHEN DOES A GENETIC DISEASE BEGIN?

A genetic disease begins when a baby is first developing inside its mother's womb. As the cells divide, something goes wrong with some of them because part of the DNA – the cell's information – from one or both parents, is faulty. The baby is then born with what is called a genetic disease. Because the genes are passed from the parent to the baby, genetic diseases are sometimes found more than once in the same family. Although the disease can be seen at birth, it can also go undetected for several years.

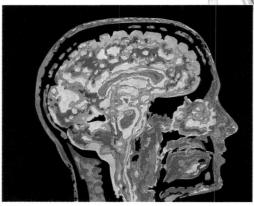

▲ Photographs taken by a brain scanner are fed into a computer and appear on a viewing screen.

◄ Photographs from a brain scan show the different areas of the brain. They also allow doctors to see if anything is wrong inside the brain.

▼ Some genetic diseases such as muscular dystrophy cause physical disability and may mean the person needs to use a wheelchair.

WHAT IS A VIRUS?

A virus is a type of germ that gets inside the body and causes an infection. Viruses are so small that they cannot be seen, and you do not realize you have one until you begin to feel ill. There are many diseases caused by viruses, such as colds and flu, mumps, measles, and chicken pox. Although these viruses can make you feel ill, your body eventually beats them and you end up feeling well again. There are other viruses however that can cause more harm, such as the virus that causes meningitis and one called the HIV virus that causes a disease called AIDS.

WHAT IS A VACCINE?

Vaccines are medicines that prevent people from catching certain diseases in the future. They are made up of dead or inactive germs, and are usually injected into the body. The body's white blood cells try to fight the mock germs, creating chemicals called antibodies. The antibodies are then in place to fight the real germs, should they ever attack you properly.

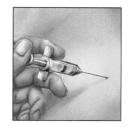

◀ A vaccine injection may hurt for a minute but it protects you for years.

WHAT ARE ANTIBIOTICS?

An antibiotic is a type of medicine that is taken to cure infections caused by germs called bacteria. They do not work on viruses which is why you are not given antibiotics for a cold or for flu. It is important not to take antibiotics too often because this may kill off the helpful bacteria that live in and protect the body.

▲ Bacteria can only be seen when they are magnified many times. The picture above shows the salmonella bacterium.

WHAT DO X-RAYS SHOW?

X-rays are taken when doctors need to find out if there has been any injury or damage inside the body. They are special photographs that see through the soft tissues of the body but not the hard bone tissue. They reveal if a bone has been damaged or broken. They can also show if some organs like the lungs and heart are working properly.

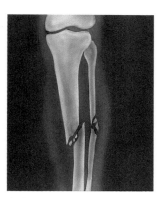

▲ An x-ray shows damage such as a broken bone.

HOW DO WE CATCH DISEASES?

Some diseases, like infections from germs, attack the body from the outside. Other diseases develop inside the body when it stops working properly – cancer and diabetes are examples of these. Luckily most diseases are not serious, but when they are there are usually medical treatments to slow down the spread of the disease and to ease any pain the disease causes.

CAN A JOINT WEAR OUT?

If you look after your body, your joints usually last a lifetime. However, some people – especially older people – have diseases like arthritis and rheumatism, which cause their joints to wear out. Operations can be done on some worn-out joints, such as the hip, knee, shoulder, and elbow, where the joint is taken out and replaced with a plastic or metal joint.

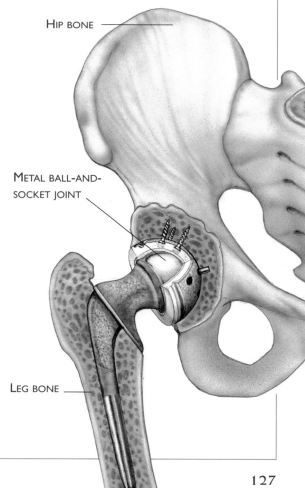

▼ Hip joints are one of the most common joints to be replaced. They are cemented into place with surgical cement, which makes them very strong and secure.

HIP BONE

METAL BALL-AND-SOCKET JOINT

LEG BONE

PART

5

SCIENCE

Atoms

WHAT IS AN ATOM? An atom is the smallest possible piece of a substance. It is so small that it cannot be broken up into anything smaller and still be the same substance. Everything in the world is made of atoms, including the air we breathe, a jumbo-jet plane, a tree, and even a human being.

ATOM

ELECTRON

NUCLEUS

WHAT DOES AN ATOM LOOK LIKE?

Atoms are so small that they cannot be seen even using the most powerful microscopes. But scientists have worked out what atoms are like. Surprisingly, an atom consists mostly of empty space. It has a small central core, called a nucleus. The nucleus is made up of two kinds of subatomic particles, called protons and neutrons. Each proton carries a positive electric charge. Neutrons have no electric charge. Circling the nucleus, and a long way from it, is a cloud of electrons. Each electron carries a negative electric charge. There is the same number of orbiting electrons as there are protons in the nucleus. As a result, their positive and negative charges cancel out, and the whole atom is electrically neutral.

▶ An atom is made up of smaller, subatomic particles. Protons and neutrons form the nucleus, and electrons travel in orbits around the nucleus. But the protons and neutrons have a structure of their own. Each is made up of three even smaller particles called quarks, held together by gluons. There are 12 different kinds of quarks, and many other subatomic particles are also made up of quarks.

LEAD ATOM

HYDROGEN ATOM

TRITIUM ATOM

HOW DO SCIENTISTS STUDY PARTICLES?

Subatomic particles are much too small to see. Also most of them move at high speeds. But they can be made to leave tracks that show where they have been. This is done using a bubble chamber. It consists of a tank of liquid hydrogen under pressure. When the pressure is suddenly released, any particles traveling through the chamber leave tracks of tiny bubbles. The bubble-chamber tracks can be photographed and then studied.

If the chamber is located in a magnetic field, the field bends the tracks of any charged particles such as protons and electrons. Some particles change into other particles after a short time. By measuring the lengths of the tracks, scientists can work out the lifetime of a particle.

▲ Using a bubble chamber, scientists can see what happens when subatomic particles collide with each other.

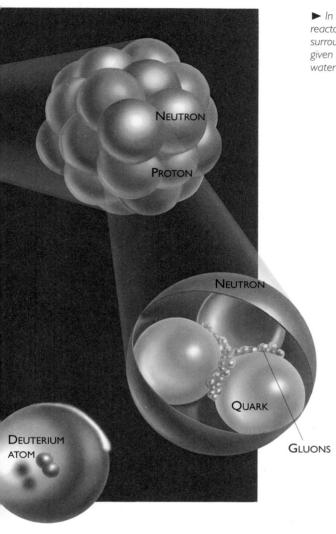

NEUTRON

PROTON

NEUTRON

QUARK

GLUONS

DEUTERIUM
ATOM

▶ *In some types of nuclear reactor, the fuel rods are surrounded by water. Radiation given off by the rods makes the water glow with a blue light.*

WHAT MAKES ATOMS RADIOACTIVE?

A heavy element such as uranium has large atoms with a large nucleus containing many subatomic particles. For example, the nucleus of one type of uranium atom contains 92 protons and 146 neutrons. Such an arrangement is unstable, and the nucleus becomes stable by 'spitting out' some particles or by giving off gamma radiation. This effect is known as radioactivity. The chief particles given off by a radioactive element are alpha particles (a cluster of two protons and two neutrons) and beta particles (electrons).

WHAT IS NUCLEAR FISSION?

Nuclear fission is the splitting of an atomic nucleus. It takes place in an atomic bomb and inside a nuclear reactor. Atoms of uranium are hit by neutrons. Some uranium nuclei absorb an extra neutron. This makes the uranium nucleus unstable. It splits into two fragments, and releases two or three more neutrons. These neutrons split more uranium atoms and the process grows as a chain reaction, releasing a huge amount of heat energy.

▶ *In nuclear fission, a uranium nucleus splits in two with the release of heat and two or three neutrons.*

WHAT ARE ISOTOPES?

An atom's nucleus contains protons and neutrons. Normal carbon nuclei for example have 6 protons and 6 neutrons, giving carbon an atomic mass of 12. There is another form of carbon with 6 protons and 8 neutrons, giving it an atomic mass of 14. The two forms, which have different numbers of neutrons, are called isotopes.

SOLAR
PROMINENCE

WHAT IS NUCLEAR FUSION?

Nuclear fusion is the joining together of two light atoms to form a heavier one, causing a release of much heat energy. It takes place in a hydrogen bomb and in the Sun and other stars. In one fusion reaction, two atoms of a type of hydrogen combine to form an atom of helium. Scientists are working to build a fusion reactor so they can use this process as a method of producing clean energy from cheap materials.

◀ *The Sun gets its enormous amounts of light and heat energy from fusion reactions that take place inside it. Sometimes large plumes of gas, called prominences, shoot out of this ball of energy.*

MOLECULES
IN METAL

Solids, Liquids, and Gases

W HAT IS MATTER? Everything is made of matter, whether it is a solid, liquid, or gas. Steel is a solid, water is a liquid, and air is a mixture of gases. Also everything is made up of atoms or molecules. The differences between solids, liquids, and gases depend on the way their atoms or molecules behave.

► *The molecules in the water surrounding the scuba diver vibrate from side to side, which is why water is a liquid. The atoms in the metal of the air bottle hardly vibrate at all, which is why the metal is a solid.*

WHAT ARE THE STATES OF MATTER?

The solid state, the liquid state, and the gaseous state are known as the three states of matter. Everything exists in one of these states. The atoms or molecules that make up a solid such as steel remain in more-or-less the same place all the time. But the atoms have a heat content and because of this they may vibrate slightly, although they do not move far. This is why a solid has a fixed shape. In a liquid such as water, the atoms or molecules vibrate more vigorously and they are free to move around. This is why a liquid takes on the shape of its container. In a gas such as air, the atoms or molecules fly around at high speed, bouncing off the walls of the container. This is why a gas exerts a pressure on its container, and why the container has to have a lid on it to stop the gas from escaping.

MOLECULES
IN AIR

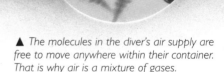

▲ *The molecules in the diver's air supply are free to move anywhere within their container. That is why air is a mixture of gases.*

▼ *When water boils in a kettle, water molecules leave the surface of the liquid and form water vapor, or steam.*

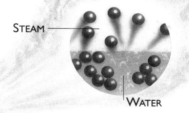

STEAM

WATER

WHAT IS EVAPORATION?

Evaporation takes place at the surface of a liquid. There, some of the liquid's molecules 'jump' clear of the surface and become a gas or vapor. Gradually the liquid dries up as more and more of its molecules turn to vapor. If the liquid is heated, its molecules vibrate faster and the liquid evaporates at a much faster rate.

WHAT IS CONDENSATION?

Condensation is the process by which a gas or vapor turns into a liquid. When a vapor is cooled, its molecules vibrate less and less. If it is cold enough, the vapor changes into a liquid. For example, when we breathe out on a frosty day the water vapor in our breath condenses into water droplets, which form a cloud of mist.

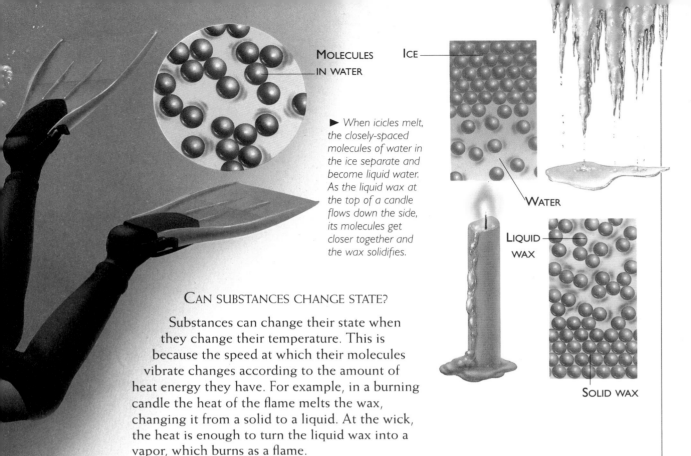

MOLECULES IN WATER

ICE

WATER

LIQUID WAX

SOLID WAX

▶ When icicles melt, the closely-spaced molecules of water in the ice separate and become liquid water. As the liquid wax at the top of a candle flows down the side, its molecules get closer together and the wax solidifies.

CAN SUBSTANCES CHANGE STATE?

Substances can change their state when they change their temperature. This is because the speed at which their molecules vibrate changes according to the amount of heat energy they have. For example, in a burning candle the heat of the flame melts the wax, changing it from a solid to a liquid. At the wick, the heat is enough to turn the liquid wax into a vapor, which burns as a flame.

HOW DOES A SOLUTION CRYSTALLIZE?

A solution is a solid dissolved in a liquid, such as salt dissolved in water. When salt dissolves, its atoms separate and move around freely in the solution. But there is a limit to how much salt an amount of water can hold. As a salt solution slowly evaporates, the water in it turns to water vapor. A point is reached when there is not enough water to hold all the salt, and the excess salt comes out of solution. The atoms that make up salt join up again and form crystals.

▼ The atoms in crystals are held in a regular pattern called a lattice. There are various types of lattice. Shown below is a hexagonal pattern, in which each atom is surrounded by six others.

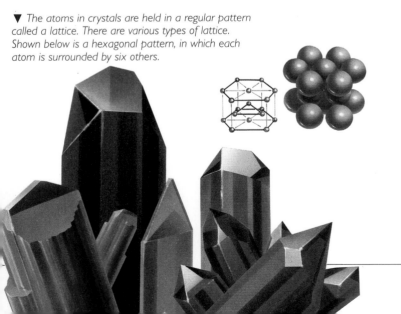

IS GLASS A SOLID?

Although glass appears to be solid, the pattern of its molecules is more like that of a liquid than a solid. For this reason, glass is known as a supercooled liquid. Over many years, it 'flows' like a thick liquid. That is why in some very old windows the glass is thicker at the bottom than at the top.

The Air

WHAT IS AIR? You do not normally notice the air you are surrounded by. Air has no color and no smell. Yet without it, all plants and animals would die. Air is a mixture of gases. The main gases are nitrogen and oxygen. Oxygen is the gas we have to breathe to stay alive. Air also exerts a pressure, and this pressure can be made to do useful work.

DOES AIR HAVE WEIGHT?

Air is a mixture of gases, and although these gases are very light they do have weight. Air also takes up space, and therefore has density, although the density is very low. When air is warmed, it expands and gets less dense. This is why warm air rises. When air is cooled, it gets more dense and falls.

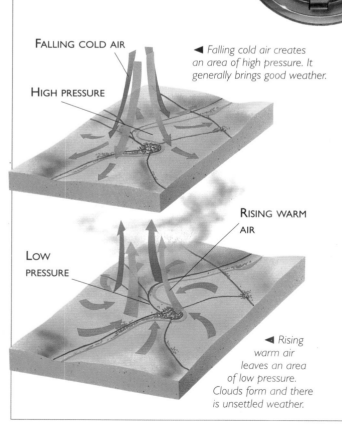

FALLING COLD AIR

HIGH PRESSURE

◀ *Falling cold air creates an area of high pressure. It generally brings good weather.*

RISING WARM AIR

LOW PRESSURE

◀ *Rising warm air leaves an area of low pressure. Clouds form and there is unsettled weather.*

CAN SOMETHING FLOAT ON AIR?

Like water, air is a fluid, and objects can float on it. To float, the object must be less dense than air – such as a balloon full of helium gas. If the object is more dense and falls through the air, it experiences a slowing-down force called wind resistance. This force is used by parachutes.

▼ *A barometer measures air pressure. Air pressure falls before rain comes, so a barometer can help to predict the weather.*

WHAT IS A BAROMETER?

A barometer is an instrument that measures air pressure. The mass of air stacked up over the Earth's surface exerts a degree of pressure on it. This is called atmospheric pressure. But higher up in the atmosphere, there is less air pressing down and atmospheric pressure is not as great. For this reason, a reading of pressure on a barometer is also an indication of altitude (height). An altimeter, which measures altitude, is just a barometer with markings showing height instead of pressure.

WHAT IS AIR MADE OF?

Air is a mixture of gases. Chief of these are nitrogen (which makes up 78 percent of air by volume), oxygen (21 percent), argon (nearly 1 percent), and carbon dioxide (0.03 percent). There are also traces of neon, helium, krypton, and xenon. Air that is polluted may contain other gases, too, such as sulfur dioxide from factories and carbon monoxide from traffic. For animals, the key gas in air is oxygen, which animals need to breathe. For plants, the important gas is carbon dioxide, which plants combine with water during photosynthesis to make sugars, which the plant uses as food. Plants also make use of nitrogen.

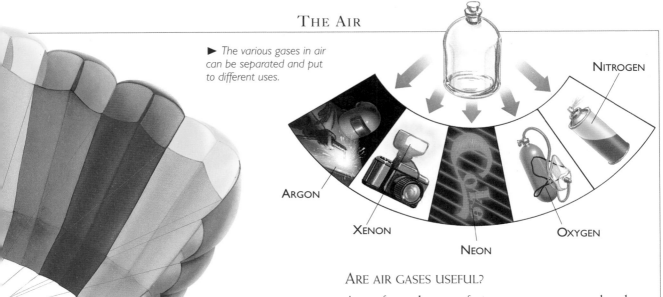

► The various gases in air can be separated and put to different uses.

NITROGEN

ARGON

XENON

NEON

OXYGEN

◄ The large canopy of a parachute ensures that it meets great wind resistance. As a result, it falls slowly.

HOW DO HOVERCRAFT RIDE ON AIR?

The technical name for a hovercraft is 'air-cushion vehicle', and this name gives a good clue as to how the craft works. Basically, a hovercraft is surrounded by a rubber curtain known as a skirt. The craft's engines drive powerful fans that pump a flow of high-speed air into the skirt. The air forms a cushion under the craft which the vehicle rides on. The hovercraft is steered using rudders similar to those on an aircraft. As well as traveling over water, the vehicle can be used to cross beaches, swamps, and even dry land, though the land needs to be smooth.

▼ A hovercraft rides over the water on a cushion of air.

ARE AIR GASES USEFUL?

Apart from the use of nitrogen, oxygen, and carbon dioxide by plants and animals, all the gases in air have industrial uses. Nitrogen is used to pressurize aerosol cans. It is also one of the raw materials in the industrial process for making ammonia. Oxygen is used in medicine, steel-making, and metal welding. Carbon dioxide is the gas that puts the bubbles in fizzy drinks. Argon forms the 'atmosphere' for welding metals such as aluminum. Neon is used in advertising signs, and xenon is the gas inside a photographer's electronic flash.

HOW IS COMPRESSED AIR USED?

Compressed air is a useful source of power. It can be either supplied in bottles of high-pressure gas, or generated where it is needed by compressors (compressing machines). Compressed air is used in pneumatic hammers and drills, which break up concrete. Commercial artists often use air-brushes, which are powered by compressed air. Divers need compressed air to breathe underwater.

▼ Powerful fans create the flow of air that inflates a hovercraft's skirt.

FAN   AIR FLOW   SKIRT

AIR CUSHION

Heat

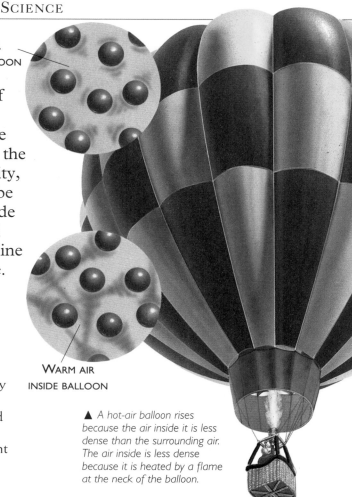

COOL AIR
OUTSIDE BALLOON

WARM AIR
INSIDE BALLOON

WHAT IS HEAT? Heat is a form of energy. In a hot object, heat is stored in its atoms. The atoms vibrate continuously, and the hotter they are the more they vibrate. Like light, electricity, and other forms of energy, heat can be made to do work. Heat engines include the steam engine and various internal combustion engines such as the gasoline engine, diesel engine, and gas turbine. All of these convert heat energy into mechanical energy.

HOW IS HEAT PRODUCED?

Heat is produced by converting a form of energy into a different kind of energy. In a fire, the chemical energy of the burning fuel is converted into heat. Electricity, another form of energy, produces heat when it flows along a wire filament and makes the wire hot. Like all other forms of energy, heat is measured in units called joules.

▲ A hot-air balloon rises because the air inside it is less dense than the surrounding air. The air inside is less dense because it is heated by a flame at the neck of the balloon.

◄ Some birds use the movement of heat to help them move. A soaring bird such as an eagle climbs without flapping its wings by spiraling up on a convection current known as a thermal.

HOW DOES HEAT MOVE?

Heat can move in three ways. Convection takes place in a body of fluid, such as a gas or liquid. When the fluid is warmed, it expands and becomes less dense. The less dense fluid rises, and cooler fluid moves in to take its place. This is the principle behind convector heaters, warming the air in a room.

All hot objects give off heat by radiation. This is how heat reaches the Earth from the Sun across the vacuum of space. We can feel radiant heat by holding a hand near a hot object.

The third way heat travels is by conduction. In any hot object, the atoms are vibrating. These atoms pass on their vibrations to their neighbors, making them hotter. In this way, heat travels along a metal bar from the hot end towards the cooler end.

▼ A hot kettle emits heat by radiation, which can be detected in a type of photograph called a thermogram.

◄ When a metal is heated, heat travels by conduction from the hot part to the cooler part.

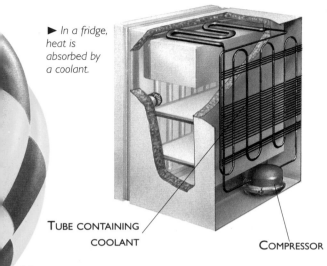

▶ In a fridge, heat is absorbed by a coolant.

TUBE CONTAINING COOLANT

COMPRESSOR

HOW DOES A FRIDGE WORK?

A refrigerator works by removing heat from its contents. A circulating ice-cold liquid, called a coolant, absorbs the heat, and the liquid changes into a gas. The gas passes through a narrow opening, which cools the gas. A compressor then changes the gas back into a liquid.

HOW DOES A VACUUM FLASK WORK?

A vacuum flask helps to keep liquids hot or cold by overcoming the three ways in which heat can travel into or out of the flask. The flask itself is a double-walled glass bottle and the thinness of the glass helps to prevent conduction. The silver coating on the glass helps to prevent radiation. Finally, the vacuum between the walls of the flask helps to prevent convection.

OUTER CASING

DOUBLE-WALLED BOTTLE

▲ A vacuum flask prevents heat moving by conduction, radiation, or convection.

HOW IS HEAT MEASURED?

Heat is measured as temperature, or the degree of hotness of an object. In a traditional thermometer, temperature is shown by the rise of a column of liquid such as mercury or dyed alcohol. A modern electronic thermometer has a thermo-electric probe. The probe generates an electrical signal when it is heated, and the amount of electric current is shown as a figure on a digital display.

HOW CAN HEAT BE KEPT IN OR OUT?

Heat can be kept in or out in several ways. One way to keep heat in is to insulate. Most insulating materials are fibrous substances that trap a lot of air. For example, glass wool is used to insulate houses and woolen clothing is used to keep people warm. Layers of similar materials can also be used to keep heat out. Protection against fierce heat is possible with a layer of a substance such as asbestos, which will not burn. It may also be painted silver so it does not absorb much heat either.

◀ A firefighter wears an asbestos suit as protection against the fierce heat of a fire.

Forces and Motion

WHEN A BALL ROLLS ALONG ON A SMOOTH SURFACE, WHY DOESN'T IT GO ON ROLLING FOR EVER? A rolling ball slows down and eventually stops because it is acted on by a force. In this case, the force at work is the friction between the ball and the surface it is rolling on. A force can move an object that is not moving, or stop a moving object.

▶ The space shuttle is launched by a large liquid-fuel rocket and two solid-fuel booster rockets.

MAIN ROCKET

BOOSTER ROCKET

SPACE SHUTTLE

HOW DO ROCKETS WORK?

When fuel burns in a rocket's combustion chamber, the hot gases that are produced exert a force in all directions. Gases pushing on the closed (front) end of the chamber cause a reaction force that acts in the opposite direction and propels the rocket upward.

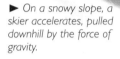

▶ On a snowy slope, a skier accelerates, pulled downhill by the force of gravity.

FORCE OF GRAVITY

DOWNWARD MOTION

DOWNWARD MOTION

FORCE OF GRAVITY

WHAT ARE THE 'LAWS OF MOTION'?

All moving objects obey the laws of motion, which were worked out 300 years ago by the English mathematician Sir Isaac Newton. Newton's first law states that an object at rest remains at rest, or an object moving in a straight line goes on moving, unless the object is acted on by a force. For example, in a game of pool or snooker, a player makes a ball move by exerting a force on it – striking it with the cue. The harder the player hits the ball, the more force is applied and the faster – and farther – the ball goes.

Every object (such as a snooker ball) has mass and when that mass is acted on by a force it accelerates (goes faster). Newton's second law of motion states that the force is equal to the mass multiplied by the acceleration. Finally, his third law states that if one object exerts a force on another object, the second object exerts an equal and opposite force on the first. This force is called the reaction.

▶ The skier keeps moving because there is little friction between the skis and the snow to work against gravity.

ARE MASS AND WEIGHT THE SAME?

Mass is the amount of substance in an object, measured in units such as pounds and ounces. An object's mass remains the same wherever the object is in the universe. However, there is a force called gravity that acts between any two objects that have mass. It draws every object on Earth towards the Earth, and the size of this force affects the object's weight (measured in units such as newtons). Because gravity varies in the universe, weight is not constant. For example, an object that weighs 60 newtons on Earth would weigh only 10 newtons on the Moon, where gravity is one-sixth of the Earth's gravity. For everyday use, weights are usually stated in the same units as mass.

▼ In a crash, forward momentum throws the driver toward the windscreen.

▼ After the impact, the car 'bounces' back and the driver is thrown backward.

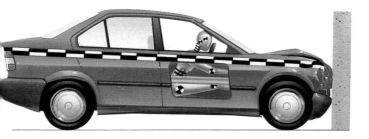

ARE SPEED AND VELOCITY THE SAME?

Speed is a measure of how fast an object moves. Mathematically, speed is the rate of change of position, or the overall distance an object travels divided by the time it takes to do so. A car that travels 25 miles in 30 minutes has an average speed of 50 mph (miles per hour). Velocity measures both speed and direction. For example, an aircraft flying towards the North Pole at a speed of 280 mph has a velocity of 280 mph northwards.

WHAT IS ACCELERATION?

Acceleration is the rate of change of velocity. A car that starts from rest and reaches a velocity of 90 mph in 30 seconds has an average acceleration of 3 miles per hour per second (each second, its velocity increases by an average of 3 mph).

◄ By turning the skis sideways, the skier creates greater friction and this force slows the skier to a complete standstill.

WHAT IS MOMENTUM?

A moving object has momentum because it has mass and velocity. To work out the momentum of an object we multiply its mass by its velocity. Because of its greater mass, a heavy truck has a larger momentum than a car traveling at the same speed. The heavy truck has more momentum at high speed than it does at a lower speed. An important law of physics states that when two moving objects collide, the total momentum before an impact is the same as after it.

Machines

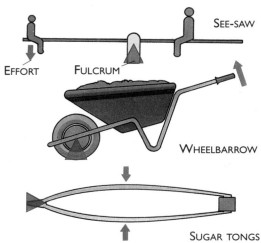

SEE-SAW

EFFORT   FULCRUM

WHEELBARROW

SUGAR TONGS

▲ *All levers have a fulcrum.
Effort is needed to move the loads.*

WHAT IS A MACHINE? A machine is any device that lets a small force (the effort) overcome a larger force (the load). One of the simplest machines is an inclined plane, or ramp. Without help a person cannot lift a 450-pound crate onto the back of a truck. But with a ramp he or she can push the crate up and onto the truck.

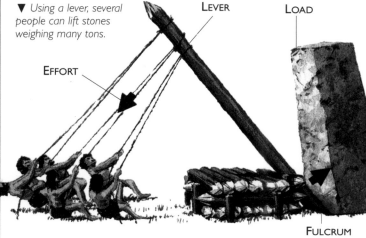

▼ *Using a lever, several people can lift stones weighing many tons.*

LEVER   LOAD

EFFORT

FULCRUM

HOW DO LEVERS WORK?

There are three classes of levers. All involve a rod or bar, a fulcrum (pivot), and places where the load and effort act. A see-saw is an example of a first-class lever. If the load is an adult sitting close to the fulcrum, a child (the effort) sitting a long way from the fulcrum can lift the adult. A wheelbarrow is a second-class lever. The load is between the effort and fulcrum. Sugar tongs are a pair of third-class levers, with the effort between the load and fulcrum.

WHAT IS A WHEEL-AND-AXLE?

A wheel-and-axle is a simple machine. One example is a windlass, such as the type used to wind up the rope to raise a bucket of water from a well. Turning the large handle or crank (applying the effort) rotates the axle, which winds in the rope to raise the bucket (the load). The longer the crank, the heavier the load the machine will be able to lift. A steering wheel and screwdriver are other uses of the wheel-and-axle principle.

◄ *All cranes make use of levers and many make use of pulleys too.*

LARGE COG
(BOTTOM GEAR)

SMALL COG
(TOP GEAR)

IS A PULLEY A MACHINE?

The answer to this question is yes and no. The simplest pulley, with only one pulley wheel, is not really a machine. This is because even without the force of friction, the effort has to equal the load in order to raise the load. In other words, it does not offer any mechanical advantage. A single pulley merely changes the direction in which the rope is pulled, changing the direction of the effort.

Unlike the single pulley, a pulley with two wheels does offer a mechanical advantage. The mechanical advantage of any machine can be calculated by dividing the load by the effort. With a double-wheel pulley, a given effort can lift a load twice as large, so the mechanical advantage is two. A three-wheel pulley has a mechanical advantage of three, and so on. With five pulleys, a child weighing only 30 pounds can lift a 150-pound adult.

WHAT ARE GEARS USED FOR?

Gears are used to change the speed or direction of a wheel's rotation. Gears have cogs with interlocking teeth. Their teeth do not have to be interlocked, but can be linked by a chain, as on a bicycle. Gears on a bicycle allow a cyclist to put the same amount of effort into pedaling, whether on level ground or a steep hill. On a steep hill a larger cog (low gear) is used. For each turn of the pedal, the bicycle does not go as far, but the effort is reduced.

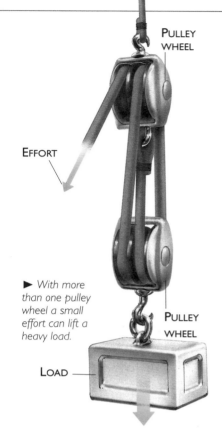

▶ With more than one pulley wheel a small effort can lift a heavy load.

PULLEY WHEEL

EFFORT

PULLEY WHEEL

LOAD

▲ Gears, or cogs, have teeth that interlock.

CRANK

PEDAL

CHAIN WHEEL

CHAIN

◀ Gears of different sizes change the speed of a wheel's rotation. Cyclists use high gears (the smaller cogs) to speed along level ground.

IS IT POSSIBLE TO MAKE A PERPETUAL MOTION MACHINE?

For centuries people have tried to build a machine that will keep going by itself. But a perpetual motion machine is impossible because no machine is 100 percent efficient. As a machine works it loses energy through friction and the heat produced by its moving parts. Every machine, therefore, needs an outside source of energy to keep going.

▼ This perpetual motion machine, like any other design, would not work because of energy losses over time.

Light

W HAT IS LIGHT? Light is a type of
energy. It enables us to see the world
around us. Light is usually given off by hot
objects, such as the Sun or the filament in
an electric light bulb. Light can be thought
of as a series of waves, with very short
wavelengths, although sometimes light
behaves as if it consists of a stream of
tiny particles.

HOW DO LENSES WORK?

Lenses work by bending rays of light – a process
called refraction. Different lenses bend the rays in
different ways. A convex lens is thicker in the middle
than round the edge. Rays from an object that pass
through a convex lens are brought together at a
focus to form an image. The image is enlarged (see
below). A concave lens is thinner in the middle than
round the edge. Rays that pass through a concave
lens diverge (move apart) and the image is reduced.

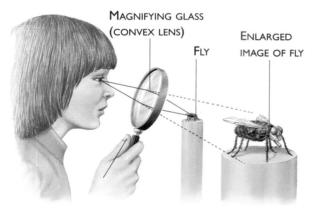

MAGNIFYING GLASS
(CONVEX LENS)

FLY

ENLARGED
IMAGE OF FLY

▲ A magnifying glass has a convex lens.
When light from an object passes through the
lens we see an enlarged view of the object.

▼ Light from a bulb comes from the
white hot filament inside. Electricity
heats the filament to about 4,500°F.

HOW FAST DOES LIGHT TRAVEL?

Light travels very fast indeed. It is the fastest
thing known. The actual speed of light is
186,000 miles per second. This means that light
from the Sun – which is 95 million miles from
Earth – reaches us in just over 8 minutes. A light
beam flashed round the world would make the trip
in less than a fifth of a second.

HOW DO MIRRORS FORM IMAGES?

Mirrors form images by reflection. When rays of
light from an object hit a polished surface, such as a
mirror, they bounce off – they are reflected. When
we look along the bounced-off rays, we see an image
of the object that appears to be behind the mirror.
The image is the right way up, but it is reversed left
to right. For example, if we look in a mirror and close
our right eye, the image seems to close its left eye.

WHAT IS A LASER?

A laser is a device that produces a powerful beam of single-color light. The light waves in a laser beam are
exactly in step with each other. This concentrates the energy of the light. The light energy can then be used
for cutting metals or even diamonds.

HOW DO FIBER OPTICS WORK?

An optical fiber consists of a hair-thin strand of glass. The outside of the strand is silvered, like a mirror. A ray of light zigzags along the inside of the strand as it is reflected off the internal surfaces. In this way, light continues to travel along the fiber even if it is bent. A bundle of fibers, called a fiber-optic cable, can carry light round corners.

Laser light traveling along a fiber-optic cable can be modulated (made to vary) so that it carries digital information. The information can be computer data, video images, and sound, or even telephone conversations. A single fiber-optic cable can carry all the calls from a large telephone exchange.

LIGHT RAY — GLASS FIBER

▶ Light rays pass through optical fibers in a zigzag path.

▼ A reflective telescope used by astronomers. It has a concave mirror, over 13 feet in diameter, which reflects light to a second mirror at the top. Light then travels back down to a third mirror, and on to a computer where the image is analyzed.

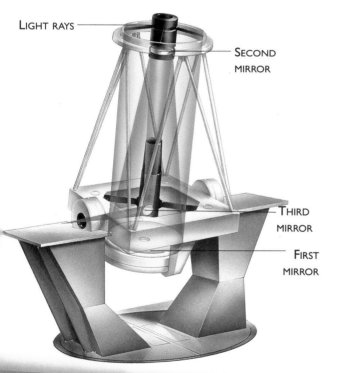

LIGHT RAYS

SECOND MIRROR

THIRD MIRROR

FIRST MIRROR

HOW DOES A TELESCOPE WORK?

There are two main kinds of telescopes – refracting and reflecting. A refracting telescope, such as the small portable telescopes used by sailors, has two convex lenses. The image formed by the front (objective) lens is further magnified by the rear (eyepiece) lens. Binoculars work in a similar way but are like two telescopes side-by-side. Mirrors or prisms 'fold' the light path internally to reduce the length of the binoculars.

A reflecting telescope, such as the large ones used by astronomers, has a curved mirror instead of an objective lens. The image formed by the mirror is directed into an eyepiece lens or camera. Astronomical telescopes use mirrors instead of lenses because large mirrors are easier to make and lighter in weight than large lenses.

HOW DOES A MICROSCOPE WORK?

A compound microscope has two lenses or sets of lenses called (as in a telescope) the objective and the eyepiece. Light, often reflected from a mirror, passes through the specimen being studied, and then through the objective lens. The eyepiece converges the light rays at the viewer's eye, which sees a highly magnified, upside-down image.

◀ The light waves in a laser beam can be directed with great accuracy.

Color

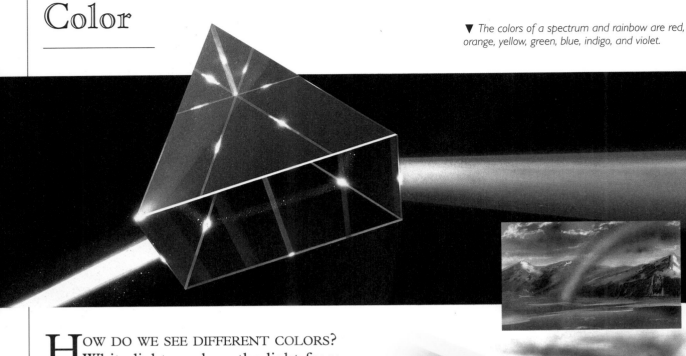

▼ The colors of a spectrum and rainbow are red, orange, yellow, green, blue, indigo, and violet.

HOW DO WE SEE DIFFERENT COLORS? White light, such as the light from the Sun, is made up of a mixture of different wavelengths. The human eye sees these different wavelengths as different colors. When white light falls on, for example, a ripe banana, all the colors (wavelengths) except yellow are absorbed by the banana. The yellow wavelength is reflected and we see it as a yellow color.

SUNLIGHT

REFLECTED COLORS

WHY DO RAINBOWS APPEAR?

A rainbow appears when sunlight shines from behind you on to raindrops in the air. The raindrops act like tiny prisms and split the white sunlight into the colors of the rainbow. The raindrops also reflect the colors down to the ground and towards you.

▼ White is made up of different colors. Black is the absence of color and appears when all colors are absorbed.

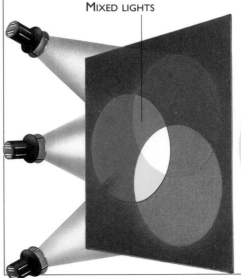

MIXED LIGHTS

MIXED PAINTS

ARE BLACK AND WHITE COLORS?

White light is a mixture of all the spectrum colors. We can prove this by mixing the three main colors of light to produce white light. Black paint shows an absence of color. Like any other objects, paints absorb colors. For example, blue paint absorbs every color except blue. If we mix the three main colors of paint, they together absorb so many colors that the mix looks black.

WHAT IS A SPECTRUM?

A spectrum is the range of colors formed when white light is split up into its component wavelengths. A spectrum appears when a beam of white light is shone through a triangular glass prism. The prism bends (refracts) each wavelength by a slightly different amount to produce the colors of a rainbow.

WHY ARE SOME PEOPLE COLOR BLIND?

We can see because inside both our eyes there is an area sensitive to light called the retina. The retina has two types of light receptors, known as rods and cones because of their shapes. Rods are used for seeing in dim light, when most things appear in shades of gray. Cones work well in bright light and allow us to see in color.

Color blindness occurs when some of the cones do not work properly. This is an inherited defect, found mainly in males. The most common type of color blindness is red-green blindness, when the person confuses the colors red and green. In the rare condition of total color blindness, the person cannot see colors at all and everything appears to be in shades of gray.

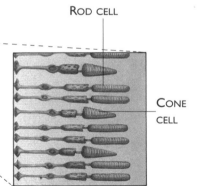

RETINA

ROD CELL

CONE CELL

▲ *In each eye there are light receptor cells for bright light and dim light.*

ARE THERE OTHER COLORS?

Human beings can only see the colors of the rainbow. But some animals can see other colors, too. Bees, for example, can 'see' ultraviolet, a color found in some flowers. Some snakes can 'see' infrared, an invisible radiation that is given off by their warm-blooded prey.

▲ *Bright colors on a peacock's feathers attract female birds.*

WHY DO SOME BIRDS' FEATHERS SHINE SO BRIGHTLY?

When light rays are reflected by objects that are very close together, such as very fine feathers, very bright colors are produced by a process called light interference. The same effect can be seen on some butterflies' wings, in soap bubbles, and in a film of oil floating on the surface of water. The colors are the result of an optical effect – they do not come from the object itself.

Sound

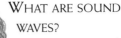

WHAT IS SOUND? Sound is a type of energy. It is produced whenever something vibrates. If the vibrations are fast enough (but not too fast) we hear the sound using sound-detecting organs in our ears. Sound travels from the sound source to our ears through the air. It travels faster through substances that are denser than air, such as wood or glass. But sound cannot travel through a vacuum, where there is no air to carry it.

▲ Sound travels like waves of water, passing energy outwards from the source of the sound.

WHAT ARE SOUND WAVES?

In the air, sound waves are pressure variations – high-pressure regions taking it in turns with low-pressure regions. They spread out from the sound source like ripples on a pond. The pressure differences are caused by vibrations that come from the source of the sound. These vibrations have a rapid to-and-fro motion. The movement in one direction squeezes air molecules closer together, causing higher air pressure. The movement in the opposite direction pushes air molecules farther apart, resulting in lower pressure.

▲ Sound waves are regions of high and low pressure.

▼ Look closely at a plucked string on a musical instrument. You will see the string vibrate. As the vibration fades, so will the sound.

VIBRATING STRING

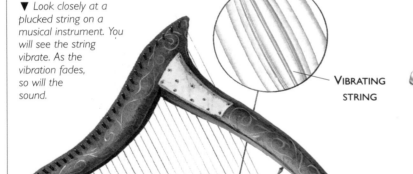

HOW ARE SOUNDS PRODUCED?

There are various ways of producing sound, all involving vibration. When a stretched string, like a guitar string, is plucked, the vibrations of the string produce sound. A string may also be vibrated by using a bow, as with a violin. When a column of air in a tube is made to vibrate, such as blowing into a recorder, it produces sound. And when a stretched drum skin or a metal cymbal are hit, they also vibrate, producing sound.

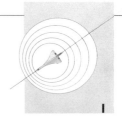

HOW DOES PITCH VARY?

Like all types of waves, sound waves have a wavelength. The pitch of a note (whether it is a high or low note) depends on its wavelength. Long-wavelength sounds are low in pitch; short-wavelength sounds are high. The number of waves per second is the frequency of a note, measured in units called hertz. A young adult human being can hear sounds between about 20 hertz (a very low note) and 20,000 hertz (a very high-pitched note).

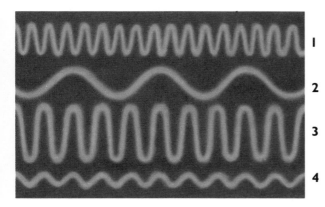

◄ *Different wavelengths: (1) short (high frequency, high pitch), (2) long (low frequency, low pitch), (3) large waves (loud sounds), and (4) small waves (quiet sounds).*

WHAT IS A SONIC BOOM?

You can hear a sonic boom when a supersonic jet, such as Concorde, flies past faster than the speed of sound. In dry air, sound travels at a speed of 1,096 feet per second. At Mach 2 Concorde is flying at twice the speed of sound. At this speed the aircraft passes by before the sound reaches you. When the sound catches up with you as a shock wave, it is heard as a sonic boom. At Mach 1 (the same speed as sound) the aircraft moves forward at the same speed as the sound waves.

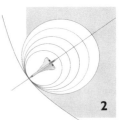

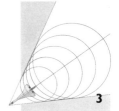

▲ *Sound waves form differently around Concorde as it flies at (1) subsonic speed, (2) Mach 1, and (3) Mach 2.*

WHAT IS ULTRASOUND?

Ultrasound is sound that has a frequency above the upper limit of human hearing – that is, greater than 20,000 hertz. Although we cannot hear such sounds, some animals can. Dolphins and some bats produce ultrasonic 'squeaks'. These animals also use a technique called echolocation – bouncing their ultrasonic squeaks off objects around them. In this way, they can detect obstacles in their path or find prey to eat.

Scientists have imitated this technique by developing sonar to find objects underwater. As with echolocation, this involves the use of ultrasonic pulses underwater to detect any echoes.

WHAT IS RESONANCE?

Any object that can vibrate gives off a sound of a particular frequency. You can make a wine glass 'sing' by running a damp finger round its rim. The frequency is the glass's natural frequency of vibration. If the sound of that frequency is aimed at the glass (from another source), it will begin to vibrate, or resonate. If the sound is intense enough, the glass may shatter, vibrating itself to pieces.

▼ *Dolphins can use ultrasonic sound to find fish in muddy waters. They can detect the size of a shoal, or even single out certain fish.*

FACTS

The first aircraft to fly faster than the speed of sound was the rocket-powered Bell X-1. In 1947, it reached a speed of 713 mph, breaking the 'sound barrier'.

Spiders can detect infrasound (sound below 20 hertz in pitch, the lower limit of human hearing). They may use it to communicate with each other.

The loudness of sound is measured in decibels (dB). Prolonged exposure to sounds of more than 120 dB (such as loud rock music) can permanently damage hearing.

Electricity

► Rubbing a balloon against a sweater charges both with static electricity. Negative charges in the balloon attract positive charges in the sweater, making them stick together.

WHAT IS STATIC ELECTRICITY?

Static electricity can be seen as electric charges that attract and repel each other. Most materials are electrically neutral – they have an equal number of positive and negative charges. But if, for example, you rub a balloon against a sweater, negatively charged electrons in the material will transfer to the balloon. The balloon will then have a negative charge of static electricity, while the sweater is left with a positive charge. The two will attract each other.

WHAT IS AN ELECTRIC CURRENT?

When a battery is connected by a length of metal wire, electrons from the metal atoms flow along the wire. This flow, from the battery's negative to positive terminals, is an electric current. Early scientists did not know about electrons, and thought electric current flowed from positive to negative.

HOW IS ELECTRICITY MADE?

There are two chief ways of making an electric current. One relies on a chemical reaction in a battery (see page 149). The other involves magnetism. In the early 1800s, the English physicist Michael Faraday noticed that when a piece of wire is moved in a magnetic field, an electric current flows along the wire. This is the principle of the dynamo, which generates electric current.

W HAT IS ELECTRICITY? Electricity is a form of energy that can be used to power many machines and devices, from electric railway locomotives to the electronic circuits in radio sets and computers. There are two main types of electricity. Static electricity is electricity that does not move. Current electricity is the kind that flows along wires as an electric current.

WHAT IS AN ELECTRIC CIRCUIT?

A circuit is a complete, uninterrupted path for an electric current to flow round. An example is a battery with wires from its terminals to a device such as a lamp or electric motor.

FLOW OF ELECTRONS   ATOMS   SWITCH

CONDUCTORS

INSULATORS

WHICH MATERIALS CARRY ELECTRICITY?

Materials that will carry an electric current are called conductors. The best conductors are metals such as aluminum, silver, and gold, although all metals can conduct electricity. Materials that will not carry electricity are called non-conductors or insulators. Insulators include glass, ceramics (such as porcelain), rubber, and most plastics. A typical electric cable has two or more copper wire conductors insulated by a covering of plastic. Some materials conduct only slightly. They are called semiconductors.

WHAT IS LIGHTNING?

Lightning is a huge electric spark. It occurs when a cloud builds up a large charge of static electricity. When the cloud comes near another cloud or the ground, a spark jumps between the two. The huge voltages make the gases in the air electrically charged, causing them to conduct electricity.

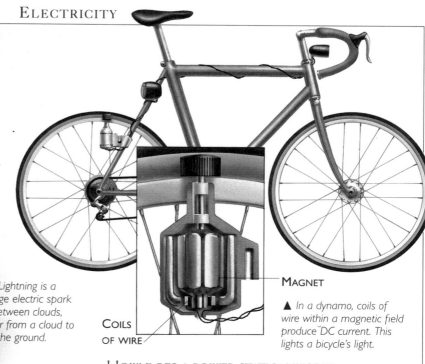

◄ Lightning is a huge electric spark between clouds, or from a cloud to the ground.

MAGNET

▲ In a dynamo, coils of wire within a magnetic field produce DC current. This lights a bicycle's light.

COILS OF WIRE

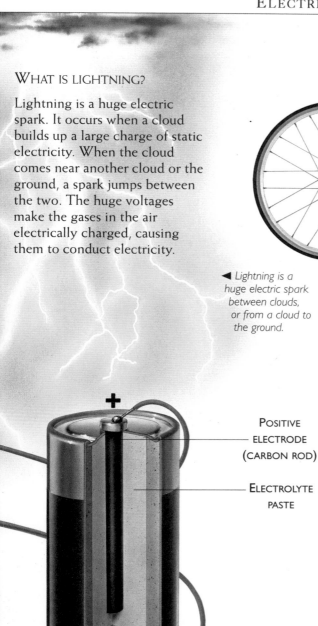

POSITIVE ELECTRODE (CARBON ROD)

ELECTROLYTE PASTE

NEGATIVE ELECTRODE (ZINC CASING)

HOW DOES A BATTERY WORK?

A battery produces direct current (DC) electricity by a chemical reaction. It has a negative electrode and a positive electrode. These are separated by a conducting solution, called an electrolyte. Chemical reactions in the battery produce electricity, which flows out of the negative electrode and on through the electric circuit, perhaps driving an electric motor or lighting a bulb on its way. It arrives back through the positive electrode.

HOW DOES A POWER STATION WORK?

A power station generates electricity for use in homes and industry. All power stations have generators called alternators, which spin round to produce alternating current (AC) electricity. But power stations differ in the way the alternators are driven. In a hydroelectric power station, flowing water makes turbines spin the alternators. Most other power stations use steam turbines to do this. The steam is produced in a boiler, which is heated by burning a fossil fuel (such as coal, oil, or natural gas) or by using the heat from a nuclear reactor.

CAN ANIMALS PRODUCE ELECTRICITY?

Some animals can produce electricity. Best known are electric fish and electric eels. Biochemical reactions in their muscles produce electricity, which creates an electric field around the animal – rather like the magnetic field around a magnet. The electric field changes when another fish enters it. The electric fish notices this change, and so can use the field to detect the presence of nearby fish. It can also use its electricity to stun a fish it wants to eat.

► An electric eel can detect other fish that enter its electric field.

Magnets

WHAT IS A MAGNET? A magnet is a piece of metal that attracts some other metals. Magnets are used in the workings of many things, such as telephones, door bells, and electric motors. Most magnets are made of an alloy (a mixture of metals) that contains iron, nickel, and steel. The metals they attract are also iron alloys. The Earth itself is like a giant magnet because there is a lot of iron at its center.

▼ Large electromagnets are used in scrap yards to lift pieces of steel.

WHAT IS A MAGNETIC FIELD?

A magnetic field is the area around a magnet in which its magnetism can be detected. With a magnet shaped like a bar, the field starts near to one end of the bar. This point is called a magnetic pole. The field curves round the outside of the bar to another magnetic pole at the other end. One magnetic pole is called north, and the other pole is called south.

▼ Unmagnetized iron (left), magnetized iron (right).

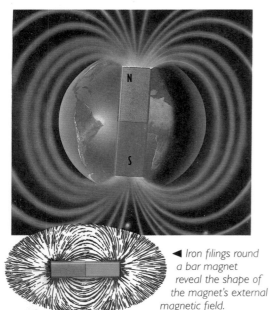

◀ Iron filings round a bar magnet reveal the shape of the magnet's external magnetic field.

HOW DOES A COMPASS WORK?

A compass has a magnetized needle, or pointer, pivoted at its center. The needle's north pole is attracted to the Earth's magnetic pole, which lies close to the geographic North Pole. This is why a magnet always points north.

HOW DO YOU MAKE A MAGNET?

In an unmagnetized piece of iron, electrons spinning round the nuclei of the iron atoms create tiny atomic magnets. Groups of atomic magnets line up with each other in regions called domains. But the domains point in many different directions, and there is no overall magnetism. If the piece of iron is placed in a magnetic field, all the domains line up with each other and stay that way when the magnetic field is removed. The result is a permanent magnet. An external magnetic field can be made by stroking the iron with another magnet.

WHAT IS ELECTROMAGNETISM?

Electromagnetism is the magnetic field made when electricity is passed through a wire. If the wire is twisted round into a coil the magnetism intensifies, and produces a magnetic field similar to that of a bar magnet. It is then called an electromagnet. If an iron bar is put inside the coil the magnetism increases even more because the iron becomes magnetic, too.

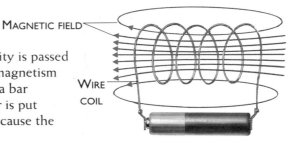

MAGNETIC FIELD

WIRE
COIL

▲ As an electric current passes through a coil of wire, a magnetic field is made.

▶ Coils of wire round an iron bar make up the electromagnet in an electric door bell.

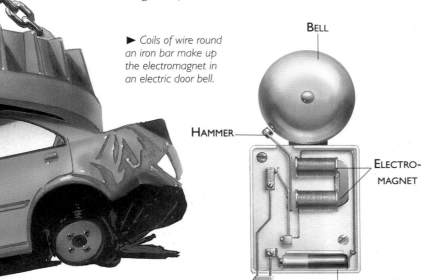

BELL

HAMMER

ELECTRO-MAGNET

BATTERY

WHAT ARE ELECTROMAGNETS USED FOR?

A small electromagnet is used in an electric bell. When an electric current flows the electromagnet's force pulls the hammer towards it so that it strikes the bell. When the current is switched off the iron in the electromagnet loses its magnetism, and the hammer falls back. Because the electric current to the magnet is rapidly turned on and off, the hammer is repeatedly pulled and allowed to fall back very quickly, which makes the 'trilling' sound for the bell.

HOW DOES A MAGLEV TRAIN WORK?

Maglev is short for 'magnetic levitation', which describes lifting something using magnets. When two magnets come together, one of two things happens. If two different magnetic poles (one north, one south) are brought together, they attract each other. But two similar poles (both north, or both south) repel each other and force each other apart. A maglev train has an arrangement of electromagnets with similar poles, one on the train and one on the track, so that they repel each other. The repulsion between the poles lifts the train slightly off the track so that it 'floats' above it. An electric motor moves the train along.

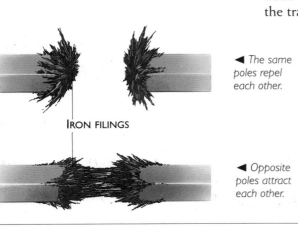

◀ The same poles repel each other.

IRON FILINGS

◀ Opposite poles attract each other.

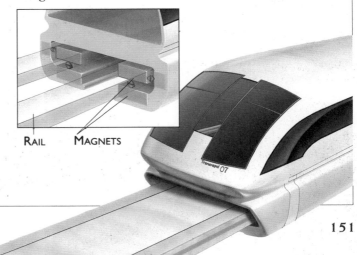

RAIL   MAGNETS

Telecommunications

WHAT IS TELECOMMU-NICATIONS? It is the science and technology of communicating, or sending messages, over a distance. It ranges from simple flag signals to international satellite communications. Some forms, such as the telegraph, the telephone, and fax machines, involve sending electrical signals along wires from sender to receiver. Other forms use radio signals to carry information.

MORSE CODE
One of the earliest telegraphs was invented in 1844 by the American Samuel Morse (below). It used Morse code, in which combinations of dots and dashes stand for letters and numbers. Coded messages were sent along telegraph wires as a series of short and long electric pulses.

ALEXANDER GRAHAM BELL
The telephone was invented in 1876 by the Scottish-born American scientist Alexander Graham Bell (above). He had the idea of using a vibrating diaphragm to produce sound after studying how the human voice is produced.

◀ Printed messages were received from Morse's telegraph as dots and dashes on a strip of paper.

▼ Intercontinental telephone calls use a satellite to receive radio signals and beam them back to a ground receiver.

HOW DO TELEPHONE CALLS CROSS THE OCEAN?
Calls between continents use communications satellites. These satellites exist in space as part of our long-distance telecommunications networks. Most are in stationary orbit. This means that they appear to stay in the same spot above Earth. In fact they orbit the Earth every 24 hours, following the Earth as it spins on its axis. Radio signals are beamed up to a satellite, amplified by its circuits, and then beamed back down to a ground receiver.

HOW DO TELEPHONE CALLS TRAVEL?

When you make a telephone call, electrical signals from your telephone travel along wires to the nearest telephone exchange. From there they travel along underground cables to the exchange nearest the person you are calling. Alternatively, the signals may be transmitted as microwave radio signals between aerials connected to each exchange. The latest systems use optical fibers to carry calls. Intercontinental calls may make use of satellite links.

◀ Many long-distance telephone calls travel as microwave radio signals between aerials on tall towers.

RECEIVER'S TELEPHONE EXCHANGE

RADIO RECEIVER

RADIO TRANSMITTER

CALLER'S TELEPHONE EXCHANGE

WHY DON'T MOBILE PHONES NEED WIRES?

Mobile phones use radio links instead of wires. The whole country is divided into small areas called cells, each with a radio transmitter and receiver. The mobile phone also has a transmitter. This sends the caller's words to the radio receiver in his or her cell. The call is then fed into the telephone network. It can also be transmitted, from any cell, to another mobile phone.

HOW DOES A TELEPHONE WORK?

The handset of a telephone has a microphone in the mouthpiece and a small loudspeaker in the earpiece. When you talk, the microphone in your telephone changes the sounds of your speech into electrical signals, which pass along the telephone line to the person you are calling. The signals then work the loudspeaker in the earpiece of the listener's telephone.

DIAPHRAGM

▼ The scanner in a fax machine converts messages and pictures into electrical pulses that travel along telephone lines.

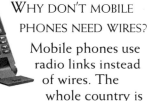

PICTURE TO BE SCANNED

HOW DOES A FAX MACHINE SEND PICTURES?

A fax (facsimile) machine contains a scanner, which scans across the out-going message or picture, picking it up as a series of closely spaced lines. The variations in light and dark picked up by the scanner are converted to electrical pulses, which are sent along a telephone line to the receiving fax machine. There, a printer reproduces each of the lines on paper to recreate the original message or picture.

MICROPHONE

▲ A telephone has a microphone to convert speech to electrical signals and back to speech.

Recording

W HAT IS RECORDING?
Recording is any
method of saving an image,
sound, or text so that it can be
seen, heard, or read later on.
Cameras record images on
photographs. Sounds may be
recorded on tapes, discs, or
CDs. Printing can record
words and pictures.

► *In a single-lens reflex
camera, a mirror reflects
light passing through the lens
into the viewfinder. In this
way, the photographer can
see exactly what the
camera 'sees'.*

VIEWFINDER
FILM

MIRROR MOVES
UP WHEN
SHUTTER OPENS

SHUTTER OPENS
TO LET IN LIGHT

APERTURE

LENS SYSTEM

HOW FAST IS A CAMERA SHUTTER?

A camera is a light-proof box with a lens on one side. The lens
focuses an image onto a film inside the camera. When a photograph
is taken, a shutter opens for only a few seconds, or even a few
thousandths of a second, to let light reach the film. The size of the
aperture – the hole through which the light enters – also controls the
amount of light. The film reacts to the light and when the film is
developed it reveals a negative image of the photograph. This can
then be turned into a positive print.

WHEN WAS PRINTING INVENTED?

Modern printing was invented in Germany in the
1400s, using the letterpress method. There are
three basic methods of printing. In letterpress,
the image to be printed is raised above the
surface of the printing plate, and the raised
areas are covered with ink. The image is transferred when paper is pressed onto the plate.

In gravure printing, the image is etched into the
printing plate. The plate is covered in ink and a
blade drawn across it. This removes the ink from
everywhere but the etched areas. Paper pressed
onto the plate picks up ink from these areas.

In lithographic printing, the image is applied to
the plate as a photograph. When the plate is inked,
the ink sticks to the image areas and not to the
blank areas between them. Paper pressed onto the
plate picks up the image.

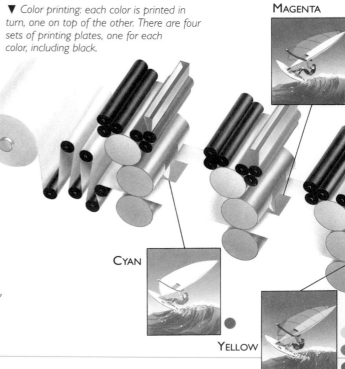

▼ *Color printing: each color is printed in
turn, one on top of the other. There are four
sets of printing plates, one for each
color, including black.*

MAGENTA

CYAN

YELLOW

TAPE
CASSETTE

ERASING HEAD   RECORDING/PLAY-BACK HEAD

◀ *A tape machine has two 'heads', one for erasing and one for recording and playing.*

HOW IS MUSIC STORED ON A TAPE?

A tape recorder stores sound magnetically. Magnetic tape winds from reel to reel past two electromagnetic 'heads' – the erase head and the record/playback head. When recording, the erase head erases any existing recording. Electrical signals from the microphone produce variations in the magnetic field of the record/playback head. These variations are 'stored' as a magnetic pattern on the tape. On playback, the same head 'reads' the pattern and converts it into electrical signals, which are changed back into sound.

▶ *Minute variations in a record groove vibrate the stylus.*

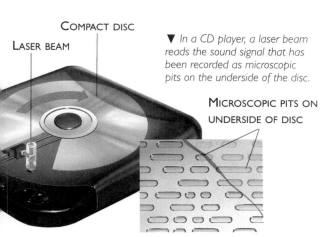

COMPACT DISC

LASER BEAM

▼ *In a CD player, a laser beam reads the sound signal that has been recorded as microscopic pits on the underside of the disc.*

MICROSCOPIC PITS ON UNDERSIDE OF DISC

HOW DO CDS WORK?

In CD recording, the electrical signals from a microphone are converted into a series of numbers or digits. These are recorded as a pattern of microscopic pits on the underside of the disc. When the disc is played, the pits produce variations in a laser beam that is reflected off the disc. Circuits change these variations back into sound signals.

HOW DO YOU MAKE A RECORD?

To make a vinyl recording, electrical signals from a microphone vibrate a cutter, which makes the grooves in a master disc. A metal copy of the master is then used to press copies in vinyl plastic.

A vinyl record has a long spiral groove on each surface. Minute variations in the width and depth of the groove match the differences in the pitch and loudness of the recorded sound. The pick-up head on a record player has a pointed crystal needle, called a stylus, that runs in the groove. The stylus vibrates up and down and from side to side as it follows the variations in the groove. The vibrations are turned into varying electrical signals, amplified, and fed to loudspeakers.

STYLUS

GROOVE

BLACK

▲ *The three colors and black combine to give all the colors of the original image.*

HOW DOES A CAMCORDER WORK?

A camcorder is a small video camera with a built-in tape recorder. The video and audio signals from the camera are recorded on tape cassettes, which can be played back through a video recorder (or through the camera) to produce pictures on a television set.

Radio and Television

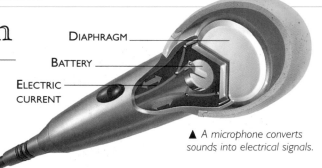

DIAPHRAGM

BATTERY

ELECTRIC CURRENT

▲ *A microphone converts sounds into electrical signals.*

WHAT IS THE DIFFERENCE BETWEEN RADIO AND TELEVISION? They both make use of radio waves – one to carry sounds and the other to carry sounds and pictures. A microphone converts sounds (audio) into varying electrical signals, and a TV camera converts images (video) into similar varying signals. A radio or TV transmitter broadcasts a continuous radio wave which is varied (modulated) by the audio or video signals. At the receiver, the broadcast is picked up by an aerial and turned back into sounds and pictures.

WHAT ARE RADIO WAVES?

Radio waves are a kind of electromagnetic radiation, as are light and X-rays. Like all waves, they have a wavelength (the distance between one wave and another) and a frequency (the number of waves per second, measured in hertz). Long and medium waves bounce round the Earth off the ionosphere. Short-wavelength microwaves travel in straight lines between points that are in line of sight of each other. But microwaves can be 'bounced' off orbiting communications satellites to increase their range.

WHAT DOES A MICROPHONE DO?

A microphone converts sounds into varying electrical signals so that they can pass along a wire or be transmitted by radio. All microphones have a diaphragm or something similar, which vibrates when struck by sound waves. The vibrations of the diaphragm are converted into electrical signals in various ways. In a crystal microphone the vibrations 'squeeze' a crystal to make it generate electrical signals. In another type, vibrations move a coil of wire in a magnetic field, setting up a current in the coil.

HOW ARE ELECTRICAL SIGNALS CONVERTED INTO SOUNDS?

The conversion is done by a loudspeaker, which uses the same principle as the moving-coil microphone described above. Varying electrical signals (usually from an amplifier) pass into a coil of wire. The coil surrounds a piece of iron attached to the center of a cone-shaped diaphragm. The varying signals in the coil make the iron vibrate, which in turn vibrates the diaphragm and so produces sounds.

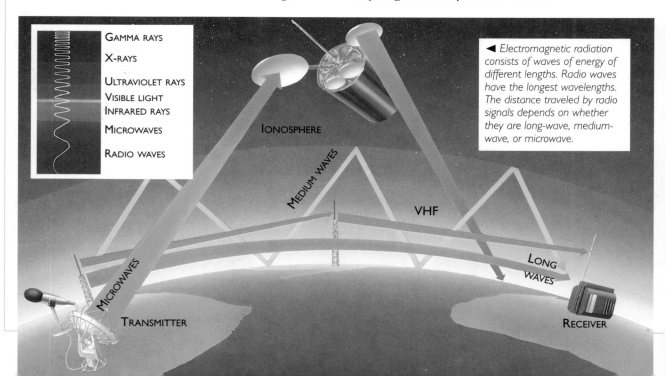

GAMMA RAYS

X-RAYS

ULTRAVIOLET RAYS

VISIBLE LIGHT

INFRARED RAYS

MICROWAVES

RADIO WAVES

IONOSPHERE

MEDIUM WAVES

VHF

LONG WAVES

MICROWAVES

TRANSMITTER

RECEIVER

◄ *Electromagnetic radiation consists of waves of energy of different lengths. Radio waves have the longest wavelengths. The distance traveled by radio signals depends on whether they are long-wave, medium-wave, or microwave.*

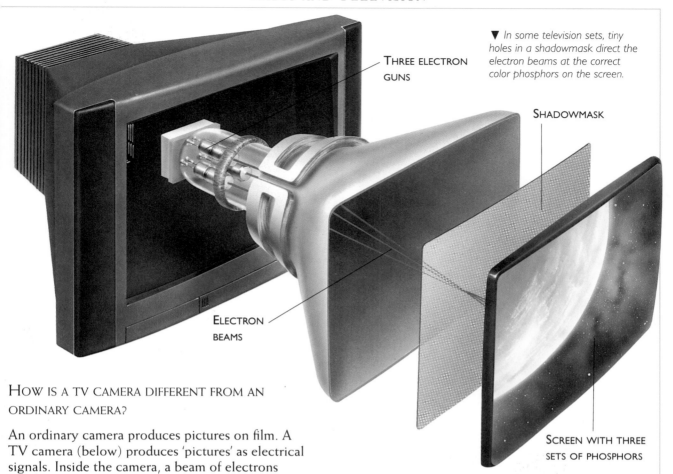

THREE ELECTRON GUNS

▼ *In some television sets, tiny holes in a shadowmask direct the electron beams at the correct color phosphors on the screen.*

SHADOWMASK

ELECTRON BEAMS

SCREEN WITH THREE SETS OF PHOSPHORS

HOW IS A TV CAMERA DIFFERENT FROM AN ORDINARY CAMERA?

An ordinary camera produces pictures on film. A TV camera (below) produces 'pictures' as electrical signals. Inside the camera, a beam of electrons scans an image focused by the camera's lens. A picture tube or a chip called a CCD (charge-coupled device) then produces an electric current called the video signal. This signal varies according to the amount of light in the image.

A color TV camera may have one or three tubes, or a CCD chip. Colored filters split the incoming light into red, green, and blue – the three primary colors of light. So the camera produces three signals, which are combined into a single video signal.

▶ *A color TV camera being used by an operator.*

WHY IS A TV SET SO BIG?

The size of a television set depends on the cathode-ray tube, which is the main part of a TV set. The front of the tube is the TV screen, so the smaller the tube, the smaller the picture. The inside of the screen is covered with a substance (phosphor) that gives off light when struck by electrons. The back of the tube has an electron gun that fires a beam of electrons at the screen. The beam scans across the screen in a series of lines, producing lighter or darker areas of the picture, according to the incoming video signal. A color TV tube has three electron guns and three sets of screen phosphors for red, green, and blue light.

WHAT WILL TELEVISIONS BE LIKE IN THE FUTURE?

Future developments include high-definition tele-vision (HDTV), which has a much clearer picture, and flat-screen TV sets that can be hung on a wall like a painting. Engineers are also using lasers to experiment with three-dimensional TV.

Computers

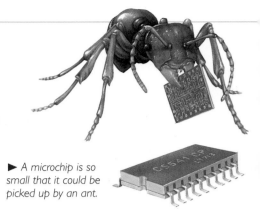

What is a computer? A modern computer is an electronic machine that deals with numbers very quickly. Unlike an adding machine (which also deals with numbers), a computer can be programmed with instructions to do various tasks. It can be programmed so that the numbers are simply used as numbers, or so that they stand for letters, words, or pictures. A computer can store information in its memory, to be used when needed.

► *A microchip is so small that it could be picked up by an ant.*

How small is a microchip?

A microchip is a thin slice of silicon about the size of a match-head. Built into the slice is a tiny electronic circuit, with transistors, diodes, capacitors, and resistors. The whole circuit – called an integrated circuit – is mounted inside a plastic block that can be plugged into other larger circuits (see above). Computers are controlled by a master chip called a microprocessor.

What is the difference between hardware and software?

The most common computers are personal computers (PCs), found in homes, schools, and offices throughout the world. There are more PCs in the world than there are motor cars. The main parts of a PC are the central processor, with its disk drives and electronic circuits, a keyboard for keying in data, and an output device such as a visual display unit (VDU) or printer. Other input devices include a mouse, which moves an indicator around the VDU screen, and a graphics tablet, which is used for drawings. All of this equipment is computer hardware.

But a computer also needs software, which is the program that sets up the machine for a particular task and enables it to carry it out. The data fed into and out of a computer is also part of the software.

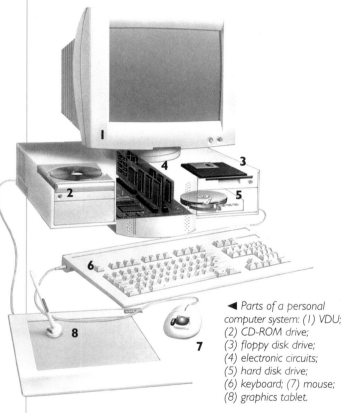

◄ *Parts of a personal computer system: (1) VDU; (2) CD-ROM drive; (3) floppy disk drive; (4) electronic circuits; (5) hard disk drive; (6) keyboard; (7) mouse; (8) graphics tablet.*

How do you 'talk' to a computer?

Computers deal in numbers, or digits. In order to program a computer, the programmer writes the instructions in a language that the computer can understand – a language made up of numbers. Examples of computer languages include BASIC (Beginners' All-purpose Symbolic Instruction Code), used by beginner programmers; COBOL (COmmon Business Oriented Language), used for business purposes; and FORTRAN (FORmula TRANslation), used by scientists and technicians.

► *Virtual reality allows a person to see, hear, and even 'feel' things that exist only in the memory of a computer.*

WHAT IS A CD-ROM?

CD-ROM stands for Compact Disc Read-Only Memory. It is a computer storage system that uses compact discs, which are 'read' by a laser beam (as with an audio CD). The stored data may include text (up to 80 million words), sounds, and still or moving images. The capacity of a CD-ROM is so large that an entire illustrated encyclopedia may be held on one disc and read using a PC with a CD-ROM drive.

HOW REAL IS VIRTUAL REALITY?

Virtual reality is a computer system that produces a lifelike reconstruction of a place or an event. The viewer wears a helmet that provides a small computer image to each eye, and sound through built-in earphones. Sensors in the helmet detect when the viewer moves his or her head, and the images change as they would in reality. For instance, the viewer can 'walk' through a building, peering round corners or going upstairs, even if the building exists only in the computer's memory. By wearing a virtual reality glove (connected to the computer), the viewer can also reach for an object and 'feel' around.

WHAT ARE COMPUTER SIMULATORS USED FOR?

Computer simulators are computers that provide a realistic environment within which a person can learn to control a machine. For example, a pilot can learn to fly a high-speed aircraft on a simulator, and even practise take-off and landing. The trainee pilot sits in a realistic cockpit. In the cockpit the pilot's movement of the aircraft's controls makes the computer tilt the cockpit and alter the surrounding images as if the pilot was in a real airplane.

WHAT IS THE INTERNET?

The Internet is an international network that links computer users throughout the world, giving them access to a vast amount of information. It is also used for sending electronic mail, making communication with people around the world easy and inexpensive.

HOW SMART IS A SMART CARD?

A smart card is a plastic card that has a microprocessor chip embedded in it. There is also a magnetic strip that identifies the user, as on an ordinary credit card. The card's microchip stores information that can be updated. For example, a person can pay in advance for telephone calls and the credit will be recorded on the microchip. Then every time the card is used, the cost of the call is subtracted from the sum in the memory.

▶ A smart card has a microprocessor to store and update information when it is used.

Medical Technology

W HAT IS MEDICAL TECHNOLOGY? It is the use of modern techniques in the prevention, diagnosis, and treatment of disorders. It includes the use of ultrasound to scan an unborn baby and laser beams to cut away unwanted tissue. Computerized X-ray scanners can take colored photographs of the inside of a patient's brain, and bionic arms and legs can be fitted to people who have lost a limb.

HOW DO MICROSCOPES HELP SURGEONS?

Microscopes have long been used in medical research to study body cells and tissues. But today, microscopes are also found in the operating theater. Surgeons use them to perform microsurgery, in which damage to very small areas is repaired with very fine instruments. The instruments are so small that they can be manipulated only by using a microscope.

▲ An electron microscope is so powerful that it can reveal AIDS viruses (the pink circles).

HOW IS SOUND USED TO SEE INSIDE THE BODY?

Sound at a frequency greater than the upper limit of human hearing is called ultrasound. When aimed painlessly into the body, it reflects off the body tissues to varying extents. The reflections can be detected and used to form an image of the tissues on a screen. Ultrasound is commonly used to check the progress of an unborn baby developing in its mother's womb.

▲ To save time, several surgeons may work together during an operation, particularly for microsurgery.

CAN A SEVERED LIMB BE STITCHED BACK ON?

Delicate surgical operations, such as the rejoining of nerves and narrow blood vessels when a severed limb is stitched back on, can now be performed using microsurgery. The surgeon uses a powerful microscope, and may have the help of a robot hand that is controlled by a computer, to make stitches with needles as fine as a human hair. The thread that makes the stitches is much finer still. Even with two or three surgeons working together, it takes many hours to perform such complicated operations.

◄ An unborn baby inside its mother's womb can be seen using an ultrasonic scanner.

HOW ARE LASERS USED IN SURGERY?

Surgeons can use the intense light of laser beams, carried along narrow fiber optic cables, to perform many intricate surgical procedures. Unwanted tissue such as a cancerous growth can be removed by a laser, causing less disturbance to surrounding tissues than the traditional scalpel method. Lasers are also used to remove birthmarks and tattoos, and to seal blood vessels to prevent bleeding.

HOW DO BIONIC LIMBS WORK?

A bionic limb – usually an arm – has battery-powered electric motors and electronic circuits that move the wrist and fingers. Some have sensors at the end where the artificial limb joins onto the stump of the missing arm. When the person tenses muscles in the stump, the action creates tiny pulses of electricity. These pulses are picked up by the detectors, amplified, and made to control the movements of the fingers. The mechanism in the hand is covered by a skin-colored glove, giving it a natural appearance.

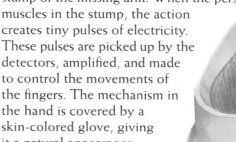

◀ *A laser beam can be aimed into a patient's ear to remove a small piece of bone that is causing deafness.*

▶ *This cutaway view of a modern artificial arm shows the electronic circuits that control its movements.*

FACTS

A type of cutter used for delicate eye operations has a blade that is a sixteenth of an inch across.

A modern bionic arm can be controlled by flexing muscles in the stump of the missing limb.

Some microsurgery operations take up to 20 hours to perform and require several surgeons, working in relays.

An ultrasound scan can sometimes tell whether an unborn baby is a boy or a girl, although most parents do not wish to be told what sex it is.

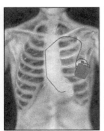

WHY DO SOME PEOPLE NEED A PACEMAKER?

The natural pacemaker is a bundle of nerve tissue in the heart that keeps our heartbeat regular. Sometimes the pacemaker fails and a person's heartbeat becomes dangerously irregular. Such a person can be fitted with an artificial pacemaker. It is a battery-powered device that produces regular pulses of electricity that pass along a wire into the heart.

CAN DOCTORS SEE RIGHT INSIDE A PATIENT'S BODY?

Doctors use an endoscope, a narrow tube that can be passed into the body, to examine the inside of a patient. Modern micro-endoscopes have a fiber optic cable to carry light as well as working channels for various instruments.

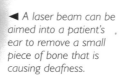

▶ *The light-carrying fiber optic cable of a micro-endoscope is only an eighth of an inch across.*

Buildings

WHICH ARE THE WORLD'S TALLEST BUILDINGS? The tallest buildings with rooms in them are the twin Petronas Towers in Kuala Lumpur, Malaysia. They each have 88 floors and are nearly 1,483 feet high. But the tallest unsupported building in the world is the CN Tower in Toronto, Canada. It is a telecommunications tower and is 1,814 feet tall.

▶ The Pompidou Center has all its pipes, lifts, and plumbing on the outside.

WHAT IS SPECIAL ABOUT THE POMPIDOU CENTER?

The Pompidou Center in Paris is built 'inside-out'. It is used for exhibitions. To create plenty of space inside the building, it was designed with all the pipe work, ventilation ducts, and even the lifts, on the outside.

WHERE IS THE HIDDEN CITY OF THE INCAS?

The Incas were native South Americans who ruled a large empire during the 1400s. Their capital city, Cuzco, was built high up in the Andes mountains. The Incas were conquered by Spain in the 1530s and their cities fell into ruins. An American explorer discovered the ruins of one Inca city, Machu Picchu, in 1911. It was built of blocks of white granite. The Incas had no machines and had to haul the huge blocks of stone up the mountain using only human muscle power. They also built terraces for growing crops on the steep mountain slopes.

▼ The ruins of Machu Picchu were discovered in 1911. The Incas (inset) had no machines to help them haul huge blocks of stone up the mountains.

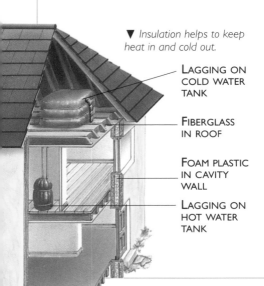

▼ Insulation helps to keep heat in and cold out.

LAGGING ON COLD WATER TANK

FIBERGLASS IN ROOF

FOAM PLASTIC IN CAVITY WALL

LAGGING ON HOT WATER TANK

HOW HAS HOUSE-BUILDING CHANGED?

The earliest houses were built of whatever materials were available locally: mud, stone, wood, or even palm leaves. If there were windows, they were merely holes in the walls. During the Middle Ages came bricks and tiles made of baked clay, and glass windows. The same materials were used until this century, when concrete blocks, steel beams, and fiberglass or foam plastic insulation were introduced. A modern house in a cool climate has many of these special features to stop the loss of heat from the building, which is a waste of energy.

CAN BUILDINGS BE MADE SAFE AGAINST EARTHQUAKES?

To reduce the damage caused by an earthquake, small buildings can be bolted to their foundations. Larger buildings in earthquake zones have rubber shock absorbers between the buildings and their foundations. The steel frameworks of tall buildings are made flexible enough to bend slightly. Heavy equipment inside a building may also be bolted down to stop it from moving.

WHAT IS SPECIAL ABOUT THE SHAPE OF THE GUGGENHEIM MUSEUM?

The Guggenheim Museum (above), in New York City, is in the shape of a long spiral ramp that winds up to a huge glass dome. The dome lets in lots of light, and the walls alongside the ramp provide lots of space for displaying paintings. The ramp is nearly 1,640 feet long, making it one of the world's longest covered walkways.

WHY ARE SKYSCRAPERS BUILT?

Until about a hundred years ago a building had to be held up by its thick outside walls and could not be much taller than 12 stories, about 246 feet high. But with the development of iron and steel frames, architects could design much taller buildings. The first skyscrapers in the world were built in Chicago in the 1880s. Soon the idea became popular in New York City, where building land was expensive and scarce. Buildings that could extend upward instead of outward were seen as the answer to the problem.

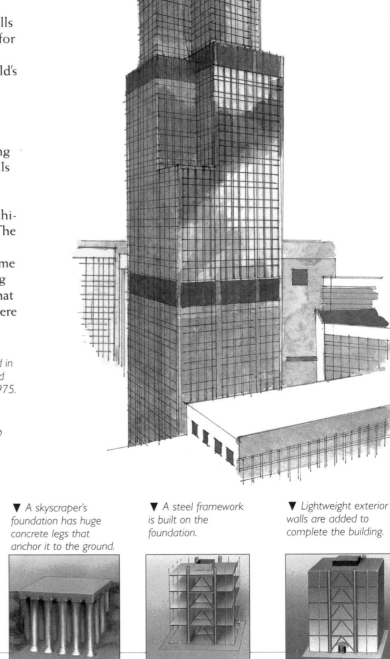

▶ The Sears Tower, Chicago, was completed in 1974. It was the highest building in the world until the CN Tower in Toronto was built in 1975.

HOW ARE SKYSCRAPERS CONSTRUCTED?

Most skyscrapers are constructed on a reinforced concrete foundation. The foundation is built on concrete legs, called piles, which are driven deep into the ground. On top of the foundation, the builders erect a strong framework, or skeleton, of steel girders. These hold up the building and its individual floors. The outer walls are lightweight and do not add to the strength of the building.

▼ A skyscraper's foundation has huge concrete legs that anchor it to the ground.

▼ A steel framework is built on the foundation.

▼ Lightweight exterior walls are added to complete the building.

Networks

WHAT ARE NETWORKS? Networks are connected transport systems involving roads, railways, canals, bridges, and tunnels. They make use of great achievements in civil engineering. Where a road or railroad has to cross a wide river, a huge bridge or a long tunnel has to be built. Where two highways cross each other, engineers build a complex junction to connect them.

HOW WERE EARLY BRIDGES BUILT?

One of the earliest and simplest bridges, over a narrow river or stream, is called a clapper bridge. These were constructed with long, flat slabs of stone on piers made of stones built on top of each other. A pontoon bridge was used to cross wider waterways. Originally it consisted of a series of many small boats moored side by side and tied together. The roadway was made from wooden planks laid across the boats.

ARE THERE DIFFERENT TYPES OF BRIDGES?

The main types of bridges are the arch bridge, the cantilever bridge, and the suspension bridge. Arch bridges made of stone or brick were among the earliest types of bridge. Modern arch bridges are built of steel or concrete. Each half of a cantilever bridge is supported at one end, built out from a pier or the bank.

▲ *Modern highways, and the bridges and flyovers connecting them, are built of reinforced concrete. Flyovers allow vehicles to change highways quickly and safely.*

WHAT IS A 'SPAGHETTI JUNCTION'?

Road engineers design complicated junctions to join highways. Slip roads curve round to make the connections. The major crossing may include a bridge that carries one highway over the other. Curved slip roads are also built at various levels so that they can cross over each other where necessary. Such a criss-crossing of road loops is sometimes nicknamed 'spaghetti junction'.

IS THE CHANNEL TUNNEL A SINGLE TUNNEL?

The Channel Tunnel runs beneath the English Channel between Calais in France and Folkestone in England. It consists of two rail tunnels side by side and a small service tunnel between them. Trains pulled by electric locomotives carry people, cars, and trucks. The tunnel has reduced the journey time from London to Paris to 3 hours, which is quicker (city center to city center) than by plane.

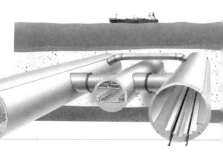

HOW DOES A SUSPENSION BRIDGE WORK?

The longest bridges of all are suspension bridges. They get their name because the roadway or deck is suspended from a pair of thick steel cables or chains slung between two tall towers. These suspension cables hang in a curve like an upside-down arch. The main cables are anchored to the banks to balance the downward pull of the suspension cables. The deck is usually made of steel and the towers from stonework or concrete.

WHO BUILT THE FIRST AQUEDUCTS?

An aqueduct is a bridge designed to carry water. It may be part of a water supply system, or it may be part of a canal and act as a bridge for carrying barges and boats. The earliest aqueducts were built of stone by the Romans in Italy and France. The most famous Roman aqueduct was built in 19BC near Nîmes in southern France.

▼ The Pont-du-Gard aqueduct, below, was built in 19BC near Nîmes, France. It consists of three layers of arched bridges.

▲ The Golden Gate Bridge spans the entrance to San Francisco Harbor. This suspension bridge is 4,198 feet long between the towers.

WHY ARE CANALS BUILT?

Before the first railways, canal networks were built to carry goods around a country. Major canals were also built as short cuts on long sea routes. The Suez Canal (between the Mediterranean Sea and the Red Sea) and the Panama Canal (between the Atlantic and Pacific oceans) are examples.

Industry

WHAT IS INDUSTRY? Industry is all the work involved in getting raw materials out of the earth, processing them, and then sometimes using them to manufacture goods. Some industries, such as the electronics industry, take small manufactured articles and assemble them to make other products. This is called light industry. Communications, farming (agriculture), and fishing are sometimes also thought of as industries.

► An offshore oil rig may have several pipes going down to holes drilled in the sea bed.

WHERE DO RAW MATERIALS COME FROM?

Many raw materials, such as ores and minerals, are extracted (removed from the earth) by mining. Coal is also mined. Oil and natural gas are extracted using drilling wells, either on land or from offshore drilling platforms. Some raw materials are extracted from air and sea water. Air contains useful gases such as oxygen and nitrogen, and sea water contains salt and other chemicals.

HOW ARE RAW MATERIALS PROCESSED?

Raw materials are processed in different ways. Metal ores are smelted (strongly heated) to produce metals such as iron and copper. Aluminum is extracted by a process using an electric current to remove aluminum from the melted ore. Crude oil (petroleum) is processed by refining. The oil is heated until it splits into its various parts, such as gasoline and kerosene.

HOT GASES

RAW MATERIALS

HOT AIR

◄ A blast furnace heats coke, iron ore, and limestone to produce molten iron.

SLAG

MOLTEN IRON

WHAT IS HEAVY INDUSTRY?

Heavy industry involves the use of large machines, usually to make large objects such as railway locomotives or space rockets. Shipbuilding is an example of a heavy industry. It mainly uses steel and other metals as raw materials. The metal pieces have to be cut and shaped, and then joined together by riveting or welding. Building a supertanker, for example, may use more than 300,000 tons of steel. Large vessels like these are usually built in sections, and then joined together.

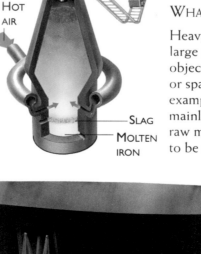

◄ A supertanker carrying crude oil to refineries.

HOW DO ASSEMBLY LINES WORK?

Traditionally, objects are made by a single worker who assembles (puts together) its various parts. On an assembly line, a line of workers stand alongside a conveyor belt, building the article as a team. A partly assembled article passes a worker, and he or she fixes one or two parts to it. By the end of the line, the article has been built.

▲ A car moves along a conveyor belt to the next stage of its production.

WHEN ARE ROBOTS USED?

Industrial robots are computer-controlled machines that can be re-programmed to do various tasks. Many industrial tasks are repetitive and boring for human workers, or they require a degree of precision that is difficult for a human to maintain for hours on end. So robots sometimes take their place. Robots can also perform tasks that are too dangerous for a human operator. And, with no need to eat or sleep, they can work 24 hours a day.

The motor manufacturing industry makes use of robots. Robots are particularly good at welding together the various pieces of the car's body shell. They may also be used to paint the finished shell, which they do without overspraying and wasting paint.

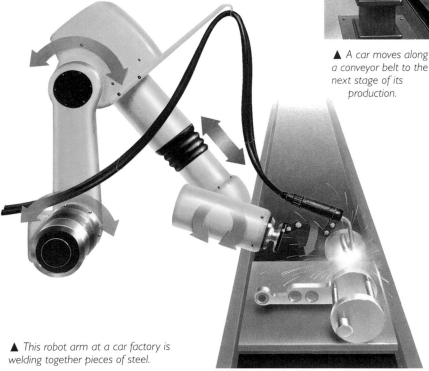

▲ This robot arm at a car factory is welding together pieces of steel.

IS THERE A CHEMICAL INDUSTRY?

Yes. The chemical industry manufactures a huge range of products, including drugs, paints, explosives, pesticides, fertilizers, and plastics, as well as chemicals for other industries to use. Some production methods are large-scale versions of laboratory processes. Others use very high temperatures and high pressures to make a useful product out of cheap and available materials.

▼ The chemical industry makes pesticides, which are sprayed onto crops.

WHAT IS FACTORY FARMING?

Factory farming is the use of factory methods in the activities of farming. In raising chickens, for example, the hens are kept in small cages. Conveyor belts supply them with food and water, and another conveyor carries away the eggs as they are laid. Many people think that it is cruel to keep animals in such cramped spaces.

Creating Energy

WHO NEEDS ENERGY? Almost everything that we do involves the use of energy. And most energy is used in the form of electricity. Factories, homes, offices, and schools use up large amounts of electricity for machines, for heating, and for lighting. Electric railways also consume a lot. Electricity is produced by converting other kinds of energy.

HOW CAN WATER PRODUCE ELECTRICITY?

In a hydroelectric power station, flowing water is used to turn turbines, which are similar to water-wheels. The turbines spin generators and this produces electricity. To ensure a constant supply of flowing water, engineers build dams across river valleys. The river water is held behind the dam, where it flows through pipes to the turbine generators.

▲ In a hydroelectric power station, water from behind a dam spins turbine generators.

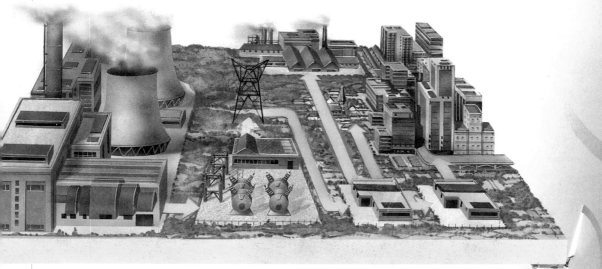

HOW DOES AN ORDINARY POWER STATION WORK?

The generators in an ordinary power station are turned by steam turbines. The steam is produced in a boiler, which is heated by burning coal, oil, or gas. The voltage of the electricity produced is then increased by transformers. This is because power lines work best with high-voltage electricity. In towns and villages, transformers at substations convert the electricity back to the lower voltage of the electric mains supply.

▲ Ordinary power stations have tall cooling towers, which release clouds of steam. The power stations burn coal, oil, or gas to boil water to make the steam. After the steam has worked turbine generators, the cooling towers convert most of the steam back into water to be used again.

CAN THE SUN PRODUCE ELECTRICITY?

Solar power is any method of using the light of the Sun as a power source, often to produce electricity. In one kind of solar power station, the Sun's rays are reflected by large mirrors onto a type of boiler in which water or another liquid is heated. This creates steam which then generates electricity. The mirrors are moved automatically so that they are always at the correct angle to the Sun. Another kind of station uses banks of solar cells to convert sunlight directly into electricity.

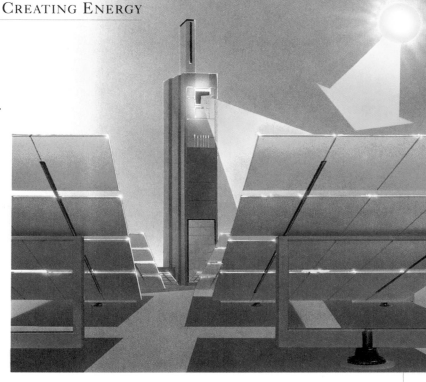

► A solar power station has large mirrors that shine the Sun's light and heat onto a boiler to make steam.

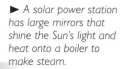

▲ Nuclear fuel rods can be dangerously radioactive and are handled by robot arms.

WHAT IS NUCLEAR POWER?

In a nuclear power station, the heat from a nuclear reactor is used to produce steam for working the turbine generators, to produce electricity. Because nuclear radiation is dangerous, strict safety precautions are taken to prevent leaks. More difficult problems concern how to dispose of used nuclear fuel and how to take apart old nuclear plants safely.

HOW DO WE USE WIND POWER?

The power of the wind can be caught using wind generating machines, which are modern versions of the old-fashioned windmill. The machine consists of a tall pole carrying a rotor, which is a three or four-bladed propeller. The bigger the propeller, the more powerful is the machine. The propellers change direction automatically so that they always face into the wind. Some wind machines have curved upright blades instead of propellers. The shaft of the rotor is connected directly to an electric generator. To obtain sufficient electricity, many machines are grouped together on high ground (where the wind is strongest) in what is called a wind farm. In very high winds, the machines are shut down to prevent them from becoming damaged if the rotors spin too fast.

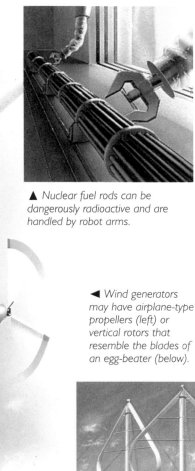

◄ Wind generators may have airplane-type propellers (left) or vertical rotors that resemble the blades of an egg-beater (below).

Cars, Motorcycles, and Trucks

WHAT DO CARS, MOTORCYCLES, AND TRUCKS HAVE IN COMMON? Firstly, they are all forms of road transport. Most are powered by internal combustion engines – either gasoline or diesel – although there are some electric vehicles. Most cars and motorcycles are used as personal transport, and both types are driven in popular motor sports. Trucks are used mainly as commercial vehicles. They have become increasingly important for transporting goods as freight-carrying railways are being used less in many countries.

► Henry Ford's Model T introduced popular motoring to the United States.

WHAT WAS THE 'TIN LIZZIE'?

'Tin Lizzie' was the nickname of the Ford Model T car. Manufactured between 1908 and 1927, it was the world's first mass produced car built on an assembly line. Because it was fairly cheap to buy and run it brought motoring to thousands of people in the United States for the first time.

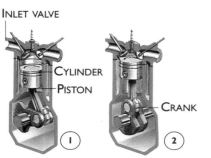

INLET VALVE · CYLINDER · PISTON · CRANK · SPARK PLUG · EXHAUST VALVE

(1) INDUCTION (2) COMPRESSION (3) IGNITION (4) EXHAUST

◄ There are four stages in the four-stroke cycle: (1) air and fuel enter the engine; (2) the air and fuel mixture is compressed; (3) a spark plug ignites the fuel and air mixture; and (4) the burnt gases leave the cylinder through the exhaust.

HOW DOES A GASOLINE ENGINE WORK?

A gasoline engine uses the expanding gases from the explosion of a mixture of air and gasoline to move a piston within a cylinder. A crank converts the up-and-down (or side-to-side) movement of the piston into a rotary movement that eventually drives the wheels of the vehicle. A car engine has a cycle of four strokes: induction, compression, ignition, and exhaust. The flow into and out of the engine is controlled by valves at the top of each cylinder.

WHY DO RACING CARS LOOK THE WAY THEY DO?

Whenever an object, such as a car or an airplane, moves along, it has to overcome wind resistance (called drag), which tends to slow down the moving object. Drag occurs because air does not flow evenly round the object but forms eddies or turbulence that slow down the air flow. Drag can be reduced by 'streamlining' the object's shape so that air flows smoothly round it. This is why high-speed vehicles such as racing cars are narrow and curved at the front and rear. Modern racing cars also have 'wings' at the front and rear which are angled so as to make air flowing over them push the car downwards onto the road.

WHAT IS THE FASTEST MOTORCYCLE?

The answer to this question depends on how you define a motorcycle. One of the fastest gasoline-engine machines from a flying start was the T120 Streamliner, ridden by American Bill Johnson. In 1962 it reached a speed of 223 miles per hour. In 1966, from a standing start, Englishman Alfred Hagen clocked a speed of 116 miles per hour on his V-twin Hagen JAP. The same year, Norman Breedlove rode his three-wheel jet-propelled 'motorcycle' over a short distance at 542 miles per hour!

▼ Racing motorcyclists lean over to turn corners at high speed.

HOW MUCH WEIGHT CAN A TRUCK CARRY?

Some modern tipper trucks can carry a load of nearly 25 tons in their high-sided bodies. The two rear axles, with paired wheels on each, are driven by a diesel engine of about 350 horsepower. A hydraulic mechanism tips the truck's body and dumps its load. This design is ideal for bulk loads such as sand and gravel, or for agricultural produce such as grain and sugar beet. For loads packed in boxes or on pallets, the best design is an articulated (sectioned) truck, which consists of a tractor unit pulling a separate trailer.

▲ Hydraulics lift a truck's body to empty its load.

▼ A racing car is streamlined to cut down wind resistance.

WHY DO TIRES DIFFER?

Tires are designed to suit the vehicle and road conditions. A road tire for a motorcycle has a high profile (narrow shape) for good resistance to wear. But a racing tire has a low profile to give extra grip as the machine goes round corners. Both racing cars and racing bikes use smooth tires when the track is dry and there is little danger of skidding. Wet-weather tires have much more tread.

HIGH PROFILE

LOW PROFILE

▲ High-profile tires are for everyday use. Low-profile tires give better grip when cornering at speed.

Trains

How MANY KINDS OF TRAINS ARE THERE? Most trains consist of a locomotive (engine) pulling a string of carriages (for carrying people) or a string of wagons or vans (for carrying goods, called freight). There are three main kinds of locomotives. Steam locomotives, first built in the 19th century, were the earliest kind. In a few places steam locomotives are still used, but they have largely been replaced by diesel or electric locomotives.

▼ In 1829, George Stephenson's Rocket reached a record-breaking speed of 29 mph.

Who built the first locomotive?

The first steam engine to run on rails was built in England in 1804 by Richard Trevithick. Locomotive design hardly improved until 1829, when George Stephenson's steam locomotive the *Rocket* won a competition for the best locomotive for the new Liverpool and Manchester Railway – the world's first passenger-carrying railroad.

▲ France's TGV trains pick up electricity from overhead wires.

WHAT FUEL DID STEAM ENGINES USE?

In Britain and most other countries in Europe, steam locomotives burned coal to heat the water in their boilers. But in the United States, most early locomotives burned wood, which was more readily available than coal. By the 1950s, many steam locomotives were designed, or had been adapted, to burn oil as a fuel. But no matter what the fuel, steam locomotives had the great disadvantage of having to carry their fuel – and water – with them. An electric locomotive does not have this problem.

◀ *In the 1870s, wood-burning locomotives pulled trains from coast to coast across the United States. They were gradually replaced by locomotives that burned coal.*

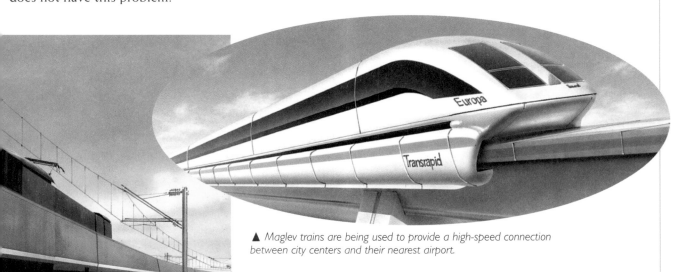

▲ *Maglev trains are being used to provide a high-speed connection between city centers and their nearest airport.*

WHAT IS A TGV?

TGV stands for the French name *Train à Grande Vitesse*, meaning high-speed train. It is an eight-carriage electric train with a locomotive at each end, and it normally runs at an average speed of about 160 miles an hour. It holds the world record for the fastest train. Its special high-speed track has no sharp curves.

HOW DOES A MAGLEV TRAIN WORK?

Maglev is short for 'magnetic levitation'. The term describes a system in which a train is held just above its track by a magnetic field, while powerful electric motors propel the train forward at high speeds. Most maglev trains are monorails, which means they run on one rail instead of two.

FACTS

The first regular use of electric locomotives began in 1890, on the City and South London underground railway.

The world speed record for a steam locomotive was set in 1938 by the *Mallard*, which pulled a seven-coach train at 125 mph.

The world speed record for a train is held by a French TGV, which on a test run in 1990 reached a speed of 319 mph.

At about 500 tons, the American 'Big Boy' steam locomotives were the heaviest locomotives ever. They reached speeds of 74 mph.

Ships and Boats

▼ A small sailing ship, the type Columbus sailed in.

WHEN WERE SHIPS AND BOATS FIRST USED?
Boats were among the earliest forms of transport. Thousands of years ago, people made simple boats from hollowed out logs or from wooden frames covered with an animal's skin. These early boats were powered by people rowing them using oars. Next the Ancient Egyptians and Arabs learned how to make sails to power their boats. Over the years, sailing ships became bigger and faster. The Age of Sail ended with the use of steam engines in ships, which had paddle wheels or propellers for propulsion. Modern ships use diesel engines, steam turbines, or gas turbine engines.

▼ Sailing is an enjoyable hobby for many people.

ARE SAILS STILL USED?

Today, nearly all sailing vessels are used for sport or leisure. Thousands of people go sailing for fun in boats that vary in size from small one-person dinghies with a single sail to large ocean-going yachts with up to ten people in the crew. Sailing boats do not pollute the atmosphere in the way other boats do, with engines that burn fossil fuels.

▶ Computers control the sails on this ship.

ARE SAILS OF ANY USE TO BIG SHIPS?

There are a few experimental ships that have sails as well as ordinary engines. The sails resemble upright airplane wings and have to be set at precisely the correct angle to help the ship along. A computer is used to adjust the sails according to the wind direction and the ship's course.

WHAT IS A HYDROFOIL BOAT?

A hydrofoil boat is one that has hydrofoils ('wings')
attached to its hull. The hull and hydrofoils are under the
water when the boat is still or moving slowly. The hydrofoils are supported on legs or struts, and have an aerofoil
shape – like an airplane's wing. The boat is driven through
the water by a propeller or water jet. As the craft gathers
speed, it rises up until the hull is out of the water and the
boat is supported on the water by the hydrofoils.
Hydrofoil boats can skim over the surface at speeds of up
to 60 miles per hour.

▲ The hull of a hydrofoil rises from the
water as the boat speeds up.

FACTS

The ship's propeller was invented
in 1836 by the Swedish-born
American engineer John Ericsson.

The first non-stop crossing of the
Atlantic Ocean by a steamship
was in 1838 by the *Sirius*, which
sailed from Ireland to New York
in just over 18 days.

The fastest crossing of the
Atlantic Ocean by a liner was
made in 1952 by the *United
States*, which took 3 days 10½
hours at an average speed of
35.6 knots (41 mph).

The largest cargo vessels are
supertankers of more than
300,000 tons deadweight,
measuring 1,132 feet in
length.

The largest ocean liner was
the *Queen Elizabeth*, which
was 1,030 feet long.

The fastest water speed
record is held by Ken Warby.
In 1978 he reached a speed
of 317 mph in the hydroplane
Spirit of Australia, on the
Blowering Dam Lake, Australia.

◄ The V foil.

◄ Shallow
draught foil.

◄ Fully
submerged
foil.

HOW DOES A SHIP'S PROPELLERS WORK?

Another name for a ship's propeller is a 'screw'. It is a good
name because a propeller 'screws' the ship through the
water. As the propeller rotates, the angled blades bite into
the water and push it backwards. The reaction to this
backward movement is a forward thrust that drives the
vessel along.

▼ A propeller screws a ship through the
water, just as a screwdriver drives a screw
into wood.

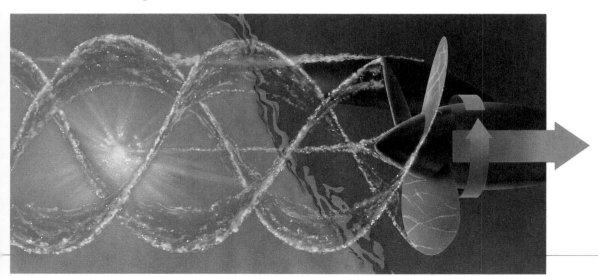

Underwater

How can people live underwater? Human beings need to breathe air in order to live, so to live underwater they have to be supplied with air. Divers carry scuba gear, which contains a supply of air. At greater depths, many people can be carried in a submarine. At the greatest depths of all, one or two people can be transported in a small vessel called a submersible.

How long can a submarine stay underwater?

How long a submarine can stay underwater depends on the way its engines work. Most ordinary submarines have battery-driven electric motors for propelling themselves underwater and diesel engines, which need a constant supply of air, for traveling on the surface. Electric motors cannot be used for long periods because their batteries need regular recharging. This is done by diesel engines on the surface.

Nuclear submarines use the heat produced by a small nuclear reactor to make steam, which drives a steam turbine engine or an electric generator. They can stay underwater for many months without surfacing.

How does a submarine dive?

Anything less dense than water floats. Anything more dense than water sinks. The ability of an object to float is called its buoyancy. A submarine can float, sink, or surface because its buoyancy can be changed, using its ballast tanks. When these are full of air, the submarine floats. When the tanks are full of water, it sinks. Compressed air pumped into the tanks forces out the water and makes the submarine rise again.

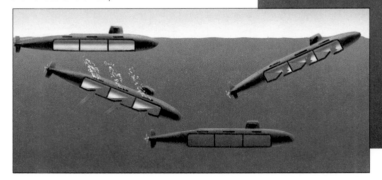

▼ Water flows into or is pumped out of ballast tanks to alter the buoyancy of a submarine. This allows it to dive or surface.

What is sonar?

Sonar detects underwater objects. It sends pulses of ultrasound through the water. If the ultrasound pulses strike an object, echoes are reflected back. The time taken for the echoes to return are a measure of how far away the object is.

▼ The two-person Sea-Link submersible can dive to 1,476 feet.

Who uses submersibles?

A submersible can carry one to three people to the deepest parts of the ocean. They are used by oceanographers (research scientists who study the ocean and the creatures that live in it) and for finding shipwrecks. Submersibles are also used to lay oil or gas pipelines and underwater telephone cables, and for maintenance work on pipelines and offshore oil rigs.

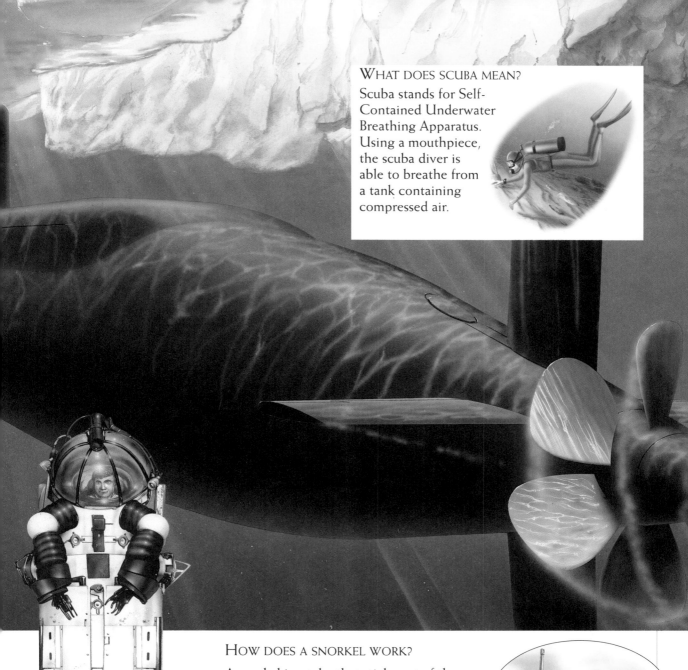

HOW DOES A SNORKEL WORK?

A snorkel is a tube that sticks out of the water to carry air to a submarine just below the surface. The air supply is needed for the crew to breathe. Naval submarines also have one or more periscopes, which allow the captain of a submerged submarine to observe other shipping, without the submarine having to surface.

▲ A submarine's snorkel takes in air and its periscope views the surroundings.

ARE DIVING SUITS STILL USED?

A modern diving suit is like a one-person submersible. It keeps the diver's air at surface pressure, allowing the diver to go deeper in safety. It moves using electric motor-driven propellers. The diver uses his or her arms to work a variety of tools.

HOW ARE SUBMERGED OBJECTS LIFTED UNDERWATER?

If a submerged object is too heavy for a diver to carry to the surface, it may be lifted by cranes on a vessel moored overhead. Water in a wreck may be blown out with compressed air (to lighten the wreck), or air bags may be tied onto the object to make it more buoyant.

Airplanes

WHAT IS AN AIRPLANE? An airplane is a powered, fixed-wing aircraft. It is unlike a helicopter, which has a rotating wing, and different to a glider, which is unpowered. Most airplanes have single wings, and are called monoplanes ('mono' means 'single'). Some small airplanes have two pairs of wings. These are known as biplanes ('bi' means 'two'). Small airplanes are usually powered by piston engines that drive propellers. Larger planes are powered by turboprops or jet engines.

HOW DOES A JET ENGINE WORK?

The jet, or gas turbine, engine drives an aircraft forward with enormous force. Air is sucked in at the front, compressed by blades, and heated with flames of burning fuel in the combustion chamber. The air is then expelled at a high speed from the back. This stream of hot air – the 'jet' – causes a thrust in the opposite direction, propelling the aircraft forwards.

HOW DOES AN AIRPLANE FLY?

The secret of airplane flight is in the shape of the wing. If you sliced through the wing, you would see that it is more curved on top than it is underneath. As the wing moves through the air, air traveling over the top of the wing has to go farther than air passing underneath. As a result, the air has to travel farther and so must go faster. Accordingly, the pressure is lower above the wing than below it. This creates lift, an upward force that keeps the airplane in the air.

LOW AIR PRESSURE   LIFT   WING

WHAT IS IN THE COCKPIT?

In the cockpit, the pilot 'steers' by means of a control column (joystick) and foot pedals. The pilot turns the top of the column around to make the aircraft roll, pulls it back to make the plane climb, or pushes it forward to make it dive. The pedals control the tail rudder, making the plane turn left or right.

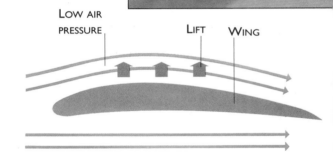

◄ *The pilot and co-pilot sit side by side in the cockpit of an airliner. Some cockpits have control wheels instead of control columns.*

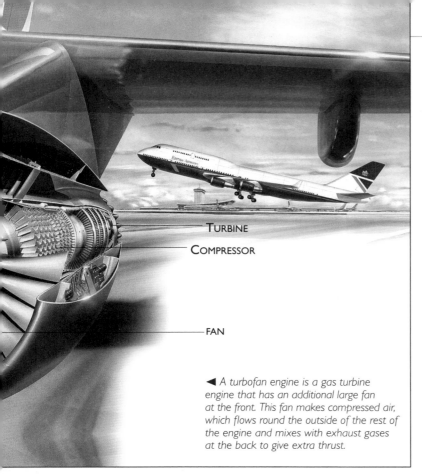

TURBINE

COMPRESSOR

FAN

◄ A turbofan engine is a gas turbine engine that has an additional large fan at the front. This fan makes compressed air, which flows round the outside of the rest of the engine and mixes with exhaust gases at the back to give extra thrust.

WHAT IS FLY-BY-WIRE?

Originally an airplane's control surfaces (the moving flaps on the aircraft that help control its speed and direction) were triggered by steel cables connected to the control column. In the fly-by-wire system installed on some modern aircraft, the control surfaces are activated by electric signals that pass along wires from the control column.

WHAT IS AN ALTIMETER?

An altimeter displays the height (altitude) of an aircraft. The simplest type, fitted to small aircraft, is like a barometer, measuring atmospheric pressure. This is because atmospheric pressure varies according to altitude.

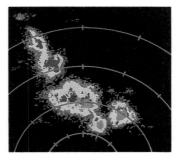

► A radar can warn a pilot of severe turbulence inside clouds ahead (shown in red).

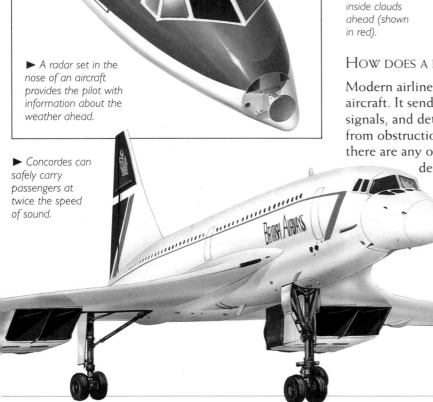

► A radar set in the nose of an aircraft provides the pilot with information about the weather ahead.

► Concordes can safely carry passengers at twice the speed of sound.

HOW DOES A RADAR WORK?

Modern airliners have a radar set in the nose of the aircraft. It sends out pulses of high-frequency radio signals, and detects any echoes that bounce back from obstructions. In this way, the pilot knows if there are any other aircraft nearby and can even detect rain and thick cloud, indicating bad weather ahead.

HOW FAST IS CONCORDE?

Concorde is currently the world's only supersonic (faster than the speed of sound) airliner. It can fly at speeds of up to Mach 2 – twice the speed of sound, or more than 1,240 miles an hour at Concorde's operating height of 49,200 feet.

Flying Machines

HOW MANY TYPES OF FLYING MACHINES ARE THERE? There are three main types. The first is the lighter-than-air craft, such as the balloon or the airship (an airship is similar to a balloon but has engines). The second main type is the fixed-wing, heavier-than-air craft, such as the airplane. Gliders are in this category, even though they have no engine. The third type has a rotating wing. The helicopter is the best-known example.

▲ The first hot-air balloon was made of paper and had a fire to heat the air inside.

WHEN WAS THE FIRST BALLOON FLIGHT?

The first piloted balloon flight took place in Paris in November 1783. Two brothers called Montgolfier made a huge balloon of paper. The air in the balloon was heated by a fire. The balloon of hot air was less dense than the air surrounding it and so it rose, carrying two passengers. A few weeks later, a French scientist flew in a hydrogen-filled balloon.

WHAT WAS THE FIRST AIRPLANE?

The first heavier-than-air craft to achieve powered flight was a two-winged (biplane) airplane called the *Flier*. It was built in the United States by the brothers Orville and Wilbur Wright, and first flew in December 1903. The first flight covered 121 feet and lasted only 21 seconds. The aircraft was made of wood and cloth, and was powered by an aluminum gasoline engine the brothers had designed.

▲ The Wright brothers' Flier had two 'pusher' propellers behind the pilot, who lay on the lower wing.

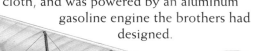

▶ The Harrier jump jet rises vertically by pointing its engine thrust at the ground.

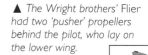

WHO MADE THE FIRST AIRSHIP?

The first airship was built in 1852 by a Frenchman named Henri Giffard. It had a hydrogen-filled gasbag resembling an elongated rugby ball, with the pilot's seat and a small steam engine slung below it. The engine drove a large propeller with two blades. The machine was called a dirigible, which is a word meaning steerable.

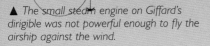

▲ The small steam engine on Giffard's dirigible was not powerful enough to fly the airship against the wind.

WHO MADE THE FIRST SOLO FLIGHT ACROSS THE ATLANTIC?

The first solo crossing of the Atlantic Ocean was made in 1927 by the American airman Charles Lindbergh. His high-winged monoplane (single-winged airplane) was called *Spirit of St. Louis*, and it took him 33½ hours to make the non-stop 3,580-mile flight.

▲ Lindbergh's Spirit of St. Louis *took more than a day to make the non-stop Atlantic crossing.*

▼ The pilot pedaled the human-powered Gossamer Albatross over the English Channel.

HOW DOES A GLIDER FLY?

A glider has no engine, and when it appears to be flying in a straight line it is in fact in a very shallow dive. To gain height, the pilot seeks out a thermal (a mass of rising warm air). The glider spirals upward in the thermal, and then returns to another long, shallow dive.

HAVE THERE BEEN HUMAN-POWERED AIRCRAFT?

There have been several air-craft driven by human muscle power. The most famous was the *Gossamer Albatross*, which in 1979 flew across the English Channel from England to France. The pilot pedaled a bicycle-type chain to turn the 'pusher' propeller.

FRONT BLADE

HOW DOES A HELICOPTER FLY?

The blades on the top of a helicopter make up the rotor — a spinning wing. Increasing the angle (pitch) of the blades as they spin makes the helicopter rise. Reducing the pitch makes it descend. If the pitch of the blades at the back of the rotor is increased, the helicopter flies forward. If the pitch of the front blades is increased it flies backward.

BACKWARD FLIGHT

CAN AN AIRPLANE FLY BACKWARD?

The only fixed-wing aircraft able to fly backward is the Harrier military jump jet. The exhaust gases from its large turbofan engine can be directed through ducts that swivel, allowing the aircraft to hover, rise vertically, or even fly backward. When the ducts are directed to the back, the Harrier can fly forward at the speed of sound.

Exploring Space

HOW ARE ROCKETS LAUNCHED INTO SPACE? Everything is held on the Earth by the force of gravity. If you throw a stone into the air, it falls back down again because of the force of gravity. But if you could throw it fast enough, it would escape Earth's gravity and go into space. This is what a space rocket does. The minimum speed needed to reach space is called the orbital velocity and, for Earth, this is about 16,500 miles per hour.

WHY DO SPACE ROCKETS HAVE STAGES?

A single rocket with enough fuel to reach space would be extremely large and heavy. Instead, rockets are built in stages, with each stage riding piggyback on the stage below it. When the first stage has burned all of its fuel, it falls away. The second-stage rocket motor then fires, pushing the craft even farther into space. There may also be a third stage.

WHAT IS A SPACE PROBE?

A space probe is a complex piece of equipment that is launched into space to investigate parts of the Solar System, such as the Moon and other planets. Most probes have panels of solar cells that produce electricity, and aerials that receive and send radio messages. In 1989 the *Galileo* probe (above) was launched in the direction of Jupiter.

HOW DO PROBES SEND PICTURES?

Pictures taken by cameras on a space probe are converted into thousands of tiny squares, called pixels. The brightness of each pixel is measured by a computer and the measurements are sent by radio back to Earth (in binary code). Then a computer on Earth reconstructs the picture.

HOW DO ROCKETS WORK?

Rockets work by reaction, which is a force that acts against another force. If you blow up a balloon and then let it go, the air inside the balloon pushes in all directions. But the air escaping through the neck – a reaction to the air pushing the other way – causes the balloon to fly away.

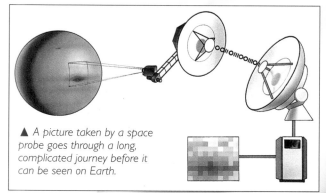

▲ A picture taken by a space probe goes through a long, complicated journey before it can be seen on Earth.

▼ The European rocket, Ariane.

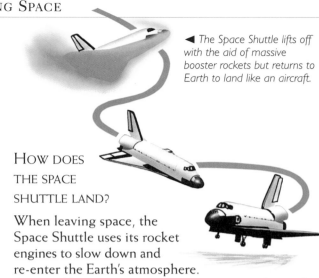

◄ The Space Shuttle lifts off with the aid of massive booster rockets but returns to Earth to land like an aircraft.

HOW DOES THE SPACE SHUTTLE LAND?

When leaving space, the Space Shuttle uses its rocket engines to slow down and re-enter the Earth's atmosphere. A special heat-resistant covering prevents the craft from becoming too hot as friction with the atmosphere heats it up. The Shuttle then goes into a long, shallow dive, while computers take over the actual landing. Lacking any power, it glides back to land on its undercarriage.

▼ A space suit protects an astronaut from the freezing cold, airless vacuum of space and from the dangerous radiation that comes from the Sun. It has an oxygen supply and a built-in radio for communicating with other astronauts and the mother ship.

CAN SPACE PROBES EXPLORE STARS?

The Sun is the nearest star to Earth. Orbiting satellites and space probes have given scientists much information about the Sun that Earth-based telescopes cannot provide. The next nearest star is Proxima Centauri, which is 4.3 light-years (25,000 billion miles) away from the Sun. So far, there is no space probe that could reach Proxima Centauri within a human lifetime.

Glossary

alternating current (AC) Electric current that flows first one way, then the other. It is the kind of electricity used in homes. *See also* direct current (DC).

arteries Tubes that carry blood away from the heart to the rest of the body. The blood contains a lot of oxygen, which the cells need for energy.

asteroid A small rocky object that revolves around the Sun.

atmosphere An envelope of gases that surrounds the Earth, the Sun, and other planets and stars.

atom The smallest particle of an element that can exist on its own. It is therefore the basic unit of all matter. Atoms have a nucleus, surrounded by orbiting electrons.

black hole A region of space surrounding a collapsed star, within which gravity is so powerful that nothing, not even light, can escape.

blood A reddish-purple liquid made up of a watery liquid (plasma) with cells (white and red) floating around in it.

carbon dioxide In the human body, a waste gas made by the cells. Blood carries carbon dioxide from the cells to the lungs, where it is breathed out into the air.

cells The microscopic building-blocks that make up the body of all organisms (plants and animals). Cells come in many shapes and sizes, and carry out all kinds of important jobs for the life of the organism.

civil engineering The building and design of large structures, such as airports, bridges, harbors, highways, and tunnels.

combustion The chemical name for burning. It is a chemical reaction in which a substance combines with oxygen, producing flames, heat, and light.

comet An object in space made of ice and dust that develops a head and one or more tails of gas and dust each time it comes close to the Sun.

compound A substance made up of two or more elements chemically bonded together. The elements in a compound can only be separated by a chemical reaction.

compressed air Air that has been squeezed until its pressure is higher than the pressure of the air around it.

compressor A machine that compresses (squeezes up) a gas such as air or the coolant gas in a refrigerator.

conservation The special work people do to help protect and preserve plants and animals and the places in which they live.

delta An area of land at the mouth of a river. It is formed from sediment that is dropped by the river as it travels to the sea.

density The density of any substance is its mass divided by its volume.

desert A very dry area of the world, which usually has less than 10 inches of rainfall a year. Most deserts are rocky or sandy.

digital Anything that takes the form of a collection of numbers (digits). Computers, for example, handle information that is in digital form.

dinosaur An ancient egg-laying reptile belonging to a group that emerged about 215 million years ago and died out about 65 million years ago.

direct current (DC) Electric current that always flows in the same direction (from positive to negative). *See also* alternating current (AC).

DNA A complicated chemical inside the nucleus of a cell. It contains specially coded instructions that are used by your cells to build your body.

earthquake Vibrations or tremors in the Earth's crust that happen after a build-up of pressure within the Earth's rocks. Most earthquakes occur along faults (breaks) in the Earth's crust.

ecosystem A living system in a particular zone of the world, in which plants and animals live together in a delicate balance with the land and weather around them.

electrode A piece of metal or carbon that releases or collects electrons in an electric circuit. An electrode connected to the negative source of electricity is called the cathode; the positive electrode is called the anode.

electromagnet A magnet made of a coil of insulated wire wrapped round a piece of iron or steel. It becomes magnetic only when an electric current flows through the coil.

electron A subatomic particle that carries a negative charge. The nuclei of all atoms are surrounded by orbiting electrons. An electric current consists of a stream of electrons flowing along a wire.

element A substance, consisting of similar atoms, that cannot be split by a chemical reaction into something simpler.

energy In science, energy is the capacity for doing work. It takes many forms, including heat, light, chemical energy, and electrical energy.

enzymes Special chemicals in the body. The digestive system, for example, has several different enzymes that attack and digest different types of food.

Equator An imaginary circle around the Earth, dividing it into two hemispheres.

erosion The break-up and removal of rocks by water, wind, and ice.

evaporation The process by which a liquid, such as water, changes into a gas when it is heated.

extinction The death of an entire species, either from natural causes or because humans killed them or destroyed their homes.

food chain A way of showing how energy is passed from one form of life to another. At the end of the chain are animals that feed on other animals that fed on other animals that originally ate plants. The energy that the plants captured from the Sun has passed along all the animals in the chain.

food web A way of showing how many different food chains (see above) link together in a complex way, so that damage to one part of the web may cause problems for the feeding of many other animals.

force Something that can move a stationary object or change the speed or direction of a moving object.

fossil The remains or trace of an animal or plant preserved in rock.

friction A force that opposes the movement of one surface against another.

galaxy A huge system of stars, gas, and dust.

gas A state of matter in which atoms or molecules are fairly far apart, move rapidly, and fill all space available.

geyser A hot spring that throws up a fountain of steam and hot water at irregular intervals.

glacier A mass of moving ice that forms from a build-up of snow. It usually moves down a valley.

gravity The force of attraction that exists between any two objects because of their masses. Gravity keeps satellites in orbit around planets and planets in orbit around stars.

habitat The kind of place in which a plant or animal lives, in balance with the climate, the soil, and the other plants and animals around it.

hormones Substances that are released from hormone glands around the body. They are involved in many processes that go on inside the human body.

hydraulic A term describing the use of pressure in a liquid to help power a machine.

ice age A period of global cooling during which ice sheets and glaciers expand.

igneous rock A type of rock that forms when molten magma solidifies.

infra-red A term describing radiation similar to light, which exists before the red end of the spectrum.

invertebrate An animal without a backbone. It is the most common type of animal on Earth.

ionosphere A layer in the upper atmosphere that contains ions and electrons. The presence of these particles makes the layer act like a mirror that reflects certain radio waves back down to Earth.

larva The young form of an animal that looks very different from the adult. A caterpillar, for example, is the larva of a butterfly.

lava Magma from inside the Earth that has escaped to the surface as a result of volcanic activity.

light-year The distance traveled by light in one year: 5.8 billion miles.

limestone A sedimentary rock composed mainly of calcium carbonate.

magma Molten (melted) rock deep within the Earth. It is usually semi-fluid.

mammal A vertebrate animal, covered at least partly in hair, which feeds its young on milk produced by the mother.

mass The amount of matter in an object. The force of gravity acting on an object's mass gives it weight.

metamorphic rock A type of rock that forms after it is subjected to intense heat and pressure.

meteor The brief streak of light seen in the sky when a tiny particle called a meteoroid plunges into the Earth's atmosphere and is destroyed by friction.

meteorite A lump of matter that survives falling from space through the atmosphere and reaches the Earth's surface.

microwave A radio wave that has a very short wavelength. Microwaves are used in satellite communications and microwave ovens.

molecule The smallest particle of a chemical compound that can exist on its own. It consists of two or more atoms held together by chemical bonds.

momentum The mass multiplied by the velocity (speed in a particular direction) of a moving object.

nebula A huge cloud of gas and dust in space.

nerves Bundles of cells that pass electrical signals to and from the brain. They allow the brain to communicate with the body.

neutron A particle that forms part of the nucleus of an atom. Unlike protons and electrons, it has no electrical charge.

nucleus In chemistry and physics, the central part of an atom, made of protons and neutrons. In biology it is the central part of a plant or animal cell, containing the genetic 'instruction manual'.

orbit The path followed by one body around another; for example, the path of the Moon around the Earth, or the path of the Earth around the Sun.

organism An individual living thing, plant or animal.

oxygen An important gas that the human body's cells need for energy. When we breathe, our lungs take oxygen from the air and pass it into the bloodstream, which carries oxygen around the body.

ozone A form of oxygen gas, produced high in the atmosphere above Earth. It helps protect living things from the Sun's damaging ultraviolet rays.

peristalsis The strong squeezing and pushing movements of the intestines' muscular walls, which help to propel food onward inside our body.

photosynthesis The chemical process by which plants make food (sugars) from water and carbon dioxide gas, using the energy of sunlight.

pollination The process by which pollen is transferred between flowers (by wind, water, or animals). Pollinated plants can form seeds.

pollution The release of waste materials that result from human activities into the air, the soil or water, where they can be highly damaging to plants and animals.

predator An animal that hunts and kills other animals to feed itself.

primate An animal belonging to the group of mammals that includes monkeys, apes, and lemurs.

prism A transparent block, usually with triangular ends and rectangular sides. A glass prism is used to split white light into the colors of the spectrum.

proton A positively charged subatomic particle that forms part of the nucleus of an atom.

radioactive A term describing an element that has atoms with nuclei that disintegrate spontaneously, causing radiation – the release of various particles and rays.

rainforest A type of forest found close to the Equator, where plentiful rain and warm temperatures throughout the year have produced a dense growth of tall trees. Many animals live in rainforests.

refraction The change in direction of a wave (such as a light wave or a radio wave) when it passes from one substance into another.

satellite A small body that travels around a planet. The Moon is the Earth's natural satellite. An artificial satellite is a manufactured device in orbit around a planet.

sedimentary rock A type of rock that forms on the seabed from material that has settled there.

skeleton The strong framework of a body, made up of bones. The skeleton allows the human body to stand and move, and protects many important internal organs.

species A group of plants or animals that are all more or less similar to one another, and which breed together, passing on these similarities to their young.

spectrum A series of wavelengths or frequencies. A light spectrum is a series of colored bands (the colors of the rainbow) produced by passing white light through a prism.

speed The rate of change in position of a moving object – that is, the distance it moves divided by the time it takes to do so.

subatomic A term describing anything that is smaller than an atom.

supernova The explosion of a star at the end of its life.

supersonic A term describing the high-pitched sounds that are beyond the range of human hearing. It also describes aircraft that fly faster than the speed of sound.

Tropic of Cancer An imaginary line of latitude around the Earth at 23.5° north.

Tropic of Capricorn An imaginary line of latitude around the Earth at 23.5° south.

Tropics An area of the world between the latitudes of 23.5° north and 23.5° south.

tsunami An ocean wave caused by an underwater disturbance such as an earthquake. A tsunami builds up to mountain-like proportions when it reaches shallow water.

tundra An ecosystem close to the arctic regions, in which the land is locked up in snow and ice most of the year, and no trees are able to grow.

ultraviolet A term describing radiation similar to light, which exists beyond the violet end of the spectrum.

universe Everything that exists; the whole of space and all the matter it contains.

vaccination Putting a 'mock' germ into the blood, so that the immune system can produce and develop defences against it in case the real, harmful germ invades.

vapor Another name for a gas. In science it describes a gas that can be turned into a liquid if enough pressure is applied to it.

veins Tubes that carry blood from the body back to the heart. They have thin walls and special flaps to stop the blood falling downward on its journey up the body.

velocity An object's speed in a particular direction.

vertebrate An animal with a backbone. Only a small number of living animal species are vertebrates.

virus A type of microbe that cannot live on its own because it feeds inside the cells of other creatures. Viral diseases include mumps, chicken pox, measles, and AIDS.

vitamins Chemicals that you need regularly in small amounts to keep healthy.

wavelength The distance between two crests or troughs in any wave motion (such as light and sound).

weight The force of gravity acting on a mass.

work In science this means the energy transferred when a force moves an object or changes its shape.

Index

Page numbers in ordinary type mean that the topic will be mentioned at least once, and there will probably be a picture too. Page numbers in *italics* mean that there is just an illustration. Page numbers in **bold** refer to main headings.